THE WORKPLACE LEARNER

THE
WORKPLACE
LEARNER

How to Align Training Initiatives with

Individual Learning Competencies

WILLIAM J. ROTHWELL

AMACOM
American Management Association
New York • Atlanta • Brussels • Buenos Aires • Chicago • London • Mexico City
San Francisco • Shanghai • Tokyo • Toronto • Washington, D.C.

Special discounts on bulk quantities of AMACOM books are available to corporations, professional associations, and other organizations. For details, contact Special Sales Department, AMACOM, a division of American Management Association, 1601 Broadway, New York, NY 10019.
Tel.: 212-903-8316. Fax: 212-903-8083.
Web site: www.amacombooks.org

This publication is designed to provide accurate and authoritative information in regard to the subject matter covered. It is sold with the understanding that the publisher is not engaged in rendering legal, accounting, or other professional service. If legal advice or other expert assistance is required, the services of a competent professional person should be sought.

Library of Congress Cataloging-in-Publication Data

Rothwell, William J.,
        The workplace learner: how to align training initiatives with individual learning competencies / William J. Rothwell.
        p.   cm.
    Includes bibliographical references and index.
    ISBN 0-8144-0674-2
    1. Employees—Training of.   2. Occupational training.   I. Title.

HF5549.5 .T7   R6598   2002
658.3' 124—dc21

                                                                    2002004843

Printing number

10   9   8   7   6   5   4   3   2   1

To my wife, Marcelina Rothwell,

who has been—and always will be—my soulmate

Contents

PART ONE

INTRODUCTION

PART TWO

UNDERSTANDING AND BUILDING INDIVIDUAL
LEARNING COMPETENCE

PART THREE

UNDERSTANDING AND BUILDING AN ORGANIZATIONAL
CLIMATE CONDUCIVE TO LEARNING

PART FOUR

THE ROLE OF THE WORKPLACE LEARNING AND PERFORMANCE PRACTITIONER

List of Exhibits

Preface

Workplace training is increasingly under attack. Managers complain that training is not as effective as they would like it to be in changing employee behavior or improving work results. At the same time, many workers complain that they do not receive enough training—or that the training they receive is offered too little or too late to be of value to them in keeping pace with today's frantic pace of organizational and technological change. Younger workers sometimes grade the quality of their organization's management by the quality of the training and development opportunities they receive, and management all too often is found wanting when measured by that yardstick. Workplace learning and performance (WLP) practitioners—whom I sometimes call "trainers" in this book as shorthand—complain that they are not appreciated and are too often asked to tackle problems that could never be solved by training. Although U.S. businesses invest somewhere in the neighborhood of $56 billion annually on training, decision makers sometimes wonder what benefits they receive from that sizable investment.

Against this backdrop, it is surprising that not more attention has been paid to *workplace learning* rather than to *workplace training. Training* is an individualized, short-term change effort intended to equip individuals with the knowledge, skills, and attitudes they need to perform their work successfully and meet or exceed customer expectations. *Learning* is an internalized change effort that individuals bring about on their own. *Life learning* helps individuals lead their lives. It is distinguishable from *workplace learning*, which helps individuals carry out their work successfully and achieve the results desired by such stakeholders as customers or clients, coworkers, organizational superiors, and organizational subordinates.

However, the tendency to focus on training rather than on learning is increasingly out of touch with reality. The issue is that much published research has focused on the competencies needed for trainers to be successful—and not on the competencies needed for learners to be successful. As a direct result of changing conditions in workplaces, changing (and less stable) employer-employee relationships, and more widely available on-demand learning opportunities produced through recent and stunning advances in instructional technology, individuals are increasingly shouldering responsibility for their own learning. To paraphrase futurist Alvin Toffler, the illiterate of the future will not be those who are unable to read or write but rather those who cannot learn.[1] Trainers, who are now called WLP professionals, must be prepared to meet this challenge in the organizations they serve.

A growing number of people today who are posing a new challenge to organizational trainers and schoolteachers alike are the *free agent learners*. These individuals aggressively pursue their own development in a way that transcends previous notions of self-directed learners. As I have often said to groups I have spoken to, "A free agent learner is like a self-directed learner on steroids." They are different because they are more likely to want on-demand learning than to return to educational providers they have used in the past. They want to meet their needs the moment they recognize them.

The future belongs to *competent workplace learners* who willingly, assertively, and (on occasion) aggressively assume responsibility for their own real-time workplace learning agenda and their own on-the-job, real-time learning process. Often the trainer (or teacher), who has traditionally served as an intermediary between learners and the subject areas that they must master, is subtracted from the equation. That means that trainers must become more masterful in facilitating learning on an individual level. It is not too fanciful to predict that free agent learning will increasingly become the norm rather than the exception, so trainers must adjust their roles to meet the needs of these free agent learners.

Traditionally, in education as in training, the lion's share of attention has been paid to teachers and to the teaching process. Teachers undergo a lengthy educational and certification process, and (in some localities) must pass a rigorous examination before they are permitted to teach in primary or secondary schools. When students fail—and when politicians, journalists, or business leaders look for scapegoats—teachers are usually held culpable. Everyone focuses attention on what happens during school time and what happens in classroom events. Very little attention is paid to what students do in the learning process, how students do it, and where they do it. (Nobody talks about certifying learners to be good learners.) Scant regard is given, for instance, to how students independently approach the learning challenges posed by their studies, how they perform their homework, how they study and apply study habits, and how much or how well they participate in classroom events. Nor does anyone pay much attention to the school's *total learning environment* (which includes not just classrooms but everything associated with a student's life at school) to see what conditions may encourage or discourage the learning process. So, when students score low on standardized tests, the blame is placed squarely on teachers. Nobody thinks to look at the learners—or at the quality of the schools' total learning environment.

And so it has been in the training community as well. Several professional associations focus on "trainers." They include the American Society for Training and Development (ASTD) and the International Society for Performance Improvement (ISPI). But no professional association for trainers focuses more broadly on reaching "learners." Yet, increasingly, the real action in gaining quantum leaps in productivity and performance improvement rests with learners, not trainers. A key driver for a rightful shift of focus from trainer to learner is the advent of e-learning, where most responsibility for the learning process rests with learners—and interactions with teachers or trainers, when they exist at all, are virtual. Nor, despite all the discussions about the need to establish learning organizations, has much attention been paid to the conditions that must be created and maintained by the organization's management so that people are encouraged to do practical, real-time learning to solve job-related problems that lead to increased organizational competitiveness, profitability, or other measures of success.

THE PURPOSE OF THIS BOOK

This book is meant to be provocative. It focuses on what it takes to develop *competent*—and what some might call *agile*—workplace learners. It is about what roles organizations should play in creating a workplace climate that encourages real-time, on-the-job learning as a key process contributing to productivity and performance.

To be clear, *competent workplace learners* are defined as *individuals who are willing and able to seize initiative for identifying their own learning needs, finding the resources to meet those needs, organizing their own learning experiences, and evaluating the results.* They are thus real-time, on-the-job learners who have mastered what it takes to "learn how to learn." To be fully effective, these learners carry out their efforts in organizations that encourage them to seize initiative for their own workplace learning.

This book offers practical, how-to-do-it advice to increase individual learning competence in employees, to reinvent workplace training so that it dovetails with (and supports) the workplace learning process, and to create organizations that encourage learning as an increasingly important means to the end of improved performance or productivity.

The scope of this book is deliberately broad. Stated succinctly, the purpose of this book is to describe what it takes to build the competence of workplace learners and what it takes for organizational leaders to establish a climate where people want to learn and can be successful in the learning process. Workplace learning is not an end in itself, but it does serve as a vehicle for achieving improved work results for organizations and improved career results for individuals.

SOURCES OF INFORMATION

Much research in the past has been directed to discovering the roles and competencies of training and development practitioners, so that academic institutions can prepare people for entry to this occupation and so that organizations can help promoted-from-within workers transition into the training and development practitioner role. But relatively little research has been focused on the roles and competencies of workplace learners and how trainers and employers can develop them.

This book began as a fanciful notion. It seemed to me to be a natural outgrowth of earlier competency studies with which I had been involved.[2] These works, of course, focused on the roles, competencies, and outputs that are essential for success in the field that has been variously called training and development (T&D), human resource development (HRD), human performance improvement (HPI) (or performance consulting), and WLP. Of course, these new names dramatized evolving paradigms about what practitioners in the field should do and what results they should achieve.

But, in time, like the Ancient Mariner in Coleridge's famous poem, I stopped everyone I met to tell them about the importance of studying the workplace learning process, the roles and competencies of the workplace learner, and the need to consider the context in which workplace learners demonstrate their learning competence. Learning competence remains a surprisingly neglected issue, both in the field once known as HRD and in public education. (However, it has not been neglected by some religions, which—in some cases, at least—equate the meaning of life with the need by the soul to learn new lessons through various incarnations.) Notably, all competency studies in the field have focused on what WLP practitioners do. It only made sense to me to start looking at what learners do. As I once quipped to a colleague, "Studying workplace training by looking at the trainer's role alone makes about as much sense to me as studying childbirth by focusing on the father's role alone."

I was greeted with surprising enthusiasm by many—but, regrettably, not by all—who stopped to hear my rhyme of the Ancient Mariner.

This book is based on two different, but related, research studies that required over four years of effort. It is the first time that the results of these research studies have appeared in published form. The purpose of those two research studies, described at length in Appendix A, was twofold. The first study investigated workplace learner roles and competencies, and the second study examined worker perceptions of the workplace conditions that encourage or discourage workplace learning. During the course of these studies, hundreds of people were interviewed. The research results, then, are grounded in the reality of actual workplace learners who represent five industry categories and nine levels of the organization's hierarchy (chain of command). Incumbents from widely varied occupational groups—ranging from a Supreme Court Justice to a garbage hauler—participated in this study. The research subjects were interviewed about their most difficult workplace learning challenges, their most common workplace learning challenges, their perceptions about what it takes to be successful in workplace learning in today's volatile workplace, and what their organizations do to encourage or discourage the workplace learning process.

THE AUDIENCE FOR THIS BOOK

The Workplace Learner: How to Align Training Initiatives with Individual Learning Competencies is written for those who wish to encourage and develop individual workplace learning competence and an organizational climate that encourages such competence. It contains information useful to people in many walks of life, since learning (like breathing) is a fundamental human process. Many people, ranging from corporate trainers to human resource executives to chief executive officers, stand to gain by reading this book.

However, many organizations are now employing a chief learning officer (CLO). The CLO's role is to facilitate and encourage learning in today's organizations and to lead the charge to focus attention on better management of workplace learning, knowledge management, and intellectual capital investment. It is the CLO who perhaps stand to gain the most from reading this book, because it is the CLO who should exert leadership to orchestrate and encourage learning for their organization and the individuals in it.

THE ORGANIZATIONAL SCHEME OF THIS BOOK

The book is organized in four major parts. Part One, which lays the foundation for the book, consists of Chapters 1, 2, and 3. Chapter 1 focuses on the past and present. It poses the deceptively simple question, worth pondering, Why is a focus on training not enough any more? The chapter differentiates key terms such as *training* and *learning* by defining them and describing their various categories. The chapter then goes on to list the problems linked to focusing on training alone without regard to learning. It explains why training and learning are sometimes confused, summarizes succinctly what is known about the trainer's role, and briefly reviews the relationships among training, learning, and performance.

Chapter 2 points toward the future. It lists trends affecting organizations, training, and learning that make a single-minded focus on training increasingly inappropriate. The chapter also emphasizes the growing importance of the workplace learner and workplace learning and describes the emergence of a new kind of learner, called the *free agent learner*.

Chapter 3 paints the landscape of workplace learning with a broad brush. It summarizes key theories of learning and explains how they are applied to workplace learning. The chapter also summarizes key points about applying learning theory to training. It then reviews what is known about individual learning styles and learning how to learn. As part of the treatment on learning how to learn, the chapter describes several previous works that have made mention of *learner competency*.

Part Two, which helps build a new awareness and understanding for readers of what is meant by workplace learning competence, consists of Chapters 4, 5, and 6.

Chapter 4, based on the first of the two related research studies I conducted, shows what happens as individuals engage in workplace learning. It emphasizes the importance of the workplace learning process and describes the steps in a model of that process. The chapter also explains how WLP practitioners may use the workplace learning process model.

Chapter 5 builds on the model described in Chapter 4. Like Chapter 4, it is also based on my original research. It defines and focuses on what roles learners play in workplace learning. The chapter then goes on to define the competencies that workplace learners must possess to be efficient and effective workplace learners. Finally, the chapter defines *output* and encourages readers to think through how workplace learning competencies can be demonstrated against the unique backdrop and context of their own corporate cultures.

Chapter 6 explains the implications of the information presented in Chapters 4 and 5, and it thus represents the culmination of Part Two of the book. The chapter addresses two important questions. First, *What are the roles of the WLP practitioner, and what are the implications of the workplace learning-process model for the roles of WLP practitioners?* Second, *What are*

some implications of the workplace learning process model for planning, con-
ducting, and evaluating formal, informal and incidental learning experiences?

Part Three focuses on the organizational setting in which the workplace learning process is carried out. Consisting of Chapters 7, 8, and 9, it
is entitled "Understanding and Building an Organizational Climate Conducive to Learning." The chapters in this part are based on the second research study, related to the first, which focused on the conditions that
organizations establish that encourage or discourage workplace learning.

Chapter 7 examines the organization's role in workplace learning. It
defines the *learning organization* and explains the related notion of *organi-*
zational learning. Finally, the chapter lists and describes the conditions,
discovered through my research, that encourage or discourage workplace
learning. Chapter 8 defines the meaning of the phrase *climate for workplace*
learning and explains how it can be measured and assessed. Chapter 9 is
the culminating chapter of Part Three, and it describes some approaches
that can be used to build an organizational climate that encourages workplace learning.

The final part, Part Four, focuses on the role of the WLP practitioner.
This part consists of Chapters 10 and 11.

Chapter 10 addresses two key questions: (1) Why should the training
department be transformed into a learning department? and (2) What
steps can guide that transformation? The chapter supplies three key reasons to transform a training department into a learning department. Then
the chapter suggests nine steps for visionary leaders to use in transforming
a training department into a learning department.

Chapter 10 also offers advice to WLP practitioners who wish to
transform themselves from traditional "trainers" into "learning facilitators." It defines a *learning facilitator* as someone who helps learners become more efficient and effective in their on-the-job, real-time workplace
learning process. The chapter provides two reasons that trainers should
become learning facilitators. The chapter also encourages trainers to reflect on their role and also to magnify their impact by encouraging supervisors and managers to serve as learning facilitators.

Chapter 11 concludes the body of the book. It offers final thoughts on
using the workplace learning model, workplace learner roles, workplace
learning competencies, and other information presented in this book. The

chapter is organized around the uses of several possible audiences for this book—including mentors and WLP practitioners, supervisors, managers and other leaders, academicians, and workplace learners themselves.

Several appendixes appear at the back of the book. Appendix A summarizes my two research studies that served as the foundation for this book. Appendix B provides my "Behavioral Event Interview Guide to Assess Workplace Learning Competence" so that you can use it to assess learning competence in your own organization. Appendix C provides portions of my transcripts from the hundreds of interviews conducted for the first study, and it is entitled "Learners' Perceptions of Workplace Learning in Their Own Words." Appendix D provides a "Behavioral Event Interview Guide to Assess Workplace Learning Climate" to help you assess the conditions that encourage or discourage workplace learning in your own organizations. Appendix E is a self-assessment instrument to help individuals assess their own learning competence. Finally, Appendix F is entitled "An Assessment Instrument for Others to Assess Individual Workplace Learning Competencies." When paired with Appendix E, it provides the foundation for conducting a full-circle, multirater (360-degree) assessment of individual workplace learning competence.

Acknowledgments

I would like to acknowledge some who have contributed to the making of this book and the research studies on which it is based. I really would like to thank everyone, but their numbers are so great that I admit at the outset that I am sure to forget someone.

First, I would like to thank a small cadre of my current or former doctoral students on the University Park campus of The Pennsylvania State University for helping me conduct literature reviews. They did so without prompting and for no credit other than the satisfaction of their own curiosity. (That is a sign of true workplace learners.) Deserving of special credit are John (Jed) Lindholm, June Wright, and Jo Stern. Jo Stern also, and separately, helped me conduct a literature review about the role of the human brain and brain chemistry in the learning process. In a separate effort, Linda Kricher prepared a paper on what she could find about learner competencies. William Wallick wrote a paper that summarized key contributions of various competency studies to training, human resource development, human performance improvement, and learning technologies. To this group I add the name of Juan Canto—an outstanding student at St. John Fisher College in Rochester, New York, who eagerly volunteered to work with me on a literature review about learning organizations—and Li Yan, who wrote a master's paper to summarize the history, research, and writings about organizational learning.

Second, I would like to thank the people who served as interviewers for the two related research studies on which this book is based. The following people, listed in alphabetical order, deserve thanks and praise for their willingness to be trained to conduct interviews and then to carry out those interviews for the first research study: Mary Abreu, Edward A. Bouquillon, William C. Butler, Teodoro M. Campos, Xiaoli Cao, Shuhong Chen, Chia-yu Chuang, Catherine Civiello, Veronica C. Conway, Susan E.

Cromwell, William G. Curley, Nancy H. Dart, Franklin E. Elliott, Patrick S. English, John E. Fibbi, Melissa Frank-Alston, Ronald A. Garner, Will Hickey, Michael A. Horst, Daryl L. Hunt, Alice Jones, Cheng-Feng Kao, Shaun C. Knight, Kristine Lalley, John E. Lindholm, Lydia M. Lockhart, Cecilia Maldonado, Pai-Hsia Shang Kuan, Patricia E. Shope, David K. Sibley, Jud F. Stauffer, Deborah J. Stern, Allen C. Stines, Dawarit Tanusuphasiri, Sandra M. Vactor, Felipe Vazquez, William Wallick, Mark Watson, Cynthia Williams, Tammy Williams-Clossen, Sakulrad Worapibulchai, June Wright, Shu-Shen Yeh, and Yu Zhanghai.

Third, I would also like to thank the following people, again listed in alphabetical order, who served as interviewers for the second research study on which this book is based: Keith Bailey, Xiaoli Cao, Angela Chen, Pat English, John Fibbi, Mike Horst, Alice Jones, Jed Lindholm, Cecilia Maldonado, Karen Peters, Ron Shafer, Jeff Spearly, Jo Stern, Dawarit Tansuphasiri, Penny Weidner, Cynthia Williams, and Tammy Williams-Clossen.

Fourth, I would like to thank several professional colleagues who took time out of busy schedules to review an early draft manuscript of this book. They are my partners professionally on too many things to list here. They are Patrick Gerity, Ph.D., Robert Prescott, Ph.D., and Joseph Benkowski, Ph.D., my coauthors on other books that have been published or that will eventually be published.

Last but not least, I would like to thank my research assistant Xuejun Qiao for her help in securing copyright permissions for this book. Although this book is not focused on her research interest—that is, executive education and development—her intense motivation to learn makes her an exemplar among workplace learners.

William J. Rothwell
University Park, Pennsylvania
January 2002

PART ONE

INTRODUCTION

Part One, which lays the foundation for the book, consists of Chapters 1, 2, and 3. These chapters:

- Define *training* and *learning*.

- List four key problems that stem from focusing on training.

- Explain why training and learning are sometimes confused.

- Review key competency studies on the trainer's role—and roles associated with that of the trainer.

- Explain relationships among training, learning, and performance.

- List fourteen trends affecting workplace learning.

- Explain why growing importance is attached to the workplace learner and to the workplace learning process.

- Define the free agent learner and explain why free agent learners are important.

- Summarize three key theories of learning.

- Review what is known about individual learning style and learning how to learn.

Chapter 1

WHY IS A FOCUS ON TRAINING NOT ENOUGH ANY MORE?

Give people fish, and you feed them for a day. Teach people how to fish, and you feed them for their lifetimes. *Help them discover how they learn—and help them improve that—and they will figure out creative new ways to fish that will empower them and others forever.*

—An Old Chinese Saying Creatively Retold

How do people learn how to learn? How does your organization encourage or discourage people to learn in ways that contribute to their on-the-job, real-time work performance and productivity? Think about these questions and complete the questionnaire in Exhibit 1-1 as a way to organize your thinking about how to answer these questions.

Read the following vignettes and, on a separate sheet, describe how *your* organization might address the key problem presented in each vignette. If you can offer an effective solution to all the vignettes, then your organization may already be tapping the full power of workplace learning and creating competent workplace learners. Otherwise, your organiza-

---

Exhibit 1-1: A questionnaire about your organization's role in workplace learning.

Directions: Read each item below. Then, in the left column, place a T for True or an F for False for each item. There are no "right" or "wrong" answers in any absolute sense.

IN MY ORGANIZATION, WE:

_____ 1.   Make an effort to help people identify their learning styles.

_____ 2.   Try to determine how much people are motivated to learn at the outset of any training experience.

_____ 3.   Devote as much time during the orientation period to training people on how they can help to orient themselves as on what they need to know as a newcomer starting out in our organization.

_____ 4.   Make it clear to people that it is their responsibility to take initiative for their own workplace learning.

_____ 5.   Pay attention to the ways that the organization encourages or discourages individual workplace learning.

_____ 6.   Place a high priority on encouraging workplace learning that will help to improve individual performance.

_____ 7.   Make an effort to *assess* individual workplace learning competence.

_____ 8.   Make an effort to *build* individual workplace learning competence.

_____ 9.   Pay attention to the efforts that individuals make to improve their own ability to learn.

_____ 10.   Believe there is a clear and indisputable relationship between workplace learning and work performance.

SCORING

Directions: Add up your scores above. For each T, give yourself a 1. For each F, give yourself a 0. Then read the comments opposite your score below:

IF YOU SCORED BETWEEN:	THEN, YOU AND YOUR ORGANIZATION SHOULD:
8 and 10	Be congratulated! You are showing sensitivity to individual workplace learning needs and abilities.
5 and 7	Work to improve how much your organization focuses attention on workplace learning.
4 or Below	Mount an effort to improve the organization's sensitivity to the needs of individuals to learn in the workplace as a means by which to help them improve their work performance.

tion's leaders may have a critical need to rethink how they are building workplace learning competence.

VIGNETTE 1

"We spent a lot of money to train our workers on ways to improve customer service," began manager Martina Smith, "but we have seen no change. We are still getting customer complaints about service. I think this is the training department's fault, really. The problem must be bad training."

VIGNETTE 2

"When I became a supervisor, nobody gave me training. I just don't understand why today's young people expect the company to train them before they do anything. Nobody has time for that. You should be prepared to roll up your sleeves and learn as you go. That's the way I did it," said Freida Fredericks, a supervisor with thirty-five years of experience in the home office of a major insurance company.

VIGNETTE 3

"I have a funny, but true, story to tell," began the accounting professor, speaking to his class. "You know, I went all the way through college without getting any work experience. I finished my Bachelor's degree, Master's degree, and Doctoral degree in accounting. Every problem I ever worked on appeared neatly printed out, with all the facts conveniently provided, in a college textbook. All I had to do was work out the problem.

"But before taking the C.P.A. exam and before I began my teaching career, I went to work for a public accounting firm to gain experience. On my first day, I was taken out into the field to do a company audit. The client ushered me into a dark and dingy back room. Waving at walls of filing cabinets, with paper spilling out of unnumbered and unlabeled drawers, the client said, "Everything you will need to conduct the audit is here. And he walked away."

VIGNETTE 4

The training director looked up from the table at his staff of six corporate trainers. He cleared his throat and began to speak, glancing around the room as he did so. "We have been asked to work on solving the problem of high turnover. You all know the problem: Last year our company had a turnover rate of 150 percent. That means all the staff turned over, and then half of their replacements were also gone by the end of the measurement period."

He waited a moment for the gravity of the problem to sink in. Then he went on. "Our exit interviews give us clues as to what the root causes of the problem might be. When people start to work here, where we have mandatory overtime for a year at a time and where people hired on Friday are asked to start that same night on the graveyard shift, they are never given proper training."

WHAT IS *TRAINING*, AND WHAT IS *LEARNING*?
KEY TERMS DEMYSTIFIED

Each vignette presented above poses a dilemma about learning. Vignette 1 shows that there is a tendency to blame training whenever behavior changes do not occur on the job. Vignette 2 shows that supervisors do not always support the need for training. Vignette 3 emphasizes how important it is to help people, particularly new hires, to learn how to learn on the job. Vignette 4 emphasizes that training can help alleviate the anxiety people feel when they enter a new job or a new organization. After reflecting on each vignette, how well positioned do you feel that your organization is in building competent workplace learners? How well does your organization establish a climate where people are encouraged to learn?

At this point, it might be helpful to begin by providing some definitions. What is *training,* and what is *learning?* What categories of training and learning might exist that could be helpful in understanding how such complex issues might be examined? This section addresses these questions.

Training Defined

Training is a short-term change effort intended to improve individual work performance by equipping people with the knowledge, skills, and attitudes they must possess to be successful in their work.[1] Training should be grounded in the work requirements and expectations of the organization's managers, customers, and other influential stakeholders.

Training cannot solve every employee performance problem. There are essentially two kinds of problems in the world: those that can be solved by training, and those that must be solved by management action. About 10 percent of all problems can be solved by training, since those problems are attributable to an individual's lack of knowledge, skill, or attitude. About 90 percent of all problems must be solved by management action, since those problems require management to change the work environment.[2]

Management action is necessary to solve problems created by the organization's work environment. After all, management controls all aspects of the work environment—including who is chosen to do the work, how they are rewarded for their performance, what work expectations are established for them to meet, what feedback they receive on what they have done, and what tools and equipment they use to do their work. No amount of training will solve a problem caused by lack of supervision, lack of organizational planning, ill-conceived reward systems that reinforce the wrong behaviors or results, or other such problems that stem from the work environment.[3]

Education is often an enabler, a means of helping people prepare for later life. It thus equips people for life learning. A key difference between training and education centers on assumptions about application. Because the unique environment for application is unknown in education, it is necessarily general. In some respects, it can be likened to the headlight beam of an automobile that cuts a broad swath. But training, which equips people to perform, should be grounded in a thorough knowledge about the work that people do and the unique corporate culture in which that work is carried out. It can thus be likened to a laser beam, which is tightly focused on giving people just what they need to be successful to do their work against the backdrop of a unique corporate culture.

Learning Defined

Learning means changing. It occurs when an individual acquires new information, skills, or attitudes. It is inherently an internal process, something that takes place in the brain. Its results can be seen, but the process itself cannot. The *American Heritage Dictionary* defines *learn* as to gain "knowledge, comprehension, or mastery of through experience or study"; "to fix in the mind or memory; memorize; to acquire experience of or an ability or skill in"; or, "to become informed of; find out."[4]

Life learning is the change that people undergo as a direct consequence of learning how to get along in the world. Individuals face unique problems at different stages of their lives, and these problems create central life challenges at each life stage. Often, these central life challenges motivate people to learn and to take decisive action to address their central life challenges. Finding a mate is, for instance, an experience for life learning. So is finding and succeeding in one's first job.

Workplace learning is a subset of life learning. It is the change that people undergo as they prepare to perform their work, as they carry out their work, or as they reflect on their work experience. It includes the knowledge, skills, and attitudes people need to perform their work tasks; what they must know, do, or feel to interact with others to achieve results; and what they come to learn about themselves and their own learning style and learning process. It also includes creative approaches to coming up with new ways to get the work done and delight customers or other stakeholders.

PROBLEMS WITH FOCUSING SOLELY ON TRAINING

Organizations establish training for many reasons. One reason is to structure the learning process. Training helps people whenever they make a change in their work by preparing them for that change. Training is a way of "pushing" information, skills, and attitudes. In contrast, learning is inherently a "pulling" process by which learners draw on their experience to acquire new knowledge, skills, attitudes, values, beliefs, and other factors that influence their ability to perform at the present and in the future. Many problems in organizations stem from focusing on training alone while ignoring individual learning. They are worth discussing.

Problem #1: Training Is Not Always Timely

Decision makers are usually preoccupied with "getting the work out." Sometimes they are so preoccupied with the task at hand that they forget that their workers may require training to learn how to use new equipment, use new technology, or meet unique customer requirements. The result is that training is an afterthought. It is not offered in a timely way at, or just before, the time the new information, skills, or attitudes are necessary for performance. If the organization is expected to structure training, then often it lags behind the changes occurring in a dynamic business environment.

But workplace learning, on the other hand, is coincident with change or even anticipatory to it. As changes are encountered, people must learn to cope with them. For instance, when new software is introduced at work, people can learn how to use it on their own. Hence, learning is a superior strategy to training. Unfortunately, organizations rarely equip people with strategies to improve how they learn effectively. Neither do educational institutions. Rather than building capacity to improve the learning process, organizations—and educational institutions—focus on transferring knowledge. The focus is thus on *what* (knowledge) rather than *how* (the learning process). At a time of increasingly rapid and radical change, such a focus is often out of step with the swiftly changing realities of workplace needs. After all, knowledge dates fast. But the learning process does not. Therefore building learner competence so that learners can master change in real time is a powerful approach—and that is what this book provides guidance to do.

Problem #2: Training Is Not Always the Right Solution

Managers are faced with many problems every day. They must be trained on models of performance analysis so they can distinguish problems that can be solved by training from problems that must be solved by management action. Because so few managers have this kind of knowledge, they sometimes seize on training as a solution to problems that it was never intended to solve.

As a simple example, consider this situation involving dress code. When a new employee in a very conservative financial services company showed up one day wearing a tennis outfit, her manager chose not to talk to her directly. Instead, he asked that a trainer conduct a session on "Wearing Appropriate Clothing to Work." All workers were then told to attend a session that trainers call "sheep dip training" because it is designed as a one-size-fits-all-regardless-of-need experience. Sometimes "sheep dip training" is done to meet legal requirements, but occasionally it is done because managers do not know other ways to solve performance problems.

Training is an expensive way to solve a problem of that kind, which might be more easily and quickly addressed if the manager would just talk to the one inappropriately attired worker.

The point here is that training is not the solution to every problem. Unfortunately, many managers do not know the difference between those problems that training can solve and those problems that require management intervention. Although managers can be trained on that difference and thus become human performance improvement practitioners, it is also possible to empower the workers themselves to diagnose root causes of human problems and select appropriate interventions.[5] When workers are empowered to find and solve workplace performance problems, they usually learn as a direct consequence of that. There is a term for that. Workplace learning that occurs as a serendipitous by-product of work experience is called *incidental learning,* which covers perhaps as much as 90 percent of all workplace learning.

Problem #3: Training Does Not Always Transfer Back to the Job

Research consistently indicates that less than 8 percent of all *off-the-job training*—that is, training conducted away from the work site—actually transfers back to the job to produce changed behavior.[6] What manager would invest one dollar and be rewarded with only eight cents in exchange for it? And, yet, that is exactly what happens when training is used by itself, without subsequent reinforcement, to change employee behavior.

Of course, there are reasons that account for this low return on training investments. One reason is simply short-term memory loss. Individuals forget about 80 percent of what they hear within forty-eight hours. If they sit through a classroom training session—or even participate in on-line training—they forget about 80 percent about two days later. The remaining 12 percent of the loss is attributable to other reasons stemming from the work environment, such as supervisors who do not hold individuals accountable for applying what they learn on the job, coworkers who ridicule new approaches, and the natural reluctance of individuals to apply new knowledge with which they have had no experience.

But the fact remains that off-the-job training does not produce much on-the-job behavior change, let alone realize the benefits stemming from improved work performance. Although on-the-job training may be a better investment, since research shows that it is consistently more likely to be applied,[7] the fact is that training alone is unlikely to produce on-the-job behavioral or performance change.

But a focus on workplace learning is entirely different. If trainers ask, *How can people be trained?* they will get one answer. But a much different answer may result when the question is posed as, *How can people be encouraged to learn a new approach?* Answering the latter question calls for a paradigm shift, a new way of thinking.

Problem #4: Training Is Not Always Sensitive to Individual Differences

American culture has long been sensitive to individual differences. That is what the current emphasis on "appreciating diversity" is all about. However, training designed as a "one-size-fits-all" experience is contrary to the distinctly American preference for individualized products, services, and (arguably) training. Of course, the trick is to find out how to use *mass customization*[8]—that is, find ways to tap into the lower costs of mass production while simultaneously modifying each product or service to meet uniquely individualized needs.

Much research has been conducted on differences in how people learn and in what styles individuals learn best.[9] And yet, when examining many traditional training courses, it is not unusual to find that no effort has been made to tailor how people are trained to differences in individual learning styles or preferences.

WHY ARE TRAINING AND LEARNING SOMETIMES CONFUSED?

Training and learning are often closely associated. Sometimes they are even confused. It is not difficult to see why. Training is what we do to help others learn. Much of it has been traditionally focused on structuring information for others to acquire. It is a means of disseminating the fruits of organizational experience, particularly to newcomers. Training efforts are often highly visible activities.

Though I show how to improve individual learning competence in Chapter 4, learning is what people do for themselves; thus, it is much more difficult to control on an organizational level. It is also much more difficult to assess. And learning is not as easy to see when it takes place individually as when it is part of organized training events.

Not surprisingly, then, some confusion is common between training and learning. If the organization sponsors training, it is assumed that people learned. That is, of course, not always the case.

WHAT DO WE KNOW ABOUT THE TRAINER'S ROLE?

Traditionally, far more attention has been devoted to studying the role played by trainers in organizational settings than to learners. It is not difficult to see why. Organizations routinely hire, promote, or transfer people into trainer roles, and they often work in a training department or a corporate university. According to the American Society for Training and Development, some 300 graduate programs in human resource development (HRD) and related fields exist to prepare individuals for occupational entry into the role of trainer, HRD professional, or workplace learning and performance (WLP) practitioner. Organizations that hire trainers and related practitioners thus have a need to find efficient ways to orient, train, and develop them, and academic institutions require a foundation for curricula on which to build academic programs intended to help people enter or advance in the field.

One result of this preoccupation with the role of trainers and related practitioners, then, is that much research has been done on what roles they should play, what competencies they should demonstrate, and what work outputs they should produce. Over the past thirty years or so, much attention has been devoted to clarifying the roles and competencies necessary for success in the field that has been variously called training and development (T&D), HRD, human performance improvement (HPI), and WLP. The differences among T&D, HRD, and WLP are summarized in Exhibit 1-2, and the differences are greater than merely providing new labels for old ideas.

People in this field have struggled to answer such questions as:

- Who are we?

- What are we doing now?

- What should we be doing?

- What roles are we playing?

- What roles should we be playing?

- How can people be prepared for entry into our field?

- What results equate to successful performance in our field?

- How can those results be measured or evaluated, both financially and nonfinancially?

- What competencies are necessary to achieve desired results?

Until recently, it was also common to base the answers to such questions on the perceptions of only seasoned, veteran practitioners of the field rather than soliciting input from such key stakeholders of their efforts as chief executive officers (CEOs), line managers, or even workers.

It is worthwhile to review what is known about the roles and competencies of T&D, HRD, HPI, and WLP practitioners. What we know about their roles and competencies is essential to understanding the need for similar knowledge about the roles and competencies of workplace learners.

(text continues on page 18)

Exhibit 1-2: Comparison of T&D, HRD, and WLP.

ISSUE	TRAINING AND DEVELOPMENT	HRD	WLP
DEFINITION *What does the term mean?*	Through planned learning interventions, training focuses on identifying and developing key competencies that enable employees to perform their current jobs.	HRD is the integrated use of training and development, organization development, and career development to improve individual, group, and organizational effectiveness (McLagan, 1989, p. 7).	WLP is the integrated use of learning and other interventions for the purpose of improving individual and organizational performance. It uses a systematic process of analyzing and responding to individual, group, and organizational needs. WLP creates positive, progressive change within organizations by balancing human, ethical, technological, and operational considerations.
HUMAN NATURE *What assumptions exist about people?*	People want and need to be instructed about their jobs to be productive.	People should be considered self-actualizing. Learning is key to self-actualization.	People want to learn and develop. People seek to achieve their potential. Learning and performance go hand in hand by helping organizations and employees reach their goals. An organization must strike a balance between its own goals and the goals of individual employees.

GOAL *What is the major goal?*	The major goal is improved knowledge, skills, and attitudes about the job.	The major goal is the integration of training and development, organization development, and career development for the purpose of achieving improved performance through planned learning.	The major goals are: ▪ improving human performance ▪ balancing individual and organizational needs ▪ building knowledge capital within the organization ▪ improving financial return.
NATURE OF LEARNING IN ORGANIZATIONS *What principles drive learning in organizational settings?*	Learning should be focused on the job performed by the individual. The results of training should be immediate, and their relationship to the job should be readily apparent.	Increased skill and knowledge about a particular set of tasks will lead to greater organizational effectiveness. Pairing an individually focused intervention (such as training) with other interventions (such as organization development and career development) best facilitates learning.	1) Learning interventions may—or may not be—appropriate for solving specific performance problems. The appropriate intervention depends on the root causes of the performance problem. 2) Continuous learning is an important organizational strategy because it builds the intellectual capital that is crucial to individual and organizational performance.

(continues)

Exhibit 1-2: (Continued).

ISSUE	TRAINING AND DEVELOPMENT	HRD	WLP
TRAINER-TRAINEE RELATIONSHIP *What is the desirable relationship between the trainer and the trainee?*	The focus of training and development is on making people productive in their jobs. Training seeks that end with a short-term focus; development seeks the same end with a longer term focus. In training and development, the primary emphasis is on isolating the knowledge, skills, and attitudes that are essential to job success and on building individual knowledge, skills, and attitudes in line with those requirements. Consequently, the trainer-trainee relationship is akin to the teacher-student model. The teacher-trainer is responsible for teaching the student-learner what he or she must know, do, or feel to be successful in the job.	HRD adopts an integrated approach to change through planned learning. It integrates the individually focused short-term learning initiative of training with group-focused learning initiatives (organization development) and with longer term learning initiatives (career development) intended to prepare individuals for future work requirements. Since training is not the sole focus of HRD, the relationship between trainer-trainee is more complex and varies with the type of change effort and with the results sought.	WLP does not focus exclusively on learning interventions. However, workers and stakeholders have major responsibility in planning instruction and, more importantly, in focusing on ways to support and encourage learning. Everyone has a role to play in that effort. The full-time WLP practitioner is a resource, enabling agent, and learning specialist who facilitates the process but does not take sole ownership of it. The learner has responsibility for taking initiative to pursue his or her own learning efforts. In WLP, the WLP practitioner and learner are partners in the learning endeavor, and both are seeking improved performance.

MEANS OF MOTIVATING LEARNING *What motivates people to learn?*	Training and development are management responsibilities because it is management's job to ensure that workers can perform their jobs properly. Employees are motivated to learn because they want to be successful in performing their jobs in keeping with management's requirements.	The integration of the following motivates learning: ■ individual motivation to learn the work through training ■ individual motivation to work effectively in groups ■ individual motivation to prepare for future career advancement.	Organizations sponsor learning because they are aware of the competitive importance of intellectual capital; individuals are motivated to learn in response to future career goals or present work needs, problems, or performance targets. Learning is work and performance focused rather than job focused, because jobs may go away but work seldom does.
NATURE OF THE FIELD OF PRACTICE *What is the nature of the field?*	Training and development focus on planned learning events.	HRD focuses on the three-fold purposes of giving individuals the knowledge and skills they need to perform, helping them formulate and realize career goals, and interacting effectively in groups.	WLP focuses on progressive change in the workplace through learning and other performance improvement strategies or interventions.
GOVERNING MODEL *What primary model best provides guidance for the field?*	Instructional systems design (ISD)	Instructional systems design, the action research model, and various career development models.	The HPI process model.

Source: W. Rothwell, E. Sanders, and J. Soper, *ASTD Models for Workplace Learning and Performance.* (Alexandria, Va.: The American Society for Training and Development, 1999), pp. 9–11. Used by permission of the American Society for Training and Development.

Leonard Nadler's Study on Training

Leonard Nadler conducted what has become known as the first occupational study of trainers in 1962.[10] For his doctoral dissertation, Nadler interviewed training directors, their subordinates, and their administrators to determine what training directors did and what know-how was needed to accomplish these tasks.[11] He looked at trainers' work tasks in terms of the expected, the actual, and the ideal. From his study, Nadler concluded that a training director typically carries out such activities as obtaining and controlling a budget; choosing, purchasing, and evaluating training equipment; leading and supervising training staff; determining training needs; planning instruction to help people meet their work requirements; delivering training; evaluating training; and sharing information about what training was planned and what was accomplished.[12] Nadler's study was foundational because it established a tradition of focusing attention on what trainers need to do to help learners in organizational settings.

The U.S. Civil Service Commission Study

In 1973, the U.S. Civil Service Commission (USCSC) conducted another key study of trainers. The study investigated what barriers needed to be surmounted to effective employee development in the federal government.[13] It was an important study because it provided a means by which to conceptualize the trainer's role in the federal government.

Using Nadler's study as a starting point, the USCSC study concluded that trainers must enact such roles as career counselor, consultant, learning specialist, program manager, and training administrator.[14] This study emphasized the role of trainer as a facilitator of the learning process.

The Ontario Society for Training and Development Studies

In March 1976, a subcommittee of the Ontario Society for Training and Development's (OSTD's) Professional Development Committee set out to investigate trainers' core competencies. The study pinpointed such trainer roles as instructor, designer, manager, and consultant.[15]

A more recent study of trainer roles was also authorized by OSTD.

Entitled *Training Competency Architecture*,[16] it describes what trainers do in terms of competencies that are akin to steps in a systematic training process. These steps include:[17]

1. Analyzing performance/training needs

2. Designing training

3. Instructing/facilitating

4. Evaluating training

5. Coaching the application of training

Although these steps are useful for guiding the actions of trainers, they do not focus attention on what learners should do.

Pinto and Walker's 1978 ASTD-Sponsored Research Study

In 1976 ASTD charged the Professional Development Committee with the task of developing a role model for HRD specialists.[18] After two years of brainstorming ideas, the committee elected to use its work as a foundation for conducting a national study of what HRD professionals actually do, rather than publish another theoretically based role model.[19] The study was undertaken to ascertain what competencies were needed for success in T&D.

Pinto and Walker defined a *role* as a set of activities performed by an individual in fulfillment of the expectations imposed by professional standards of behavior or employer position requirements.[20] They defined *competencies* as the specific skills knowledge, abilities, and other attributes, such as values and attitudes, necessary for effective role performance.[21]

This study was important because it collected information from 2,790 practitioners in the United States and other nations. It was thus grounded in the daily reality of the actual work. The study became a foundation for many similar studies that followed as the field evolved.[22] But like studies that came before it and studies that followed, it continued to emphasize what trainers should do rather than the learner's role.

McLagan's 1983 ASTD-Sponsored *Models for Excellence*

In 1981 the Professional Development Committee of ASTD commissioned a Training and Development Competency Study. Eventually entitled *Models for Excellence*,[23] its key purpose was to establish relevant T&D roles, competencies, and outputs. Patricia McLagan, the voluntary study director, worked with a team to discover the competencies that would define performance excellence for training and development professionals.[24]

McLagan's methodology consisted of a series of related research studies that were specially designed to:

1. Determine the domain of the T&D field.

2. Determine the key roles for the T&D field.

3. Identify the major environmental forces expected to affect the field in the near future.

4. Identify the critical outputs which the T&D function is expected to produce.

5. Identify the critical competencies for the T&D field.

6. Develop behavioral anchors for the competencies.

7. Cluster the roles to reflect common competency requirements.[25]

Ultimately, McLagan's *Models for Excellence* defined training and development as a specialty within the human resources field. The study provided a future-oriented perspective to help T&D professionals select, manage, and develop professionals in the field. Additionally, the results of the study defined training and development work in terms of results or outcomes rather than tasks and activities, which was the focus of many other studies.[26] The study identified T&D as one of nine specialty areas in the human resources field that consisted of 15 roles, 32 competencies, and 102 outputs. Although this study was a major contribution to the training field, it did not give equal emphasis to the learning process or to the key role played by learners.

McLagan's 1989 ASTD-Sponsored *Models for HRD Practice*

The third major competency study, called the *Competencies and Standards Study,* was commissioned by ASTD in 1987 to update, and expand upon, the results of the 1983 study. Known today as *Models for HRD Practice,*[27] it differed from the 1983 study in key ways. Specifically, the 1989 study covered the field of HRD rather than just training and development. Of significance was this paradigm shift from focusing on training to a more expansive view of the field. HRD was defined as the *"integrated use of Training and Development, Organization Development, and Career Development to improve individual, group, and organizational effectiveness."*[28] *HRD roles* were defined as roles that individuals in HRD will perform in the future and that encompass the range of responsibilities and functions that define HRD work.[29] The study listed future forces likely to have a significant impact on HRD and HRD professionals, eleven HRD roles, seventy-four HRD outputs, thirty-five HRD competencies, ethical challenges facing HRD professionals, and quality requirements by output.[30]

Although more expansive than the studies preceding it, *Models for HRD Practice* did not treat the learner's role in HRD. But it did begin to show how important the workplace environment can be in encouraging (or discouraging) the change process that planned learning efforts are intended to facilitate.

Rothwell's 1996 *ASTD Models for Human Performance Improvement*

The fourth major ASTD-sponsored competency study was *ASTD Models for Human Performance Improvement,*[31] which was revised and republished later in a second edition.[32] The study followed the tradition of Pinto and Walker,[33] McLagan and McCullough,[34] and McLagan.[35] The study was intended to lay the foundation for future work on HPI.[36] HPI was defined as *"the systematic process of discovering and analyzing important human performance gaps, planning for future improvements in human performance, designing and developing cost-effective and ethically justifiable interventions to close performance gaps, implementing the interventions, and evaluating the financial and nonfinancial results."*[37] Of significance, the study again adopted a more expansive view of the field than earlier works focused on HRD or, before that, training.

This study was important because it suggested that a broader, more systematic view was on the horizon. Directed as much at line managers and employees as at trainers, it emphasized shared responsibility for performance improvement among different stakeholder groups in organizations.

I began the study by preparing an extensive review of literature on relevant competencies. Next, I gathered a panel of experts to select the competencies that they believed were most relevant to the study of human performance improvement. I identified four roles tied to human performance improvement work and identified thirty-eight competencies. As in the studies that preceded it, *Models for Human Performance Improvement* directed its attention to those who seek to improve performance. But it did not emphasize what performers do or how the learners master what they do.

Piskurich and Sander's 1998 *ASTD Models for Learning Technologies*

The fifth major ASTD-sponsored competency study was *ASTD Models for Learning Technologies*.[38] The study specifically examined the modifications in the roles and competencies that HRD professionals are required to make to enable them to manage cutting-edge workplace learning technologies. It also examined the organizational forces potentially affecting the use of technology as applied to learning in the future. It was a modification of the 1989 *Models for HRD Practice* and was focused on the new challenges that HRD professionals must face to design, develop, and deliver e-learning applications.

Rothwell, Sanders, and Soper's 1999 *ASTD Models for Workplace Learning and Performance*

ASTD Models for Workplace Learning and Performance is the most recent ASTD-sponsored competency study of the field.[39] It was not intended to update McLagan's study of HRD. Instead, it had the more ambitious goal of reinventing the HRD field in light of new thinking about HPI.

WLP, the new name for the field once called T&D, HRD, and HPI, was designed to stimulate a shift toward bridging the gap between activity and results. WLP was defined as "*the integrated use of learning and other interventions for the purpose of improving individual and organizational performance. It uses a systematic process of analyzing performance and responding to individual, group, and organizational needs. WLP creates positive, progressive change within organizations by balancing human, ethical, technological, and operational considerations.*"[40] The research questions guiding the study centered on the current and future competencies required for success in WLP as perceived by practitioners, senior practitioners, and line managers. The research methodology used to conduct this study was similar to earlier ASTD-sponsored studies, except that part of this study was conducted and data were collected for the first time on the World Wide Web. Data were collected from twenty-eight nations. The study identified seven workplace learning and performance roles. But it did not identify roles or competencies of the learners. Instead, its attention—like that of its forerunners—was on those who facilitate the learning process.

A Final Point

It is worth emphasizing that in all the time that ASTD has been sponsoring research on the role of practitioners—who have variously been called "trainers," "human resource development professionals," "human performance improvement specialists," and "workplace learning and performance professionals"—nobody has sponsored and carried out research on the roles and competencies of learners. Although the trainer's role is undoubtedly important and will always remain so, the learner's role is of at least equal importance. What the learner does affects the trainer, the HRD practitioner, the HPI practitioner, and the WLP practitioner—and vice versa. These issues are addressed in Chapters 4 to 11.

WHAT ARE THE RELATIONSHIPS AMONG TRAINING, LEARNING, AND PERFORMANCE?

Performance—understood to mean *results* or *outcomes*—does not just happen on its own. It is, instead, the culmination of meaningful efforts. To achieve those efforts, individuals must demonstrate behaviors and take action, whether planned or unplanned, to achieve results. *Learning* is an important means to the end of achieving results, since people continuously improve themselves from what they learn and how they learn. "*Learning*," write Hergenhahn and Olson, "refers to a change in behavior potentiality, and *performance* refers to the translation of this potentiality into behavior."[41] In fact, some recent research suggests that learning curves are themselves appropriate depictions of—and possibly even predictors of—performance improvement.[42] Learning has been shown to play a key role in other elements of organizational performance.[43]

Training, on the one hand, is an organizationally sponsored effort to organize or plan learning. But learning, on the other hand, is the core process itself. Although performance is not limited to what humans do—since machines, capital, and technology may also be regarded from the standpoint of how they contribute to performance—learning is a key feature in what makes organizations competitive, and learning that occurs in real time and on the job is increasingly important.[44] After all, who can dispute that the organization's leaders, themselves guardians of organizational strategy, learn through the process of doing, and do while in the process of learning? The key focus of this book, and the research on which it is based, examines the competencies of workplace learners.

SUMMARY

This chapter defined *training* to mean *a short-term change effort intended to improve individual work performance by equipping people with the knowledge, skills, and attitudes they must possess to be successful in their work.* It defined *learning* to mean *a change that occurs in an individual as he or she acquires new information, skills, or attitudes.* The chapter pointed out several key problems with focusing on training alone without regard to learning:

1. Training is not always timely.

2. Training is not always the right solution.

3. Training does not always transfer back to the job.

4. Training is not always sensitive to individual differences.

The chapter also explained that training and learning are sometimes confused because they are related processes. A focus on training is not always sufficient or appropriate to bring about change. A better approach is to focus on how people learn and give them the means to learn on their own. Only in that way can individuals keep pace with dynamically changing organizational conditions and the explosion of information and knowledge.

This chapter traced the evolution of the traditional trainer's role from T&D through HRD, HPI, and WLP. Essentially, the traditional trainer's role has evolved to encompass any solution to the root cause(s) of human performance problems. The goal is to achieve improved work results more than to rely on specific interventions, such as training. The evolution of the trainer's role can be seen by examining the research conducted on what people in the field should do. Unfortunately, scant attention has been focused on workplace learners. This book is meant to fill that void.

Chapter 2

WHAT THE FUTURE HOLDS IN STORE

It has become commonplace to note that change has become the only constant. That is as true for the field now known as WLP as it is for any other field. The future will not necessarily be like the past or present.

But what will the future hold in store by way of trends that affect organizations, training, and learning? Why is workplace learning an issue of growing importance? What new kind of learner may be emerging to challenge traditional assumptions about the learner's role in the learning process? This chapter addresses these questions. By doing so, it emphasizes the need for new information about workplace learners.

TRENDS AFFECTING ORGANIZATIONS, TRAINING, AND LEARNING

In *ASTD Models for Workplace Learning and Performance*, Sanders, Soper, and I defined a *trend* as "a recurrent phenomenon that takes place over time and gives rise to speculation on the future" and a *trends analysis* as "an examination of these phenomena and speculation on the likely impact they will have in the future."[1] Many studies have been conducted to surface trends and describe their probable impact on organizations, on WLP professionals,[2] on HPI,[3] on human resources,[4] and on similar topics.[5] But few studies have examined the likely impact of such trends on the workplace learning process or on the workplace learner. It is worthwhile to spend a moment to reflect on possible trends that may influence the growing importance of workplace learning.

Trend 1: Partitions Between the Workplace and Other Spheres of Life Are Falling Down

Technology has both the advantage and disadvantage of knocking down communication barriers. E-mails are sent internationally with ease; cellular phones hooked to satellites make everyone reachable, even to a depth of one hundred feet below the ocean or on the surface of the moon, at all times; and wireless technology enables people to communicate anywhere and anytime.

This trend will continue. With the advent of even more advanced technology—such as broadcast-quality videoconferencing from the desktop—human experts will be instantly available on demand. Workplace learning will become divorced from place alone and will be just as likely to occur in an automobile, on the sofa at home, or in an airplane as behind a desk, on a production line, or in front of a computer screen. In many places this has already happened, as definitions about what constitutes the workplace have shifted to include "anywhere and anytime." As a result of this trend, workplace learners will feel free to seek out useful information to guide their performance whenever they need it. By implication, learning will be just as likely to occur during recreation as during purposeful work activity. It must increasingly be available on demand.

Trend 2: Increasingly, Individuals Must Take Charge
of Their Own Learning

The old rubric that "the division between schooling and work life has fallen" will yield to the new rubric that "individuals must increasingly take charge of their own learning rather than leave that responsibility up to others." Schools and training departments will increasingly become as interested in showing people how to become more effective in their learning processes as how to master subject matter and improve performance. The learning process itself will be increasingly recognized as critical to both individual and organizational competitive success. For individuals, it will be critical as a means to keep their knowledge and skills current in the midst of a continuing, and expanding, explosion of knowledge, information, and ideas. For organizations, it will be critical as a means to find ways to harness the benefits of experience—and even find ways to simulate or induce artificial experience (scenarios) that will permit people to anticipate as well as react to change. Current interest in knowledge management and intellectual capital is nothing more than recognition that the fruits of experience, and creativity, are critical to present and future organizational and individual competitiveness.

Trend 3: Instructional Technology Will Encompass All Senses and
Will Be Paired with Expert Systems

Until now, applications of instructional technology have largely been focused on the senses of sight and touch. Learners have viewed computer screens and interacted with keyboards or touch-sensitive screens. Recently, with the advent of improved sound cards, hearing has been gradually added as another dimension.

But, in the future, all senses will be engaged in the workplace learning process, both as a means of engaging learner interest but also in an effort to engage the seven intelligences that relate to learning.[6] Expect enhancements focused on applications intended to expand the use of sight, touch, and hearing and new efforts to engage the senses of taste and smell. Applications of virtual reality, which is gradually becoming more sophisticated, will permit learners to experience a "simulated world" that can engulf all the senses and give learners opportunities to "practice" before they are even required to perform or in real time just before they perform. Already that is used in some places.

Learning applications will also appear in unusual, or at least hitherto unexpected, places. With the advent of the wireless Web, palmtops and personal digital assistants (PDAs), people will have access to learning assistance in real time. Moreover, the ability to miniaturize television screens and embed them in eyeglasses, for instance, will make access to real-time coaching a possibility.

Trend 4: More Workplace Learning Will Occur in Real Time

As partitions fall between workplace learning and other spheres of life, learners will increasingly expect real-time gratification when they recognize the importance of learning something new or experience curiosity. They will be less patient to wait for planned learning events. So-called *teachable moments*,[7] when individuals are primed to learn because they face an immediate problem, will be transformed into *learnable moments* when people seize initiative to act to meet their own learning needs. They will increasingly take proactive steps on their own to "surf the Web," "network with others," or take other proactive steps to learn *what* they want, *with whom* they want, *when* they want, *how* they want, and *where* they want. They will also determine *why* they want to learn.

Advances in instructional technology will only accelerate this trend. As noted above, learners equipped with miniaturized computers in their glasses or sewn into their clothing can access real-time coaching before and during performance, and feedback immediately following performance. Learning will increasingly be recognized as an integral part of doing, and doing will be recognized as an integral part of learning. Also, group learning experience will shift from occasions to disseminate knowledge gained in the past to opportunities for generating new ideas and new information that can lead to breakthroughs in performance improvement.

Trend 5: Workplace Learning Will Assume Broader Definitions

Traditional, and artificial, distinctions between "training" and "working" will vanish in the future, since both will share "learning" as a common

denominator. As a consequence, workplace learning will become synonymous with any effort from which people learn either deliberately (through
a planned means) or accidentally (through unplanned means) as serendipitous by-products of experience. Workplace learning will thus include not
only traditional training efforts but also what people learn from whom
they have worked with, what customers or clients they have served, what
products or services with which they have dealt, under what time lines or
deadlines they have performed, in what geographical regions they have
worked or with what geographically based clients they have dealt, how
they have performed, and why they have worked in the areas in which
they have worked. The challenge will be to channel this learning into useful directions and to track who has demonstrated competencies in these
work-related areas.

Trend 6: Advances in Neurophysiology Will Yield New Insights into the Learning Process

As medical science advances to unlock the secrets of brain physiology,
brain chemistry, and even the role of genetics in learning, expect to see
such knowledge applied to the learning process. Already many advances
have been made to explain how the brain works and how that may affect
learning. Expect more advances as scientists examine the way chemicals
work in the brain and influence the senses and the intellectual faculties.

Trend 7: Individuals Will Increasingly Seek Employers Who Encourage Learning

Employers will increasingly find that workers are looking for more than
competitive wages and favorable working conditions. In a bid to maintain
employability at a time when "career resiliency" is key to an individual's
survival and success and at a time when the "employment contract" between worker and organization is viewed as only a day-to-day or even
minute-to-minute covenant, individuals will act in their own self-interest
and will prefer employers that encourage learning that will enhance future
employment prospects of individuals both inside and outside the organization. Employers who encourage learning—and act to manage it and sup-

port it in ways that contribute to work performance while also enhancing individual workers' marketplace employability—will find themselves at a competitive advantage for attracting and retaining the most talented people who possess the most exciting new ideas. For this reason, then, decision makers will find it necessary as never before to take proactive steps to:

- Create learning organizations.

- Make the learning and developmental objectives of work assignments as important as the performance results to be achieved (so that it is clear "what's in it" for the learner/worker), perhaps through ongoing applications of action learning.

- Establish, maintain, and enhance organizational conditions that support workplace learning through competitive management of training, tuition reimbursement, work assignments, and other means by which to help individuals develop themselves.

Trend 8: Organizations Will Increasingly Seek Individuals Who Are Willing to Take Charge of Their Own Learning

Corporate executives will consider learning and development as important tools for lowering costs and improving performance. Organizations will manage knowledge capital to preserve their intellectual assets.

As a corollary to that, decision makers in organizations will increasingly seek individuals who are willing to take charge of their own learning, be proactive, and cultivate their talents both for the organization's benefit and for their own benefit. Decision makers will have less tolerance for people who must be "mandated" to participate in planned or unplanned learning experiences and will increasingly seek people who are highly motivated—on their own—to seek out and manage their own learning.

Trend 9: WLP Practitioners Will Increasingly Become Facilitators of Learning, and Their Competencies Will Be Dependent on Learner Competencies

Gone are the days when WLP practitioners—or trainers—are to be regarded as corporate schoolmarms. If individuals are to be more self-directed in their learning, then WLP practitioners must increasingly become facilitators and helpers to encourage that. They will assist line managers, teams or work groups, and individuals to assess their own needs, formulate their own measurable objectives, forecast their own desired results, select or create their own instructional media and materials or resources, seek out those resources, and evaluate results. In doing so, WLP practitioners will function more as change facilitators and enabling agents to help others meet their own needs in real time. At the same time, the success of WLP practitioners will increasingly be viewed as a function of how successful individuals are in creating and maintaining cutting-edge skills, achieving measurable results, and coming up with creative ideas to solve real-time work problems.

Trend 10: Organizations Viewed as Learning Organizations Will Become Synonymous with High-Performance Workplaces

In the future, distinctions between high-performance workplaces and learning organizations will become less apparent. High-performance organizations will become synonymous with, and interchangeable with, learning organizations. Performance and learning are converging. Increasingly, an organization's competitiveness (and thus performance) is synonymous with its ability to unleash human potential, harness human creativity, manage knowledge assets, win the talent war for attracting and retaining talent, and preserve and cultivate intellectual capital.

Trend 11: Links Between Learning and Performance Will Become More Apparent, More Measurable, and More Convincing to Traditionalists

Say the word *learning* today, and too many people think of their schooling or their planned training experiences. In the future, however, even traditionalists will not deny that learning occurs more often before and during work, or as a by-product of experience, than it does as an activity that is somehow set apart from work. At the same time, a research base is building that shows correlations between various definitions or aspects of learning and various definitions or aspects of performance.[8]

Trend 12: Work Groups and Teams Will Become One of Many Vehicles by Which to Organize and Direct Learning Experiences

Some years ago, when Cyril Houle explored the reasons why people undertake learning projects,[9] he discovered that some people pursue learning for a social purpose, some people pursue it for the sheer love of knowledge itself, and some people pursue it to meet life-related or work-related goals. Increasingly, as work and learning become integrated and occur in real time, individuals will look to "natural family groups"—such as their work groups or teams—as a natural grounding place and context for learning experiences. As a consequence, approaches such as action learning,[10] or the goal-based scenario,[11] will become increasingly common. These approaches rely on teams or groups as a context for cross-development of individuals and group learning.

Trend 13: Learning Ability, Not Educational Attainment, Will Become a Measure of Success

Educational attainment is not necessarily the same as learning ability. Educational attainment is measured by amount of schooling, not by openness to learning and change, motivation to learn, or facility in the learning process. That distinction will become increasingly apparent. It will give rise to mounting attention to focus on learning ability (or "learning agility") rather than on less appropriate measures such as years of schooling, because a person's success is ultimately tied to her learning ability. The challenge will be to find a way to measure that ability or agility.

Trend 14: Cross-Cultural Differences in Learning Styles Will Be More Widely Explored

Cultural norms influence the workplace learning process as much as those same norms influence work habits, attitudes about authority, attitudes about performance (and how it should be achieved), appropriate rewards for performance, and other key workplace issues. In China, for instance, traditional views of schooling—which favor an "expert" model where the "teacher" is highly respected and is never questioned—are yielding to more Westernized views of "learners as self-teachers." However, cross-cultural differences in learning styles—and in gender communication styles affecting such styles—are likely to be the focus of increasing attention in the future.

Many trends point toward the growing importance of workplace learning. Take a moment to organize your thinking about these trends and how your organization is adapting to them or coping with them. Use the worksheet in Exhibit 2-1 to help you do that.

THE GROWING IMPORTANCE OF THE WORKPLACE LEARNER AND WORKPLACE LEARNING

Workplace learning is becoming key to individual and organizational competitive success. Of course, not all learning contributes to performance, and not all learning occurs in workplace settings. However, it is increasingly clear that, at a time of rapid change and superheated global markets, the razor-thin margin of difference between success and failure is the ability to "outlearn" competitors—that is, the ability of individuals and organizations to marshal their resources to adapt to change and to master (or anticipate) the competencies required by that change.

Why is it important to focus on workplace learning? Why is it important for WLP practitioners to examine what is known about learning how to learn? This section addresses these questions.

The Importance of Focusing on Workplace Learning

Performance does not just happen on its own; rather, it is the result of meaningful efforts. To achieve those efforts, individuals must take action, whether planned or unplanned, to achieve results. Learning is an important means to the end of achieving results, since people continually improve themselves from what they learn and how they learn.

However, a convergence of trends is making the role of the learner more important. Rather than focusing exclusively on the roles, competencies, and outputs essential to success for trainers, HRD professionals, or WLP practitioners, we must balance our attention with an equally impor-

Exhibit 2-1: A worksheet on trends pointing toward the growing importance of workplace learning.

Directions: Many trends point toward the growing importance of workplace learning. Use this worksheet to organize your thinking about these trends and how your organization is coping with them. For each trend listed in the left column below, describe what the trend means to you and your organization in the center column. Then, in the right column below, describe what you believe you and your organization should do to meet the challenges posed by the trend.

THE TREND	WHAT DO YOU THINK THE TREND MEANS TO YOU AND YOUR ORGANIZATION?	WHAT DO YOU BELIEVE YOU AND YOUR ORGANIZATION SHOULD DO TO MEET THE CHALLENGES POSED BY THE TREND?
1 *Trend 1*: Partitions between the workplace and other spheres of life are falling down.		
2 *Trend 2*: Increasingly, individuals must take charge of their own learning.		
3 *Trend 3*: Instructional technology will encompass all senses and will be paired with expert systems.		
4 *Trend 4*: More workplace learning will occur in real time.		
5 *Trend 5*: Workplace learning will assume broader definitions.		
6 *Trend 6*: Advances in neurophysiology will yield new insights into the learning process.		
7 *Trend 7*: Individuals will increasingly seek employers who encourage learning.		

(continues)

Exhibit 2-1: (Continued).

THE TREND	WHAT DO YOU THINK THE TREND MEANS TO YOU AND YOUR ORGANIZATION?	WHAT DO YOU BELIEVE YOU AND YOUR ORGANIZATION SHOULD DO TO MEET THE CHALLENGES POSED BY THE TREND?
8 *Trend 8:* Organizations will increasingly seek individuals who are willing to take charge of their own learning.		
9 *Trend 9:* WLP practitioners will increasingly become facilitators of learning, and their competencies will be dependent on learner competencies.		
10 *Trend 10:* Organizations viewed as learning organizations will become synonymous with high-performance workplaces.		
11 *Trend 11:* Links between learning and performance will become more apparent, more measurable, and more convincing to traditionalists.		
12 *Trend 12:* Work groups and teams will become one of many vehicles by which to organize and direct learning experiences.		
13 *Trend 13:* Learning ability, not educational attainment, will become a measure of success.		
14 *Trend 14:* Cross-cultural differences in learning styles will be more widely explored.		

tant question: *What roles, competencies, and outputs are essential to success for workplace learners in learning experiences?* After all, the success of WLP practitioners depends on roles played by learners themselves and by decision makers who establish the organizational conditions that influence workplace learning. Indeed, the part played by individuals in their own learning is becoming more important as technology enables information to be made available to anyone at any time and at any place. At the same time, increased understanding of learners' roles, competencies, and outputs could contribute to fresh perspectives about the theory and practice of WLP.

The Importance of Examining the Workplace Learner

If leaders are only as effective as the followers they serve, then perhaps it is also true that WLP practitioners are only as effective as the learners they serve. Similarly, if the roles, competencies, and outputs of effective WLP practitioners can be identified, then it should also be true that the roles, competencies, and outputs of effective workplace learners can also be identified. Of course, there is one key difference: WLP practitioners often hold distinctive positions and titles in organizational settings. But workplace learners cut across the boundaries of all job categories and hierarchical levels. Studying the roles, competencies, and outputs of the workplace learner thus calls for an examination of *metacompetence* that, by definition, means competence that cuts across industries, hierarchical levels, occupations, and jobs.[12] Much has been written about adults as learners,[13] of course, and it can be summarized in a few key points (see Exhibit 2-2). However, even those points have been challenged—and particularly open to challenge has been the view that *all* adults tend to become more self-directed as they reach maturity.[14]

THE EMERGENCE OF THE FREE AGENT LEARNER

Self-directed learning. Problem-based learning. Distance learning. The new worker. Although these words and phrases evoke many ideas and feelings, they come together to create something new—free agent learning. Free

Exhibit 2-2: What do we know about adult learning? A summary.

"As adults mature, they prefer self-direction."

"Adults learn better from experience than from listening to others."

"Adults are motivated to learn when they experience a need."

"Adults want to learn only what they can immediately apply."

"When conditions are right, adults seek out and demand learning experiences. More often than not, adults seek out learning experiences to cope with life-changing events."

"Motivation to learn can be increased. If you can stimulate curiosity about the subject matter, demonstrate early on that the learning will be immediately useful, and ensure low risk for learners, you can convert some of the uncaring."

"The learning experience should be problem-centered."

"The learning experience should acknowledge and be relevant to the learner's personal goals for the program."

"Preprogram assessment is important."

"The learning design should promote information integration. To remember and use new information, adults need to be able to integrate it with what they already know."

"Exercises and cases should have fidelity. Adults are not enthusiastic about far-fetched cases and artificial exercises. They prefer activities that are realistic and involving, that stimulate thinking, and that have some (but not too much) challenge."

"Feedback and recognition should be planned."

"Adults tend to take errors personally and to let them affect their self-esteem."

"Curriculum design should, where possible, account for learning-style differences."

"Design in transfer strategies."

"Create a safe and comfortable environment."

"Facilitation is more effective than lecture."

agent learners (FALs) take the initiative to learn on their own. They do not need (or necessarily want) trainers, because they organize and structure their own learning experiences to solve the immediate problems they face. When free agent learners show up on the job, they pose a unique new set of challenges for the WLP professional.[15]

What is an FAL? What are the characteristics that distinguish an FAL from other learners? What have FALs looked like in the past, and what will they look like in the future? What trends shape the future for free agent learning? This section addresses these questions.

What Are Free Agent Learners?

FALs take their own initiative to seek out knowledge, skills, or attitudes to meet their needs without necessarily relying on support, or assistance, from immediate supervisors or institutional providers (such as WLP professionals or educators) and without relying on planned learning experiences organized and scheduled by others. FALs, like their free agent counterparts in the sporting world, will not necessarily stay with any team, organization, or lengthy series of courses just because that is where they started. Just as many of today's workers refuse to permit their careers to rest in the hands of their immediate supervisors, the same workers also refuse to sit passively by and permit their learning experiences to be managed by trainers or WLP professionals. They want to—and do—take charge of their own learning. Their model? The quick and easy access to the huge information available on the World Wide Web. They want information, and learning, immediately accessible to them to solve real-time problems and meet immediate learning needs. However, a key challenge they face is sifting through the immense amount of information that is available to find useful knowledge that can be applied to solving the immediate work and life problems they face.

In short, FALs want immediate solutions to life or work-related problems. They are driven, highly ambitious people who are not attracted to organizationally sponsored learning experiences—such as training courses that are not offered conveniently at times, places, or formats that suit them. Like the customers of online merchandising, FALs want on-demand learning that they can access whenever they want it, however they want it, and wherever they want it.

Perhaps a glimpse of a free agent learner in action will give you a sense of how FALs think and act. If they confront a problem, they seek the fastest means to get a solution. They do not sign up for a training course because that usually takes too long. Instead, they turn immediately to coworkers for answers or else go immediately to the Web. They know how to ask people questions to get the information they need when they need it. They also know how to use search engines on the Web to find practical, useful information. (Of course, really skilled FALs have discovered metasearch engines where they can skim many search engines at once.) They are searching for immediate learning on demand, and their unarticulated assumptions about their learning are comparable to a search engine where they can plug in key words and find resources immediately to satisfy their needs. They have less patience for lengthy learning experiences than their predecessors over long time spans. Instead, they want learning in bite-sized chunks that can be skimmed with the same ease of access as a television sound bite. They will gravitate to the practical more than the theoretical, and they define practical as what helps them find employment or advancement in their careers.

Because they do not feel bound by the rules—and other barriers—limiting attendance at training courses or other experiences sponsored by their organizations, they are not the darlings of traditional trainers, who think courses are the preferred learning methods. Nor do FALs like training that is offered in organized time slots for participants who have been officially nominated to attend training by their immediate supervisors. FALs are a quantum leap beyond the self-directed learners who have commanded the attention of traditional trainers for years. FALs are aggressive learners who want their needs met immediately and are comfortable about seizing the initiative to meet their own needs.

What Are the Characteristics of Free Agent Learners?

FALs have several distinctive characteristics that distinguish them from other learners:

First, they want information on demand, and they also want learning resources just in time to help them. They do not want to wade through lengthy courses, either onsite or online.

Second, they are persistent. They are tenacious enough to wade through useless information on the Web to find want they need. They stick to it. They do not give up. Their approach is to leap with agility from one source to another, just as Web users jump from one Web site to another until they find something useful to them. They learn the same way some television viewers use the remote to flip through channels, skimming (and watching) many programs simultaneously.

Third, they are more highly motivated for their own purposes than most people or most learners. When they have a problem or sense a need, they jump into action. They possess a degree of self-confidence that is lacking in many people.

It goes without saying that they are less impressed by branding than are many learners. They do not care whether the information they desire is offered by Harvard University, Phoenix University, or a private vendor. Speed and usefulness are what they care about most. They do not care whether the information is available from the training department of their company, a Web site, or a book. In fact, they do not care whether they find what they want from a vendor with no credentials. However, they usually start with Web-based resources and go from there. Why is that? One reason is that they can access huge amounts of information in a short time, looking for people, books, or Web sites that will help them solve their pressing problems or meet their immediate needs. The source of information is less important to them than the time. They prize anything that quickly helps them solve their problems and instantly meet their learning needs.

They are also problem-oriented. They usually do not learn for fun, though they may occasionally learn out of curiosity. As they investigate a problem, they will search broadly and then more specifically. As they progress in this investigation, they may look at information just to see how useful it might be to them.

FALs structure their own knowledge and skill acquisition. Although other learners may need instructional designers to chunk information into meaningful segments or sequence it in logical order, ensuring that prerequisites are met before the learner is led on, FALs willingly accept chaotic information. They are willing to piece it together like someone working on a jigsaw puzzle. They may ask other people for help in doing that, but they are usually far along in collecting information by the time they request assistance.

FALs are skilled in using technology. They may start researching a problem on the Web because of its ease of accessibility, but they eventually branch out to find other technologies of use to them. Their mastery of other resources—software, hardware, people, books, training courses, and so forth—may come later.

What Did the Twentieth-Century Free Agent Learner Look Like?

The twentieth-century FAL was a *self-directed learner*, as described by Cyril Houle, Allen Tough, Malcolm Knowles, and other authors of the adult education movement. Such learners willingly take charge of their own learning.

In *The Adult Learner: A Neglected Species*,[16] for instance, Malcolm Knowles provides a classic description of the adult learner. The same characteristics typified the twentieth-century FAL. Such learners need to know why they should learn before they begin. They possess a strong self-concept, value their own experience, and are problem-driven in their approach to learning. They want to learn only those things for which they perceive that they can immediately use.

What Will the Free Agent Learner in the
Twenty-First Century Look Like?

Twenty-first-century FALs are virtual learners. They are a quantum leap beyond the old-style twentieth-century FAL. Such learners want learning on demand. They use technology as a tool to achieve that end. As technology advances, FALs will also advance. They use PDAs, wireless modems, cell phones with Web access, and other technological advances to find immediate answers to daily, even minute-by-minute, problems they confront. They often want practical information but are willing to patiently skim through huge volumes of information to find what they want. Their impatience is with technology: They want faster Web connections, faster modems, faster hardware, and a Web that operates like commercial television with the information search capabilities of the Library of Congress.

The demographics of twenty-first-century FALs will eventually become more diverse than the early adopters of the twentieth century. They will be found in all age groups, all educational levels, and all geographical locations. Men and women will be more equally distributed. FALs will be well represented in all fields.

What Trends Will Shape the Future of Free Agent Learning?

The future of the FAL will be shaped by technology, demographic change, and institutional offerings.

Technology will be a major driver of change for FALs. Like many e-customers, FALs want easier-to-use (and artificially intelligent) search engines, easy-to-use screens, easy-to-access information, easy-to-use help, blended sources of information (human, electronic, print, and so on), and immediate online access to automated and human help. The marriage of multiple technologies—video, Web, and wireless technology—will give rise to learners who want and even demand learning to be accessible at any place, at any time, and in any format.

People are not born as FALs. They become that way. Changing age is probably not a factor in free agent learning.

It is true that younger people in the United States are often more comfortable with using technology than their elders. Whereas the parents of today's children grew up with television, today's youngsters are growing up with the Internet and the Web. About ten years from now, the first cohorts of the so-called baby boom will reach age 65. Many will seek second careers in telecommuting, necessitated by the inadequacies of retirement plans. If anything, then, older people and younger people alike will form a bimodal distribution of FALs who want to learn in real time on the Web. Many will find jobs, and carry them out, online. They will expect learning experiences to match their lifestyles.

How Will Institutional Offerings Affect the
Shape of Free Agent Learning?

FALs find distance education and learning more appealing than traditional classroom courses. One reason is density. Distance education—and specifically e-learning—can be linked to many resources. That is done less often in classroom settings.

Institutional offerings of distance education programs, defined as "a collection of innovative approaches to the delivery of instruction to learners who are remote from their teacher,"[17] continue to experience phenomenal growth. That is driven, in part, by the demands of today's FALs. Pam Dixon estimates that some 5 million to 7 million people currently participate in some form of planned distance learning program.[18] Estimates vary of how many such programs exist, ranging from 93 accredited programs to 700 programs.[19]

How well have these programs been working? According to one source:[20]

> *Preliminary findings from a number of studies have been quite positive: The U.S. Office of Technology Assessment, which is sponsored by the U.S. Congress, has found in several reports that distance learners do as well or better in their courses and on achievement tests than traditional students. Dr. William Souder taught the same graduate-level course simultaneously at two traditional campuses, Georgia Tech and the University of Alabama, and one online school, National Technical University, and found that distance students not only learned more but also gained social skills and a network of student peers.*
>
> *And annual comparisons done by the University of Phoenix have consistently found that distance students perform as well or better in their classes, and interact with the instructor and each other more, than their campus-based peers. There have been similar findings in numerous small, less formal studies.*

It is important to emphasize, however, that FALs use many methods other than distance education or learning. They are, for instance, superb in their ability to network with other people. In fact, anyone who takes aggressive initiative to learn on his own is an FAL, and so the number of FALs more nearly approaches the total of all Internet and Web users than it does the smaller number of distance education participants. Many children are inveterate FALs. (So are many WLP practitioners.)

What will the future hold in store? I predict:

- **Shorter Courses.** Since FALs want learning packaged and delivered on demand, the pressure will be on providers to make experiences short, to the point, and practical.

- **More Personal Contact.** FALs want high touch as well as high tech. Providers will get away from electronic page turners and clunky Web pages. They will become more skilled at finding ways to structure information for easier access and more contact between individuals and groups. That will include a range of approaches— including listservs, newsgroups, and even television integrated with online learning. The aim will be online *interactivity*, already shown to be key to success in e-learning applications.

- **Use of Technological Innovations.** Canny WLP professionals will learn how to distinguish their educational offerings from others. They will build them around problems and solutions or problem-oriented questions and solution-oriented answers rather than linear sequences that start with theory, history, or definitions.

- **Increasing Recognition of FALs and What They Mean for WLP Professionals.** More WLP professionals will become aware of FALs and will take steps to cater to them. Many of the same approaches used to cater to e-customers will probably work for e-learners.

- **More Use of Electronic Performance Support Systems or Low-Tech Counterparts.** Electronic performance support systems (EPSS),[21] which put everything performers need at their fingertips, are particularly appealing as a technological solution for FALs. So are expert systems that document how more experienced performers have solved problems.

Summary

This chapter focused on the future. It identified fourteen key trends affecting organizations, learning, and training. To list them:

- **Trend 1:** Partitions between the workplace and other spheres of life are falling down.

- **Trend 2:** Increasingly, individuals must take charge of their own learning.

- **Trend 3:** Instructional technology will encompass all senses and will be paired with expert systems.

- **Trend 4:** More workplace learning will occur in real time.

- **Trend 5:** Workplace learning will assume broader definitions.

- **Trend 6:** Advances in neurophysiology will yield new insights into the learning process.

- **Trend 7:** Individuals will increasingly seek employers who encourage learning.

- **Trend 8:** Organizations will increasingly seek individuals who are willing to take charge of their own learning.

- **Trend 9:** WLP practitioners will increasingly become facilitators of learning, and their competencies will be dependent on learner competencies.

- **Trend 10:** Organizations viewed as learning organizations will become synonymous with high-performance workplaces.

- **Trend 11:** Links between learning and performance will become more apparent, more measurable, and more convincing to traditionalists.

- **Trend 12:** Work groups and teams will become one of many vehicles by which to organize and direct learning experiences.

- **Trend 13:** Learning ability, not educational attainment, will become a measure of success.

- **Trend 14:** Cross-cultural differences in learning styles will be more widely explored.

The chapter also emphasized the growing importance of focusing on the workplace learning process and the workplace learner. It described the emergence of *free agent learners* (FALs), defined as learners who take their own initiative to seek out knowledge, skills, or attitudes to meet their needs without relying on support, or assistance, from immediate supervisors or institutional providers (such as WLP professionals or educators) and without relying on planned learning experiences organized and scheduled by others. FALs, like their counterparts in the sporting world, are not bound to any team, organization, or lengthy series of courses.

Based on all the topics addressed in this chapter, it is clear that a focus on training is not enough. It is high time that workplace learners should become at least an equal focus of attention.

Chapter 3

WHAT IS KNOWN ABOUT LEARNING?

The single, most important educational gain in America in the last fifteen or twenty years has been the fact that 20, 30 or 40 million Americans have learned how to use a PC. Now isn't it amazing? They didn't go to school to learn that. How did they learn? They learned first from pimply-faced kids in Radio Shacks, who sold the first machines and said: "You push this button over here." Then they brought the machines home and then they played with them and then they said, "Gee," they needed to know more, so they called a guru. Who was a guru? A guru was a neighbor or a co-worker who had bought a machine one week before them. He was now, or she was now, the expert. What happened was, through an informal process of people-to-people learning, an enormous bank of skills was distributed through our society. No school. Schools didn't matter in that process. Virtually none. *That says to me, if we understood people-to-people learning, and distributed intelligence, we could transform and accelerate the learning processes in fabulous ways that have nothing to do with schoolrooms and seats* [emphasis added].

—Alvin Toffler, Interview, *Star Tribune*. Copyright 1996 *Star Tribune*.
Republished with the permission of the *Star Tribune*.

If organizations are to create empowered and competent workplace learners, it is appropriate that decision makers begin by considering what is known about the learning process. That is, of course, an enormous topic. Think of it as a map with an unusual topography. This chapter provides a "big picture" overview of what is known about learning generally.

It thus charts the landscape. The chapter summarizes key theories of learning, explains the implications of learning theory for training, reviews briefly what is known about brain physiology and brain chemistry as they affect the learning process, and summarizes what is known about such diverse topics as learning style and learning how to learn. This chapter thus provides essential background information for an examination of workplace learner competencies and organizational conditions that encourage or discourage the workplace learning process.

SUMMARIZING KEY THEORIES OF LEARNING AND ADULT LEARNING PRINCIPLES

To have a meaningful discussion about workplace learning and the role of the workplace learner, WLP practitioners, chief learning officers, and others must first have some understanding of the learning process itself. That is, of course, an immense topic. If training can be dated from prehistoric times, when one-on-one instruction was used to pass knowledge from one generation to the next,[1] learning in the broadest sense must predate even that. After all, human beings would not exist as a species if evolution, a form of biological learning, had not occurred.

Although many theories have been proposed to explain the learning process,[2] three have emerged as predominant. They are:[3]

1. Behaviorism

2. Cognitivism

3. Constructivism

Each warrants a brief description.

Behaviorism

Three key assumptions govern behaviorism.[4] First, the external environment is key to understanding human behavior, since people are influenced by their environment. This is the notion of *environmentalism*. Second, human behavior lends itself to analysis by examining external events. This is the notion of *objectivism*. Third and finally, the consequences of human actions affect behavior. This is the notion of *reinforcement*. "Reinforcement and the concepts that are developed from reinforcement—stimulus control, chaining, shaping, competing and enhancing repertoires, and interpersonal and intrapersonal behavior," writes Cooper, "are central to behaviorism."[5]

Behaviorism has many implications for WLP practitioners. According to *The ASTD Reference Guide to Workplace Learning and Performance*, practitioners should:[6]

- Reinforce learner behavior 100 percent of the time after the first few responses, but then gradually switch to partial reinforcement.

- Make learning experiences as individualized as possible.

- Avoid punishment. Simply ignore or do not reinforce inappropriate behaviors.

- Keep learners active, since repetition of appropriate responses is generally important to behaviorists.

- Encourage practice.

- Motivate learners by clearly explaining the link between learning and achieving goals.

Cognitivism

Cognitivists concern themselves with insight and understanding, with the individual's ability to make meaning and draw conclusions from the stimuli presented by the external world. Originating in the work of Wolfgang Kohler, the cognitive view can best be understood as centering around the importance of *insight*, an instant flash of recognition.[7] Although a stimulus is important, it is only important to the extent that people perceive it to be.

On the basis of the work of the cognitivists, I advise WLP practitioners to:[8]

- Emphasize learner understanding more than behavioral change.

- Present a step-by-step model of an entire process first and then relate parts to the whole.

- Help learners solve problems, because unsolved problems create uncomfortable ambiguity for learners.

- Structure learning problems so learners perceive the most important features first.

- Emphasize the meaningfulness of the learning event and its importance in achieving desired goals.

- Provide frequent feedback to learners to confirm appropriate responses or correct inappropriate ones.

- Allow learners to establish or participate in establishing instructional goals.

- Encourage creative thought.

Constructivism

In contrast to the behaviorists and the cognitivists, who directed their attention to the world outside the learner, constructivists focus their attention on the world inside the learner.[9] Whereas behaviorists and cognitivists see the external environment as of primary importance in shaping meaning, constructivists believe that "reality is determined by the senses of the knower."[10] Indeed, constructivists see learning as integrally related to problem solving and personal discovery. To learn effectively, individuals need a supportive environment that encourages such problem solving and discovery. In this theory, learner goals are not preestablished—as is often true of training or other instruction based on behaviorist or cognitivist theories; rather, they are negotiated between the individual and others, and learning activities are not sequenced in any preferred way but are organized to make information available to the individual on demand. Technology is thus an enabler for the learner that encourages her to access, store, and retrieve needed information in real time and for immediate applications. Electronic performance support systems, expert systems, hypermedia, and other technologically based ways of manipulating information on demand make technology a servant to individual problem-oriented, discovery-focused learning in real time.

REVIEWING WHAT IS KNOWN ABOUT BRAIN PHYSIOLOGY AND BRAIN CHEMISTRY AS THEY AFFECT LEARNING

Since the 1960s,[11] a virtual explosion of research and writing has been focused around the study of the human brain.[12] The human brain has long fired the imagination of educators and corporate trainers alike. That is particularly apparent in recent years, as many books have been published about possible applications of what is known about the human brain to enhance the teaching and learning process.[13] Educators and trainers have long held out hope that as additional information is acquired about the physiology and chemistry of the human brain they could take advantage of it to make their lives easier by improving the efficiency and effectiveness of the learning process—and perhaps even accelerating it. At the same time, of course, a deeper understanding of the brain would empower individuals to take greater charge of their own learning destinies, fueling the self-improvement movement so apparent through efforts to improve dieting, exercising, vocabulary building, and much more. Of particular interest has been the function of brain anatomy, brain chemistry, and memory. These issues, since they have important implications for workplace learning, are worthy of review. However, in truth it must be said that applications of this new knowledge to effective practices in teaching and learning are still in their infancy. Much remains unknown.

Sperry's research identified two spheres of the brain.[14] The right hemisphere, he believed, controlled emotion and creativity. The left hemisphere controlled logic and rationality. Subsequent research has revealed that brain functioning is really much more complex than that rather simplistic explanation.

It is worthwhile to review, even if only very briefly, what is known for sure about the human brain. It is clear that parts of the human brain do control all the senses. This is important. After all, the brain's physiology does control what people learn, how they learn, what they remember, how long they remember, and how they process and use information. And brain chemistry often mediates, and enhances, the physiological process. What is more, the more that different senses are appealed to during the learning process, the more likely it is that learners will remember what they learned.

Although a complete review of the brain is beyond the scope of this book, what follows below is a list of important points about what we know about the brain:[15]

- The brain's ability to produce new brain cells accounts for the brain's ability to learn and thereby keep itself up-to-date.

- Mind and body work together. Their interrelatedness is just now becoming fully apparent and appreciated. For the brain to be used to best effect, individuals must pay attention to their body—and particularly the blood flow from the heart. The brain is not separate from the body. Instead, mind and body work together to help people be attentive, solve problems, and remember solutions.

- Exercise is essential to keep the brain healthy, and physical movement is linked to the learning process.[16]

- It is worth emphasizing that, for the brain to function most effectively in the learning process, individuals must feel emotionally at peace. Strong emotions—particularly stress—can be harmful to the learning process.[17]

- The sense of sight seems to engage the brain most effectively.

- To be most effective, the brain must be treated to proper sleep, nutrition, and exercise. The brain does not age in the same way that the body does. People can be mentally alert at any age. Only Alzheimer's may affect that adversely late in life. But continued stimulation of the brain keeps people sharp regardless of age, and occasional relaxation is also important.

Although it is difficult to do this topic justice in such a brief format, the above list summarizes the key points you need to be familiar with for the purposes of this book.[18] For more detailed information on the brain, see Ned Hermann's *The Whole Brain Business Book* (New York: McGraw-Hill, 1996).

SUMMARIZING WHAT IS KNOWN ABOUT LEARNING STYLES AND LEARNING HOW TO LEARN

This section reviews several important topics related to learning. The first section defines learning styles and explains why they are important. The second section focuses on what is known about learning how to learn. Related to the second topic is previous work that has made mention of *learner competence*, a key issue related to the purpose of this book.

Learning Styles

"*Learning style*," write Dixon, Adams, and Cullins, "addresses an individual's preference for learning."[19] Learning style has commanded much attention since the 1970s. The reason is that "interest in studying learning style in adults arose out of an awareness of differences in how people learn and a hypothesis that somehow learning outcomes would be better if these differences were planned for in designing instruction."[20] It is clear, after all, that individuals prefer different approaches to the learning process. If learning experiences only could be designed in ways that keyed in to those preferences, learning would be more effective.

Although many instruments have been developed to measure learning style, perhaps best known is Kolb's Learning-Style Inventory (LSI).[21] Kolb's instrument is based on a theoretical framework. After individuals have completed the instrument, their scores are plotted along a grid that identifies the learner as a Diverger, Assimilator, Converger, or Accommodator.

> *Divergers* are concrete/reflective learners. They focus their interest in others, and they prize diverse viewpoints. They tend to be emotional and have an active imagination.
>
> *Convergers* are abstract/active. Relatively unemotional, they apply deductive reasoning. They are particularly good at matching the right solutions to the right problems.
>
> *Accommodators* are concrete/active. They prefer deeds to words. They like risk taking, dealing with people, and intuitive problem solving. They tend to be impatient, wanting immediate results.

Assimilators are abstract/reflective. The opposite of accommodators, assimilators prefer analysis to what they regard as hasty action. Capable of feeling "analysis paralysis," they eschew risk taking, like dealing with things more than with people, and insist on facts rather than intuition in their problem-solving efforts.

Despite the popularity of Kolb's instrument and other writings on learning style, research has yet to bear out that instruction can be effectively tied to individual learning style—or that individuals, once familiar with their learning styles, can take advantage of their knowledge.

Learning How to Learn

Are there competencies that account for success in workplace learning and that, if enhanced, could improve the ability of individuals to learn in those settings? Although these are intriguing questions, literature searches on the Internet conducted around such keywords as *learning competency* or *learning competencies* turn up few references. However, several books refer to these terms.[22]

WLODKOWSKI

In *Enhancing Adult Motivation to Learn*,[23] Wlodkowski included a chapter on building learner competence. Wlodkowski addressed learner competence from two perspectives. First, he examined the desire of adults to achieve competence and their pursuit of learning as a means to that end. Second, he focused on "the personal feelings and beliefs that the process of learning can enhance or decrease in the learners themselves while they are learning."[24] He supported this view with references to scores of other researchers who have concluded that the adult developmental process and adult learning needs are strongly rooted in a quest for competence both as a result of learning and during the learning process.[25] Learning competence is thus equated with individual independence.

Wlodkowski went on to examine different incentives and rewards that can serve as motivators for learning. He equated the long-term process of building competence and self-determination with learning. As he concluded, "When adults see themselves as the locus of causality for their learning they are much more likely to be intrinsically and positively motivated."[26]

Wlodkowski also examined learner responsibility. He observed that "there are more than a few important things that can enhance adult competence" and that these "may be things that the learners know about but [that] we as instructors do not . . . such as creativity or cooperation. In some instances, they may be part of the human experience that learners and instructors share because they have worked and accomplished something together."[27] Wlodkowski supplied the following list of "strengths and assets that learners often possess" that can benefit the learning process:[28]

- Writing skills

- Thinking skills

- Physical skills

- Experience

- Planning skills

- Cooperativeness

- Personal traits

- Creativity

- Verbal skills

- Math skills

- Knowledge base

- Sense of humor

- Organizational skills

- Helpfulness

- Significant actions

- Leadership skills

This list may serve as a useful starting point for pinpointing workplace learner competencies, though Wlodkowski provided no further elaboration on how these competencies were arrived at, how they might be used, or how they could be evaluated other than to note that they might result "from the total human experience of the learning situation."[29] As he envisioned them, then, they are more of a consequence of learning experience than the enablers to help the process.

GORDON

Jack Gordon, who defined learning "as something you are *doing,* rather than as something being done to you by an instructor,"[30] differentiated between enabling skills and learning skills. *Enabling skills* help the learning process. They include problem solving, reading, communication skills, active listening, time management, goal setting, decision making, group dynamics, giving and receiving performance feedback, and teaching skills. Gordon, however, did not further break down learning skills into components. He simply indicated, following Robert Smith,[31] that the problem-solving process equates to learning how to learn. Gordon believed that any enabling skill listed above could also be listed as a learning skill.

Gordon expanded his point by stating that "learning also cannot be synonymous with consciousness, in the sense that our brains have no off-switch and are busy processing 'new' information taken in by our senses every moment of every day. In other words, learning can't be something that everybody's doing all the time. Learning must be something, as opposed to everything. It must be a specific portion of a task."[32] If learning is viewed as an activity or task—"something to be worked at"[33]—then that is a first step toward learning how to learn and toward viewing workplace learning competency as a discrete process rather than as a process that occurs within and across most or all other mental processes.

In reviewing what is known about learning how to learn, Gordon describes *metacognition* as monitoring one's own learning.[34] It is an individual's ability to identify a task goal, select and use appropriate ways to achieve the goals, monitor one's own progress, and make adjustments to strategies in pursuit of the goal as they are needed. Put simply, *metacognition* is one's ability to understand one's own learning process well enough to self-monitor and self-regulate it.[35] Learning how to learn is thus a topic that has commanded growing interest in recent years.[36]

Related to workplace learning is *career resilience*, which refers to an individual's ability to adapt to dynamic circumstances affecting his career and employment—even when those circumstances are discouraging, disruptive, or discontinuous.[37] In the wake of the corporate downsizing and reengineering trend of the 1980s, 1990s, and early 2000s, individuals have found that it is essential for them to be self-reliant and self-directed in their approach to learning, career development, and training.[38] In the wake of organizational upheavals, the new employer-employee covenant means that employers and employees share responsibility for ensuring an individual's continued employability inside and outside the organization.

The topic of maximizing learning is becoming increasingly important. As Gordon writes, "I can see in the next decade [someone starting] a magazine like *Training*, but for the guy on the other side of the chalk. A magazine that covers the skill of learning instead of the skill of training. What a healthy person you'd have sitting there! What a dangerous person!"[39]

HARTLEY

More recently, Darin Hartley suggested that individuals who attempt online learning must possess unique competencies. Although there is no evidence that Hartley's work is based on research, he does emphasize that online learners should be results-oriented, be willing to take initiative, be willing to seek information, demonstrate self-efficacy, demonstrate flexibility, be capable of learning "on the fly," and be goal-driven.[40] These characteristics, he submits, are essential competencies for those learners who want to be successful in using technologically supported instruction. What is interesting about this work is the confirmation that learners are increasingly oriented to on-demand learning—what is referred to in this book as free agent learning.

VAN HORN AND REED-MORRISSON

Barbara H. Van Horn and Laura Reed-Morrisson examined the essential competencies for adult learners. Directing their work for the benefit of adult educators, and particularly of those who specialize in Adult Basic Education (ABE), they undertook a literature-based study. The goal of the study was to provide a foundation for the practice of education in Pennsylvania. In reporting their results, Van Horn and Reed-Morrisson list the adult learner competencies in three levels "mirroring the commonly used designations of basic (Level 1), intermediate (Level 2), and advanced (Level 3) skill achievement."[41] They defined Level 1 as the equivalent of grades 0 to 4, level 2 was associated with the skills of grades 5 to 8, and Level 3 was associated with the skills used from grades 9 on.[42]

Exhibit 3-1 illustrates the adult learner competencies for Level 1 from the Van Horn and Reed-Morrisson study. The learner competencies for all three levels are too lengthy to provide here. But the exhibit does show how learner competencies were presented in the report.

Based on the Van Horn and Reed-Morrisson study, it does not seem to be unreasonable to suppose that there could be a *hierarchy of adult learner competencies*. As Exhibit 3-2 illustrates, the first three levels of adult learner competencies are foundational. These are the competencies reported by the Van Horn and Reed-Morrisson study. They provide the basis for other, more advanced learner competencies essential for success by experienced, educated, incumbent workers engaged in the workplace learning process. My research, then, focused on level 4 as it is depicted in Exhibit 3-2. Essential for individuals to be successful as incumbent workers and as real-time, on-the-job, workplace learners, the competencies needed for workplace learners are described in Part Two of this book.

SUMMARY

This chapter provided a "big picture" overview of what is known about learning generally. In doing so, it presented necessary background information for decision makers who are interested in empowering competent workplace learners to take charge of their own workplace learning process. The chapter summarized key theories of learning and the implications of learning theory for training. It also reviewed, in simple terms, what is known about brain physiology and brain chemistry as they affect the learning process as well as what is known about learning style and learning how to learn. Of particular note, the chapter reviewed what little information exists about learner competence.

The chapters in Part Two are based on the author's original research. They introduce a new model of the workplace learning process. They also describe the roles and competencies of the workplace learner.

Exhibit 3-1: Adult learner skills competencies: level 1 basic.

COMMUNICATION		READING
READING GOAL		On achieving Level 1 reading competencies, the learner will use basic word recognition and comprehension skills and strategies to read simple materials on familiar topics.
1		Use word recognition skills to decode, pronounce, and comprehend the meaning of familiar words and of new words introduced through instruction.
	1.1	Recognize selected words by sight (sight vocabulary).
	1.2	Apply basic symbol/sound correspondences for the letters of the alphabet to pronounce and identify words (phonics skills).
	1.3	Apply basic language patterns (for example, syllables, common affixes) to pronounce and identify words.
	1.4	Use context clues to identify familiar words.
	1.5	Use references (for example, dictionary, glossary) as source of information about unfamiliar words in text.
2		Demonstrate fluency in reading orally from familiar materials.
3		Demonstrate knowledge of principles of alphabetization.
	3.1	Apply knowledge to arrange selected words in alphabetical order.
	3.2	Apply knowledge to locate information listed in alphabetical order (for example, names, and/or businesses in telephone book; words in dictionary).
4		Demonstrate knowledge of vocabulary in selected instructional contexts.
	4.1	Identify and comprehend the meaning of basic functional (that is, life skills), occupational, and content-specific (that is, academic) vocabulary.
	4.2	Use context clues and the meaning of common affixes to select or infer the meaning of unfamiliar words and to distinguish meanings of homographs and words with multiple meanings.
	4.3	Apply vocabulary knowledge to comprehending text on familiar topics such as those introduced through instruction.
5		Read and interpret common signs, symbols, and abbreviations.
	5.1	Identify and interpret basic social and survival signs (for example, classified ads, clothing labels, road signs, and alpha-numeric codes, such as aisle numbers).
	5.2	Identify and interpret common safety codes and symbols.
	5.3	Identify and interpret commonly-used abbreviations (for example, weights, measures, and sizes).
	5.4	Apply knowledge of signs, symbols, and abbreviations to comprehend and perform simple tasks (for example, recipes, prescriptions, public signs, laundering labels).

6		Read and interpret simple documents (that is, tables, schedules, charts, graphs, maps, forms).
	6.1	Locate information in simple documents.
	6.2	Follow directions for completing common documents (for example, forms, schedules).
	6.3	Interpret abbreviations commonly used in documents.
	6.4	Apply knowledge of simple documents to perform basic tasks.
7		Demonstrate literal and inferential comprehension of simply written materials.
	7.1	Identify directly stated main ideas.
	7.2	Identify inferred main ideas.
	7.3	Locate directly stated details (for example, examples, facts, descriptions, reasons) that contribute to understanding the main idea.
	7.4	Paraphrase and summarize (for example, retell, recall, or explain) information in simple texts.
	7.5	Draw conclusions based on details in the text.
	7.6	Identify and interpret basic figurative language (for example, similes, metaphors) and idioms.
8		Apply basic comprehension-monitoring (metacognitive) strategies.
	8.1	Use pre-reading strategies (for example, prediction, questioning, prior knowledge).
	8.2	Use comprehension checking strategies (for example, rereading, self-questioning).

COMMUNICATION		**LISTENING**
LISTENING GOAL		On achieving Level 1 listening competencies, the learner will use basic listening skills to interpret orally presented information on familiar topics.
1		Demonstrate knowledge of basic oral communication conventions.
	1.1	Understand and respond to common nonverbal gestures (for example, eye contact, facial expressions, gestures, and conversational pauses).
	1.2	Listen attentively (for example, demonstrate attentiveness through nonverbal or verbal behaviors).
	1.3	Demonstrate understanding of everyday conversation, stories, and other kinds of oral communication by paraphrasing or retelling.
2		Apply active listening skills to simple verbal messages.
	2.1	Follow simple oral instructions.
	2.2	Order or re-order information to modify a task based on changes in simple oral instructions.
	2.3	Demonstrate understanding of information received through situations in which the speaker is not present (that is, telephone, audiotaped information).
	2.4	Identify the main idea of a verbal message, conversation, and other oral communication.
	2.5	Paraphrase and summarize (for example, retell, recall, or explain) orally presented information.
	2.6	Draw conclusions based on details provided orally.

(continues)

Exhibit 3-1: (Continued).

	2.7	Use intonation, rhythm, and stress to determine speaker's intent.
	2.8	Analyze information (for example, relevance to issue, author's purpose and point of view).
3		Apply basic comprehension-monitoring (metacognitive) strategies.
	3.1	Use comprehension strategies (for example, prediction, questioning, prior knowledge) to prepare for active listening.
	3.2	Seek repetition or ask questions for clarification of orally presented information.

COMMUNICATION	WRITING
GOAL	On achieving Level 1 writing competencies, the learner will communicate information on familiar topics using direct, concise, and clear writing and will complete simple documents accurately and completely.

1		Demonstrate basic knowledge of the alphabet and spelling of familiar words.
	1.1	Identify and write upper and lower case letters of the alphabet from memory.
	1.2	Write basic words that are spelled orally.
	1.3	Spell familiar basic words that are pronounced orally.
	1.4	Approximate spelling of unfamiliar words that are pronounced orally.
2		Apply basic principles of language mechanics in written work.
	2.1	Use basic principles of capitalization (for example, proper nouns, first words in sentences, days of the week, the word "I").
	2.2	Identify and use common punctuation marks (for example, period, comma, apostrophe, question mark, and exclamation point).
	2.3	Recognize and apply standard English usage for common verbs and pronouns.
3		Complete basic writing tasks accurately.
	3.1	Write names and addresses correctly (for example, spacing, spelling, punctuation, capitalization).
	3.2	Write simple lists, notes, and messages legibly and accurately.
	3.3	Fill out basic forms and documents legibly and accurately.
	3.4	Write a variety of complete simple sentences including statements, questions, and commands.
	3.5	Write a basic paragraph including a main idea statement and several (2-3) supporting details.
4		Demonstrate knowledge of basic concepts about writing.
	4.1	Identify and apply basic purposes for writing (that is, communicate information and ideas).
	4.2	Identify basic audiences (for example, friend, employer, school personnel), and identify appropriate writing styles.
	4.3	Identify procedures for producing final document (for example, pre-writing/brainstorming, drafting, revising, reflecting on impact of writing on audience).

COMMUNICATION	SPEAKING
GOAL	On achieving Level 1 speaking competencies, the learner will speak clearly and with basic understanding of standard grammar and syntax to communicate information and ideas on familiar topics.

1	Use questioning strategies effectively to obtain or clarify information.	
	1.1	Ask for basic assistance or information.
	1.2	Ask simple clarification questions (for example, about job tasks and instructions, about errors on bills), or repeat/paraphrase words or phrases for clarification.
2	Use explanatory language and basic persuasive language effective to communicate information.	
	2.1	Explain own or others' actions including reasons and/or simple procedures/processes.
	2.2	Teach others how to perform simple task (for example, explain steps in a process and/or give directions).
	2.3	Accurately report on activity or facts about selected situations (for example, report an emergency, describe own or others' health condition).
	2.4	Communicate information clearly via telephone/voice mail.
	2.5	State a personal opinion clearly and effectively.
3	Participate in basic conversation or discussion.	
	3.1	Use appropriate conversational techniques (for example, interrupting or including other people in a conversation) and behaviors.
	3.2	Respond appropriately to others' requests, criticisms, or praise (for example, respond to supervisor's comments about quality and timeliness of work)
	3.3	Participate in discussion or interview, asking and answering questions and volunteering information as appropriate.
4	Demonstrate knowledge of basic concepts about effective speech.	
	4.1	Identify procedures for preparing a simple oral presentation (for example, identify audience, identify purpose and basic concepts to communicate).
	4.2	Employ appropriate use of language (that is, grammatically correct, audible, clear enunciation) and nonverbal behaviors (for example, eye contact, gestures).
	4.3	Determine audience's understanding of presentation by observing verbal and nonverbal cues.

NUMERACY	
GOAL	On achieving Level 1 numeracy competencies, the learner will apply basic arithmetic functions to solve familiar mathematical problems.

1	Recognize numbers and demonstrate basic computation skills.	
	1.1	Identify, classify, and write numeric symbols as numbers and as words.
	1.2	Count and associate numbers with quantities, including recognizing correct number sequence.

(continues)

Exhibit 3-1: (Continued).

	1.3	Identify basic information needed to solve a simple mathematical problem.
	1.4	Recognize basic mathematical concepts (that is, simple properties, patterns, fractional parts, even-odd, multiples).
2		Compute using whole numbers.
	2.1	Identify place values.
	2.2	Add and subtract whole numbers involving simple borrowing and carrying.
	2.3	Recognize and use basic multiplication and division facts to complete mathematical problems.
	2.4	Multiply and divide whole numbers.
	2.5	Average whole numbers.
	2.6	Identify commonly used key words and determine which operations are required to solve simple word problems.
3		Apply numbers as used with dates, times, and temperature.
	3.1	Interpret meanings of dates, times, and temperature.
	3.2	Calculate solutions to simple problems involving dates, times, and temperature.
	3.3	Interpret typical uses of numbers in documents and in consumer settings (for example, travel and appointment schedules, receipts, etc.)
4		Use coins and currency.
	4.1	Identify names and values of common coins and currency.
	4.2	Recognize symbols for currency, such as ($) and (.).
	4.3	Add and subtract decimal fractions in context of currency.
	4.4	Interpret typical uses of numbers in documents and in consumer settings (for example, price tags, check books, receipts, etc.).
5		Measure.
	5.1	Recognize, use, and measure linear dimensions.
	5.2	Recognize, use, and measure basic geometric shapes and angles.
	5.3	Recognize, use, and measure weight, area, and volume.
	5.4	Select, use, and interpret basic problem-solving tools (for example, calculators, computers, mathematical tables, and instruments such as rulers, scales, gauges, and dials).
	5.5	Calculate solutions to simple problems involving distance, weight, and volume.
	5.6	Interpret typical uses of numbers in documents and in consumer settings (for example, maps, nutritional information, recipes).
6		Estimate.
	6.1	Estimate arithmetic results without a calculator prior to calculations (for example, estimate sales tax or tip on service).

	6.2	Use estimation to check the reasonableness of results.
	6.3	Compare and round whole numbers.
7		Use common mathematical documents.
	7.1	Interpret basic charts, graphs, schedules, tables, and/or diagrams.
	7.2	Construct basic tables, charts, schedules, diagrams, and graphs.
HIGHER ORDER SKILLS		
GOAL		On achieving Level I higher order skills competencies, the learner will apply problem-solving, decision-making and other critical thinking skills to familiar situations or topics.
1		Demonstrate basic problem-solving and decision-making skills.
	1.1	Identify and define simple problems to be solved.
	1.2	Identify and define goals and restraints concerning simple decisions to be made.
	1.3	Identify, locate, and collect basic information needed to resolve problems or make decisions.
	1.4	Identify potential solutions for problems or decisions using collected information.
	1.5	Analyze information (that is, relevance to problem or issue, bias, etc.).
	1.6	Identify potential impact of information on solving problems or making decisions.
	1.7	Evaluate progress, revising solutions or seeking assistance if necessary.
2		Demonstrate basic critical thinking skills.
	2.1	Identify and analyze components of a simple process, procedure, or system.
	2.2	Draw conclusions or make predictions about a simple process, procedure, or system.
	2.3	Evaluate the effectiveness of a simple process, procedure, or system.
EXTENDED LITERACY		
GOAL		On achieving Level 1 extended competencies, the learner will use basic knowledge and skills applied to familiar situations or topics.
1		Locate and use appropriate resources to solve basic problems and make decisions.
	1.1	Identify and access basic sources of information and assistance.
	1.2	Identify and use basic reference materials (for example, indices, dictionaries, technology-based systems, etc.) to locate information.
	1.3	Choose resources consistent with a specific task (for example, reference materials, technologies, individuals or organizations).
	1.4	Identify and use basic test-taking strategies.
2		Demonstrate ability to apply basic interpersonal skills.
	2.1	Negotiate with group to set and achieve goals.

(continues)

Exhibit 3-1: (Continued).

	2.2	Negotiate with group to arrive at mutually acceptable solutions to simple problems to make decisions.
	2.3	Assist others in a group (for example, identify learning needs, use techniques appropriate for group members).
	2.4	Value and respect others regardless of culture (for example, ethnicity, religion, physical attributes, etc.).
3		Demonstrate ability to apply basic organizational and management skills.
	3.1	Identify and prioritize personal and educational goals.
	3.2	Develop and use simple physical system of organization (for example, notebooks, calendars, lists, etc.).
	3.3	Manage time, money, materials, space, and people as ways to organize personal life (for example, roles as family member, worker, citizen).
4		Demonstrate basic understanding of common systems.
	4.1	Identify systems (for example, family, educational, workplace, government, health, religious) commonly encountered and individual's role within each.
	4.2	Describe basic purposes and functioning of common systems.

Source: Barbara Van Horn and Laura Reed-Morrisson, *Adult Learner Skills Competencies: A Framework for Developing Curricula in Adult Contexts and Linking Instruction to Assessment* (University Park, Pa.: The Institute for the Study of Adult Literacy, 1996–97). Federal Grant Contract Number 98-7008. Funder of project: Bureau of Adult Basic and Literacy Education. Used by permission.

Exhibit 3-2: A hierarchy of learner competencies: learning how to learn.

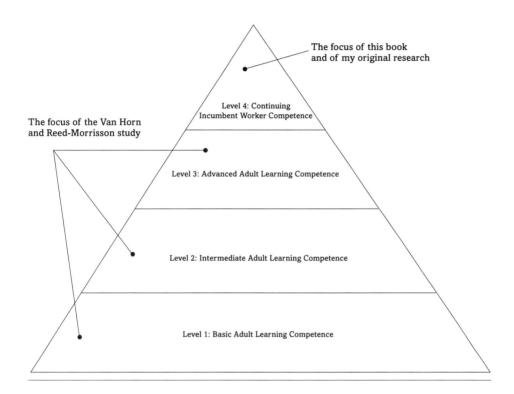

UNDERSTANDING AND BUILDING

INDIVIDUAL LEARNING

COMPETENCE

Part Two, comprising of Chapters 4 through 6, is the heart of the book. This part introduces a way to conceptualize the workplace learning process, describes the roles and competencies of workplace learners, and explains how to use this information to improve workplace learning. This new information is based on the first of two related research studies that serve as the foundation for this book.

More specifically, the chapters in this part:

- Emphasize why it is important to understand the workplace learning process.

- List nine steps in the workplace learning process.

- Explain how workplace learners and WLP practitioners may use the model of the workplace learning process.

- Define *role* and explain why roles are important.

- List and describe four key roles for workplace learners.

- Relate the roles of workplace learners to the workplace learning process.

- Define *competency* and explain why competencies are important.

- List the competencies associated with workplace learning.

- Define *output* and explain why outputs are important.

- Provide a process for identifying workplace learning outputs.

- Describe important implications of the workplace learning process, workplace learning roles, and workplace learning competencies for WLP practitioners.

Chapter 4

What Happens in the Workplace

Learning Process?

This chapter addresses three key questions: (1) Why is it important to understand the workplace learning process? (2) What model can help understand the steps that an individual or group undergoes as the workplace learning process is experienced? (3) How can the model be used by workplace learners and WLP practitioners? The chapter describes each step of the workplace learning process, explaining how people learn in workplace settings, and offers suggestions on applying this knowledge.

Why Is It Important to Understand the
Workplace Learning Process?

Many models have been described to guide the development of training. Perhaps best known is the Instructional Systems Design (ISD) model, introduced and perfected by the U.S. military.[1] Training based on that model has been shown to be rigorous and results oriented. At least forty versions of that model have been introduced. Exhibit 4-1 depicts one version of the model.

This model is immensely useful in guiding the steps of a training project from start to finish. The implication of the model is clear: training should be based on analysis. Preceding the application of the model, trainers should take care to distinguish problems that can be solved by training from those that must be solved by other interventions. Once it is clear that a problem exists that lends itself to a training solution, then several key questions should be considered:[2]

1. What are the learner needs?

2. What kind of people will participate in the training?

3. In what kind of setting will they apply what they learn in the training?

Exhibit 4-1: A model of steps in the ISD process.

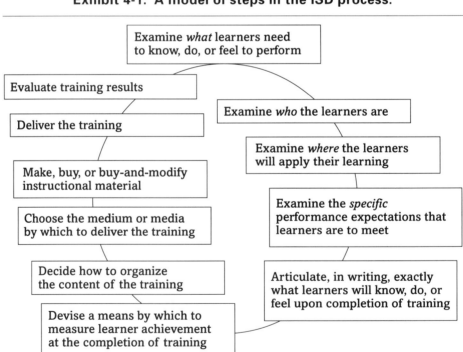

Source: William J. Rothwell and H. C. Kazanas, *Mastering the Instructional Design Process: A Systematic Approach*, 2nd ed. (San Francisco: Jossey-Bass, 1998). This material is used by permission of Jossey-Bass, Inc., a subsidiary of John Wiley & Sons, Inc.

4. Exactly what must they know and do to perform effectively?

5. What should they know, do, or feel following the training?

6. How will their learning outcomes be measured or assessed?

7. How should the training be organized so that they can learn?

8. What approaches or instructional strategies should be used to help them learn?

9. What materials are needed to facilitate the learning process?

10. How should the results of the training be evaluated?

After these questions have been answered, the training can then be tested out and delivered.

The only problem with the ISD model is that it focuses on what trainers should do.[3] It does not clarify what the learner should do. It encourages the wrongheaded notion that learning is the responsibility of the trainer rather than making clear that learning is the responsibility of the learner.

But if trainers, HRD, or WLP practitioners knew how individuals engage in the learning process, they could cast the process from the learner's, rather than the trainer's, standpoint. That could lead to profound changes in the way that learning opportunities are designed. But, as it is, the ISD model implies that entire process rests squarely on the shoulders of trainers. However, as work settings become more dynamic and as individuals become more aggressive in their pursuit of real-time learning to help them meet real-time needs, the ISD model—which will always in some form remain useful to trainers—needs to be paired up with a corresponding model of the workplace learning process. When it is, training can be "pushed" while learning can be "pulled." The result can be a more powerful impact on individuals and groups.

STEPS IN THE WORKPLACE LEARNING PROCESS

How do individuals learn in the workplace? In short, what does the workplace learner *do*?

I set out to answer these questions. The resulting model of the workplace learning process is based, in part, on writings from many sources.[4] However, it has also been field-tested with learners and refined through discussions with practitioners.

In the workplace learning process, the learner:

- Experiences a triggering circumstance.

- Recognizes the importance of learning.

- Experiences curiosity about the issue or circumstance that triggered learning.

- Seeks information.

- Processes the information.

- Converts that information into what is useful to the individual and thereby internalizes it into short-term and/or long-term memory.

- Applies the knowledge in the future.

- Reflects on what was learned and may apply that newly acquired knowledge to new situations.

- May experience a double-loop trigger, which means a stimulus to reflect on the learning process, and evaluation of the learning process.

These steps are shown in Exhibit 4-2. It is important to emphasize that *not all steps in this model occur in every learning situation, nor do all steps necessarily occur in a step-by-step or linear fashion.* It is also important to emphasize that each step listed above can occur on any or all of three domains—that is, cognitive (associated with thinking),[5] affective (associated with feelings, beliefs, and values),[6] or psychomotor (associated with doing).[7] The domains are summarized in Exhibit 4-3.

Each domain shown in the exhibit was originally intended to help instructors by classifying the type of instructional objectives that they were trying to achieve. But these domains serve another purpose. In effect, they create categories for human learning. Think of each domain as represent-

Exhibit 4-2: The workplace learning process.

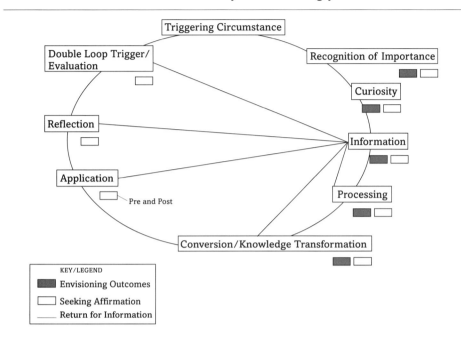

ing an aspect of *what* people can learn. These can be useful to learners as well as trainers because they suggest what aspect of learning an individual may focus attention on during the learning process. Each step of the workplace learning process is described in more detail in the sections below.

Step 1: Experiencing a Triggering Circumstance

A *triggering circumstance* is anything that prompts people to notice something. Think of it as a *stimulus*, that which creates conditions in an individual that support learning. (See Exhibit 4-4 to read about what one workplace learner had to say about triggering circumstances.) The stimulus may be evoked by external events, people, or situations. Alternatively, it may be evoked by the memory of past events, people, or situations. When encountering a triggering circumstance, workplace learners say to themselves, "What is this?"

Exhibit 4-3: The psychomotor, cognitive, and affective domains.

	THE COGNITIVE DOMAIN	THE AFFECTIVE DOMAIN	THE PSYCHOMOTOR DOMAIN
Most Complex	Evaluation *Definition: Behaviors associated with judging the value of ideas*		Nondiscursive Communication *Definition: Behavior associated with the ability to use the body to express emotion*
	Synthesis *Definition: Behavior associated with assembling a whole from parts*	Characterization by a Value or Value Complex *Definition: Behaviors that are linked to beliefs strong enough to dominate an individual's total life philosophy*	Skilled Movements *Definition: Behavior associated with advanced, learned movements—such as ability to perform surgery.*
	Analysis *Definition: Behavior associated with breaking down material into parts and recognizing the way they are organized*	Organization *Definition: Behavior linked to the development of a value system*	Physical Abilities *Definition: Behavior associated with qualities that must be improved for further psychomotor development.*
	Application *Definition: Behavior associated with using what has been learned*	Valuing *Definition: Behavior linked to internalizing preferences*	Perception *Definition: Movements in response to stimuli*
	Comprehension *Definition: Behavior associated with understanding messages*	Responding *Definition: Behavior associated with participation*	Fundamental Movements *Definition: Basic movement, such as walking*
Least Complex	Knowledge *Definition: Behavior associated with remembering*	Receiving *Definition: Behavior linked to paying attention*	Reflexes *Definition: Involuntary movement, such as breathing*
	Source: Bloom, B. (1956). *Taxonomy of educational objectives: The classification of educational goals: Cognitive domain.* New York: David McKay.	Source: Krathwohl, D., Bloom, B., and Masia, B. (1964). *Taxonomy of educational objectives: The classification of educational goals: Affective domain.* New York: David McKay.	Source: Harrow, A. (1972). *A taxonomy of the psychomotor domain: A guide for developing behavioral objectives.* New York: David McKay.

Source: Vincent Miller, *The Guidebook for International Trainers in Business and Industry* (New York: Van Nostrand Reinhold, 1979). Used by permission of the publisher.

Exhibit 4-4: Triggering circumstances in the words of a workplace learner.

A president and general manager of a hotel described in my study what is necessary to be "triggered" to learn: "You have to be open to the aspects of competition and to new trends breaking in the industry. Be a curious observer so that always you can create a product people want at a price they want. If you are a manager, you should create a nonthreatening work environment so that people feel achievement from what they learn. To be effective learners, people should be attentive and interested and willing to trust others and be open to new ideas and new ways of doing things. They should be willing to take action to blast through the hierarchy and keep an aggressive, questioning mind both in researching industry trends and in observing what is gaining in the hotel industry in the USA. . . ."

Source: The direct quotation above is taken from an interview respondent in William J. Rothwell, "Models for the Workplace Learner." Unpublished research report, Copyright 2000 by William J. Rothwell, Ph.D. All rights reserved.

Typical triggering circumstances include:

- Work problems

- Personal crises

- Organizational crises

- Perceived opportunities for improvement

Other possible triggering circumstances have been identified in *The Teaching Firm* and by the Center for Creative Leadership.[8] Many examples of triggering circumstances are listed in Exhibit 4-5.

Triggering circumstances have much to do with answering the question, "What prompts people to learn in the workplace?" Cyril O. Houle found in a classic research study of twenty-two people that individuals initiate learning for three primary reasons. Although no individual represents an ideal type of learner and no two people respond to the same stimulus in exactly the same way, individuals can be categorized into three primary types:[9]

1. The *goal-oriented*, who establish their own reasons for learning and seek that goal

2. The *activity-oriented*, who enjoy participating in planned learning activities such as courses

3. The *learning-oriented*, who pursue knowledge for its sake for the sheer love of learning

---

Exhibit 4-5: Examples of triggering circumstances.

- Feel a need to learn more about a problem, issue, or opportunity and conduct individualized needs assessment.

- Hear a complaint from a customer.

- Teach a class.

- Try to perform a task and fail.

- Try to perform a task and do it only moderately well.

- Hear questions posed by others.

- Watch someone else struggle with an activity, issue, or problem.

- Make sense out of data.

- Experience challenges stemming from life stages (such as adolescence, early adulthood, midlife crisis).

- Experience challenges stemming from life events (such as birth of child, death of parents).

- Grapple with barriers to learning (such as lack of time, money).

- Experience challenges stemming from the job (as a whole) or from specific work tasks (building, tearing down, trouble-shooting, repairing, evaluating).

- Experience challenges stemming from other people in the workplace (customers, supervisor, coworkers).

- Receive feedback from other people about oneself or performance of self.

- Experience a personal or professional crisis (divorce, job loss, employer bankruptcy).

- Establish a goal.

- Create a vision.

- Notice an opportunity for improvement.

- Feel a need to be with or interact with other people.

- Feel a need to pursue knowledge for its own sake.

- Watch others struggle with a challenge.

- Read about problems experienced by others.

- Examine how others feel about an event or situation.

- Consider an issue.

- Note issues affecting organizational strategy.

- Recognize deficiency in a standard operating procedure.

- React to existing changes in the external environment.

- Anticipate expected changes in the external environment.

- Consider changing job requirements.

- Find oneself in a new setting.

- Find oneself with new people or with new responsibilities.

- Counsel other people in crisis.

These learner categories essentially identify needs or desires that prompt people to learn.

As a simple example, think about a time when you were prompted to learn something new in the workplace. Perhaps you encountered a new software application with which you were unfamiliar. Or perhaps you were assigned a work project that required you to acquire new information. These are examples of triggering circumstances. Use the worksheet in Exhibit 4-6 to help you organize your thinking about occasions when people might be triggered to learn.

WLP professionals can use this theory by giving learners an activity or a difficult situation at the opening of a training or other planned learning experience to trigger learning.

**Exhibit 4-6: A worksheet to organize your thinking
about triggering circumstances.**

Directions: Use this worksheet to help you organize your thinking about triggering circumstances, the first step in the workplace learning process. Answer the questions appearing
below. There are no "right" or "wrong" answers in any absolute sense, though some answers
might be more useful or insightful than others.

QUESTIONS

1	Under what conditions in your organization might individuals be "triggered" to learn in real time on the job? What major work challenges face people? How are they responding now?
2	What triggering circumstances have encouraged people to learn on their own in your organization in the past? If you do not know, who might you ask to find out?
3	How can your organization best create triggering circumstances to encourage learning in the future?

Step 2: Recognizing the Importance of Learning

Individuals are continuously bombarded with stimuli from their environment. But they act only when they recognize that there is some reason to
do so. (See Exhibit 4-7 to read about what one workplace learner had to
say about recognizing the importance of learning.) Consequently, *recognizing the importance of learning* is the manifestation of a "felt need," a sense
that there is "something in it for the learner" to attack a learning problem
or seize a learning opportunity. This step, then, is linked to arousal and
motivation and a sense that a reward, tangible or intangible, will result
from taking action to learn. It is in this step where "attitude toward learning" becomes critical. Without it, the workplace learner progresses no far-
ther and simply ceases action.[10]

Exhibit 4-7: Recognizing the importance of learning in the words of a workplace learner.

A church missionary from my study explained what it takes to be effective as a workplace learner and in doing so he described succinctly what is involved in recognizing the importance of learning: "*Desire.* Because if you want a thing bad enough to go out and fight for it, to work day and night for it, to give up your sleep and your time for it. If only the desire of it makes your arm strong enough never to tire from it, if life seems all empty and useless without it, and all that you dream and you scheme about is for it gladly, you will sweat for it, plan for it, pray for all your strength for it. If you'll simply go after the thing that you want with all your capacity, strength, faith, hope and confidence. If neither poverty nor cold, [*nor lack of*] nourishment, nor sickness of your body or brain can turn you away from the aim that you want. If doggedly and grimly you bring your best to it, you'll get it."

Source: The direct quotation above is taken from an interview respondent in William J. Rothwell, "Models for the Workplace Learner." Unpublished research report. Copyright 2000 by William J. Rothwell, Ph.D. All rights reserved.

Workplace learners experience this step in the workplace learning process when they:

- Think about career goals in the context of a problem, issue, or opportunity.

- Listen to other people describing similar problems (which tends to reinforce and affirm to the individual that such an issue is important).

- Identify how many people are involved (which also tends to reinforce importance).

- Manage time (which, when a problem or issue tends to affect time, can emphasize to the individual how important it is). WLP professionals may encourage this by giving activities with tight deadlines.

Of course, learners may recognize importance in other ways, and some are summarized in Exhibit 4-8. Use the worksheet in Exhibit 4-9 to help you organize your thinking about occasions when people might recognize something in the workplace as worthwhile to learn about.

As a simple example, think about a time when you realized that you had just heard something of value to you in solving a current problem you

---

Exhibit 4-8: Recognizing the importance of learning.

- Think about career goals in the context of the problem, issue, or opportunity.

- Listen to other people describing similar problems.

- Identify how many people are involved.

- Present a list of work tasks in descending order of importance to work success.

- Manage time.

- Ask questions to clarify the importance of an issue or problem.

- Review similar situations or occasions from the past.

- Visualize what will happen if the problem is not solved or the issue is not addressed.

- Examine what is best for the most people.

- Examine what is best for key stakeholders.

- Prioritize an activity within existing time frames and resources.

- Compare what is happening in a situation with what should be happening based on organizational policy or procedure.

- Establish and clarify goals.

- Figure out new requirements for a job.

- Find oneself in a leadership role.

- Experience a trigger from instinct, intuition, imagination, or social networking.

- Recognize importance by watching others and wanting to imitate what they do.

- Identify how many people are involved.

- Calculate what will be lost by not learning or not adapting.

- Estimate the severity of the problem or issue or estimate the value of the opportunity.

- Connect more than one related issue.

- Connect more than one unrelated issue.

---

face. Perhaps you were looking for a job and overheard someone talking about various Web sites that list job opportunities and resumes. That would be an example of recognizing the importance of learning, and in this situation the focus would be on the importance of online job searching.

Step 3: Experiencing Curiosity About the Issue

Issues, problems, or opportunities may be recognized as important. But they will not stimulate an individual to learn unless they also excite curiosity. (See Exhibit 4-10 to read about what one workplace learner had to say about experiencing curiosity.) *Curiosity* is the feeling of a need for more information, a desire to pursue that information in quest of a solution or a confirmation of the importance of an opportunity. *Experiencing curiosity about the issue* is thus a third step in the workplace learning process model.

Organizations can spark curiosity about an issue by having learners:

- Read in-house materials.

- List or identify sources of information or problems that need solutions.

- Develop strategies for resolving workplace conflicts.

- Look for the experience of other people.

- Interact with coworkers.

Any or all of these events may further pique learners' curiosity, prompting them to seek more information about the issue of interest to them. See Exhibit 4-11 for more examples of how to pique curiosity. Use

---

Exhibit 4-9: A worksheet to organize your thinking about recognizing the importance of learning.

Directions: Use this worksheet to help you organize your thinking about recognizing the importance of learning, the second step in the workplace learning process. Answer the questions
appearing below. There are no "right" or "wrong" answers in any absolute sense, though some
answers might be more useful or insightful than others.

QUESTIONS

1	How much are people in your organization thinking about career goals in the context of a problem, issue, or opportunity? Ask some people to find out, and then record the notes in the space below.
2	How do people in your organization recognize the importance of learning, particularly in real-time, on-the-job situations?
3	How can your organization encourage the recognition of what is important to learn in the future?

the worksheet in Exhibit 4-12 to help you organize your thinking about occasions when people might experience curiosity.

As an example, imagine that you were about to take a trip abroad on business. You read an airline magazine that tells you that you can purchase CD-ROMs that will help you learn a foreign language—and that will even permit you to practice your pronunciation. If that situation piqued your curiosity, it would exemplify the step labeled "experiencing curiosity about the issue."

Step 4: Seeking Information

Seeking information is the step in the workplace learning process model in which learners undertake an active search for sources of information that may help them solve the problem, find out more about the situation, or

---

Exhibit 4-10: Experiencing curiosity in the words of a workplace learner.

The vice president of sales of a toy company in my study described what is meant by experiencing curiosity: "First, regardless of your experience, don't have a closed mind to new ideas. You can always learn something new from a fresh or different perspective. Don't be shortsighted and react impulsively, but take the time to analyze a situation and look at it from your perspective and the other side. Draw from all resources within your organization. Understand others' strengths and liabilities. Encourage subordinates to take responsibility and make decisions so they can learn and grow. Don't think you have all the answers. Working in toy sales, I am in a constantly changing environment and need to keep abreast of retailers' financial conditions, mergers and acquisitions, buyer changes, competition, product knock-offs, rates of sale, fashion and entertainment trends. I gather information from my rep network and/or buyers on a regular basis. One might consider it gossip from the industry grapevine. 'Did you hear ABC Company is introducing product x,' but it is the latest information in the business. Through store visits and reading trade publications, I'm also exposed to what is new in the industry. This information is then used to direct the company's product development process and make appropriate sales recommendations to buyers."

Source: The direct quotation above is taken from an interview respondent in William J. Rothwell, "Models for the Workplace Learner." Unpublished research report. Copyright 2000 by William J. Rothwell, Ph.D. All rights reserved.

---

affirm that an opportunity exists. Workplace learners who undertake this search have engaged in a *learning project*, defined as a definable effort to discover new information of value about a problem, goal, issue, or vision. Theorist Allen Tough found that adults undertake, on average, about one or two major learning projects each year and that some individuals pursue as many as fifteen to twenty. "It is common," Tough wrote, "for a man or woman to spend 700 hours a year at learning projects."[11] Tough discovered that "about 70 percent of all learning projects are planned by the learner himself [or herself], who seeks help and subject matter from a variety of acquaintances, experts, and printed resources."[12] Learners, Tough went on to note, tend to pursue their learning in a project-oriented approach. Tough defined such projects as "*episodes*, adding up to at least seven hours. In each episode more than half of the person's total motivation is to gain and retain certain fairly clear knowledge and skills, or to produce some other lasting change in himself [*or herself*]."[13]

Many approaches may be used by learners to seek information. Planned learning experiences—such as structured on-the-job or planned off-the-job training programs—actually comprise a relatively small percentage of such information-gathering approaches. More commonly, learners in pursuit of knowledge will:

Exhibit 4-11: Experiencing curiosity.

- Read in-house materials.

- List sources of information or expertise.

- Develop strategies for resolution of workplace conflicts.

- Look for other people's experience.

- Interact with coworkers.

- Formulate questions to be answered about an issue or problem.

- Apply creative thinking by combining two unlike issues.

- Research existing sources of information.

- Find out what stakeholders think and feel about the issue or problem.

- Collect data/information about the issue or problem.

- Ask others for assistance and background on an issue, problem, or opportunity.

- Develop a laundry list of possible solutions to a problem.

- Develop a laundry list of possible ways to study a problem, issue, or opportunity.

- Search for information about how exemplars perform the work or task.

- Feel a sense of wonder about the issue, problem, or opportunity.

- See, hear, touch, taste, or smell the need to learn.

- Identify a sense of "what's in it for me" to learn.

- Experience a sense that it is worthwhile to learn and is of benefit to learn.

**Exhibit 4-12: A worksheet to organize your thinking about
experiencing curiosity about an issue.**

**Directions: Use this worksheet to help you organize your thinking about experiencing curiosity
about an issue, the third step in the workplace learning process. Answer the questions appearing below. There are no "right" or "wrong" answers in any absolute sense, though some answers might be more useful or insightful than others.**

QUESTIONS

1	Workplace learners may experience curiosity about an issue whenever they encounter some reference to it while they read in-house materials, list or identify sources of information, develop strategies for resolving workplace conflicts, look for the experience of other people, or interact with coworkers. Any or all of these events may further pique learners' curiosity, prompting them to seek more information about the issue of interest to them. Which materials does your organization use to spark curiosity?
2	What prompts curiosity among people to learn more about an issue in your organization? Ask some people to find out.
3	Which materials and methods can your organization start using to spark curiosity?

- Ask other people—particularly their coworkers.

- Watch others.

- Listen to what others say.

- Read available information pertaining to the topic.

- Experiment with a new approach on their own ("play").

Learners thus seem to prize immediate gratification. They typically want quick and useful answers to their questions, and they want information that is tailor-made as closely as possible to the conditions they face in solving the problem or pursuing an opportunity for improvement. When searching for a solution to a problem, they have little patience for wading through unnecessary information or vague, theoretical interpretations.

Other specific events or activities that workplace learners may use in this step of the workplace learning process are listed in Exhibit 4-13. Use the worksheet in Exhibit 4-14 to help you organize your thinking about ways of seeking information.

Suppose that you are handed a new assignment by your immediate supervisor to implement an enterprise resource program (ERP) in your organization. If you began skimming the Web for information and asking other people what they knew about ERPs, you would be engaging in an example of this step.

Step 5: Processing Information

Processing information refers to the steps taken by workplace learners to classify and organize the information they have gathered. This step can take place both concurrently with information-gathering and following information-gathering efforts. It is an individual's process of beginning to internalize and make sense of information. (See Exhibit 4-15 to read about what one workplace learner had to say about processing information.)

During processing, the workplace learner may ask other people how they have processed the same or similar information and what sense they have made of it. Processing may occur on one or more than one level. These are mental processes representing levels in the cognitive, affective, and psychomotor domains (see Exhibit 4-3). Some key events or activities linked to this step are shown in Exhibit 4-16. Use the worksheet in Exhibit 4-17 to help you organize your thinking about ways of processing information.

Imagine that you have been assigned to investigate the use of a new technology for your organization. You would undoubtedly have to search for information about it. Once you had done so, you would organize that information. In that situation, you would be demonstrating the step in the workplace learning process of processing information.

Exhibit 4-13: Seeking information.

- Study models of successful programs.

- Develop a list of tasks for possible actions.

- Check, download, and access e-mail.

- Talk to other people.

- Read text and articles.

- Scan the environment of the organization.

- Scan the environment of the occupation.

- Scan the environment of the industry.

- Search the topic or issue on the Internet or on the World Wide Web.

- Attend training sponsored by the organization.

- Read a book.

- Watch a video.

- Question others.

- Listen to others.

- Watch others.

- Develop a list of tasks in an activity.

- Visit locations where the issue or problem is relevant.

- Scan the environment.

- Generate surveys.

- Collect information about the issue or problem.

(continues)

Exhibit 4-13: (Continued).

- Find and review literature/written material about the issue/problem.

- Contact other workers.

- Envision desired outcomes.

- Assemble a broad array of opinions on the issue, problem, or opportunity.

- Study successful solutions in other settings (formal or informal benchmarking).

- Check records.

- Explore media-based material for relevant information.

- Experience the problem, issue, or opportunity through firsthand experience that is not planned (learning is a by-product).

- Attend meetings or conferences to seek information on an issue or problem.

- Participate in formal training.

- Hear something that another person did not intend to say or did not mean.

- Attend internal or external workshops.

- Participate in on-the-job training.

- Make presentations.

- Participate in panel discussions (live or on-line colloquy).

- Attend conferences.

- Attend teleconferences.

- Attend videoconferences.

- Participate in credit college courses.

- Use multimedia instruction.

- Participate in simulations, case studies, or games.

- Use self-pace tutorials (print or multimedia).

- Read newsletters.

- Read listservs.

- Participate in rotation programs.

- "Shadow" exemplary performers.

- Interview exemplary performers to find out what they do, how they do it, and what resources they use.

- Serve on crossfunctional task forces.

- Participate in on-the-spot huddling sessions on a specific problem or issue in the work setting or close to the work setting.

- Participate in job exchanges with other organizations.

- Participate in outside-the-organization events (such as charity drives, church groups).

- Participate in professional associations.

Step 6: Converting Information

Converting information completes the learner's process of internalizing what was learned. During this step in the workplace learning process model, workplace learners draw conclusions about the relative importance of the information they have gathered, draw conclusions about what that information means, hypothesize how that information may be applied, and store what they consider to be essential information in short-term and long-term memory. Some key events or activities linked to this step in the workplace learning process model are listed in Exhibit 4-18. Use the worksheet in Exhibit 4-19 to help you organize your thinking about ways of converting information.

Suppose you participated in a benchmarking experience in your or-

---

Exhibit 4-14: A worksheet to organize your thinking about seeking information.

Directions: Use this worksheet to help you organize your thinking about seeking information, the fourth step in the workplace learning process. Answer the questions appearing below. There are no "right" or "wrong" answers in any absolute sense, though some answers might be more useful or insightful than others.

QUESTIONS

1	Planned learning experiences—such as structured on-the-job or planned off-the-job training programs—actually comprise a relatively small percentage of information-gathering approaches. More commonly, learners in pursuit of knowledge will ask other people—and particularly their coworkers. They will also watch others, listen to what others say, read available information that may pertain to the topic, and experiment with a new approach on their own ("play"). How do people in your organization seek information most often? Ask some people to find out.
2	What approaches to seeking information are most effective in your organization? Ask some people to find out.
3	How can your organization improve the ability of workers to seek information in the future?

Exhibit 4-15: Processing information in the words of a workplace learner.

A program secretary in a university department in my study summarized how she processes information: "Learning can be fun. Make a game of it. It can be like putting a puzzle together—with some of the pieces gone. When you find the missing pieces, you can see the big picture. Focus in on the big picture and try to see where you fit in. Learning to get organized and using the resources that are available can only streamline the process and lower the stress level of the project through to completion."

Source: The direct quotation above is taken from an interview respondent in William J. Rothwell, "Models for the Workplace Learner." Unpublished research report. Copyright 2000 by William J. Rothwell, Ph.D. All rights reserved.

Exhibit 4-16: Processing information.

- Sort information found for relevance to the issue at hand or problem being investigated.

- Discard the irrelevant.

- Consider past experience with the issue or problem.

- Develop a tentative list of desired outcomes for yourself.

- Develop a tentative list of desired outcomes for others.

- Relate to yourself or others how the issue at hand relates to other issues, problems, or activities.

- Create a procedure.

- Examine/analyze an existing procedure.

- Design meetings with members on the team.

- Develop a prototype of the solution to a problem.

- Develop a goal to be achieved.

- Identify what resources will be needed to implement a solution.

- Generalize information for possible application to other problems, issues, or opportunities.

- Establish a preliminary structure by which to make sense of information.

- Present information to others to gain their opinions.

- Process what was learned during practice.

- Question exemplars about what they learned.

Exhibit 4-17: A worksheet to organize your thinking about processing information.

Directions: Use this worksheet to help you organize your thinking about the ways individuals process information in your organization. Processing information is the fifth step in the workplace learning process. Answer the questions appearing below. There are no "right" or "wrong" answers in any absolute sense, though some answers might be more useful or insightful than others.

QUESTIONS

1	How do people in your organization process information most often? Ask some people to find out.
2	What approaches to processing information are most effective in your organization? Ask some people to find out.
3	How can your organization improve its ability to help individual workers process information?

---

ganization to identify best practices used by another organization, and you then worked with a team to transform the notes you took on a benchmarking field trip into recommendations for making changes to work processes in your organization. As you did that, you would be demonstrating the process of converting information.

Step 7: Applying the Knowledge in the Future

Knowledge without application rarely endures in short-term memory. Indeed, for information to be consolidated most effectively, the learner must apply it somehow. It is for this reason that so-called hands-on application is so important. Applying the knowledge in the future thus refers to the step in which workplace learners try out what they have learned. (See

---

Exhibit 4-18: Converting information.

- Develop activities and assessments according to standards and desired outcomes.

- Create activities.

- Create practice sessions.

- Guide others through the process.

- Evaluate how well transfer of learning has occurred ("double-check understanding").

- Identify and record the names of individuals or other sources of information that could help during application.

- Create opportunities to practice.

- Create opportunities to evaluate variations on the solution.

- Plan for application.

- Budget for application.

- Make sure the right people are in place for application.

- Make sure the right tools and equipment are available for application.

- Communicate with stakeholders about application if there is a need to garner support and ownership from others for the workplace learning effort.

- Estimate the costs and benefits of application to the individual and to the organization.

- Take notes from the experience and draw conclusions from it.

- Create a presentation to deliver to individuals who are knowledgeable about the issue, problem, or opportunity.

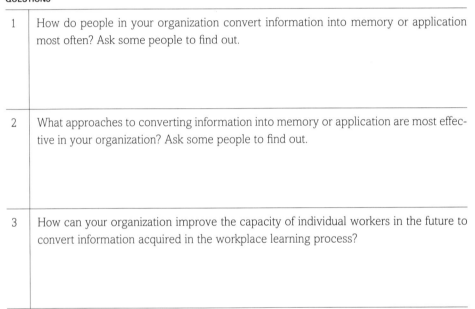

Exhibit 4-19: A worksheet to organize your thinking about converting information.

Directions: Use this worksheet to help you organize your thinking about the ways individuals convert information into memory or application in your organization. Converting information is the sixth step in the workplace learning process. Answer the questions appearing below. There are no "right" or "wrong" answers in any absolute sense, though some answers might be more useful or insightful than others.

QUESTIONS

1	How do people in your organization convert information into memory or application most often? Ask some people to find out.
2	What approaches to converting information into memory or application are most effective in your organization? Ask some people to find out.
3	How can your organization improve the capacity of individual workers in the future to convert information acquired in the workplace learning process?

Exhibit 4-20 to read about what one workplace learner had to say about applying the knowledge that was learned in the future.)

Without application, knowledge is soon extinguished. Some key events or activities linked to this step in the workplace learning process model are listed in Exhibit 4-21. Use the worksheet in Exhibit 4-22 to help you organize your thinking about ways of applying the knowledge in the future.

As a simple example of "applying the knowledge in the future," suppose that you were sent to a conference by your organization. When you returned, you wrote up a report about how you could apply on your job what you had learned at the conference. Then, you actually did so. As you applied that knowledge, however, you also made creative changes to what you learned to adapt the new knowledge to your organization's corporate

---

Exhibit 4-20: Applying the knowledge in the future in the words of a workplace learner.

A hotel switchboard operator in my study explained what it means to apply knowledge in the future: "I could never learn anything out of a book. I always needed hands-on experience. I would learn the job fundamentals and then with the experience I could do the jobs very well. I have even done jobs that required a college degree and performed them very well. You have to become part of the organization and be part of the team and learn all you can."

Source: The direct quotation above is taken from an interview respondent in William J. Rothwell, "Models for the Workplace Learner." Unpublished research report. Copyright 2000 by William J. Rothwell, Ph.D. All rights reserved.

---

culture. If you did that, you would be demonstrating the step in the workplace learning process of applying the knowledge in the future.

Step 8: Reflecting on What Was Learned and Applying That New Knowledge to New Situations

Reflecting on what was learned and applying that new knowledge to new situations is essentially a process of evaluating what was learned. (See Exhibit 4-23 to read about what one workplace learner had to say about reflecting on what was learned.) Not all individuals reflect on what information they have gathered or what they learned from applying such knowledge to specific or new situations. However, those who do are called *reflective practitioners*. By reflecting on what they have learned, they can often draw creative conclusions about additional issues to be explored, surface additional hypotheses to test out in practice, pinpoint additional feedback to seek from others, and exercise creative thinking. Some key events or activities linked to this step in the workplace learning process model are listed in Exhibit 4-24. Use the worksheet in Exhibit 4-25 to help you organize your thinking about ways of reflecting on what was learned and applying that new knowledge to new situations.

Think about a time when you were confronted by a work challenge and you dimly recalled having heard or read something about that challenge. Perhaps you were trained at one time on conducting employment interviews, but you did not have any job openings in your work unit at the time you received the training. A year or two later, after you quit that organization and joined another, you find that you must conduct employ-

(text continues on page 100)

Exhibit 4-21: Applying the knowledge in the future.

- Analyze the difference between what you have learned and what happens in application.

- Develop a budget.

- Use information relevant to an issue in practice.

- Train or mentor other people based on the fruits of an individual's experience.

- Give feedback to others about what they have done.

- Demonstrate how information is used in practice.

- Give an example or tell a story about how information is used.

- Develop a process to deliver the information to other people.

- Design a program or experiment.

- Formulate or test alternative solutions to the problem or other views of the issue.

- Deliver information to others.

- Try hands-on experiments.

- Pilot test a solution.

- Modify opinions based on experience, as the experience is taking place.

- Demonstrate by example.

- Make a mistake.

- Do something by accident.

- Do something spontaneously.

- Work for a difficult supervisor.

- Work with difficult coworkers.

- Work on a team.

- Work individually.

- Work with a difficult customer, supplier, or distributor.

- Set up something new.

- Shut down something that is not working.

- Turn around a failing enterprise.

- Juggle multiple, related projects simultaneously.

- Juggle multiple, unrelated projects simultaneously.

Exhibit 4-22: A worksheet to organize your thinking about applying the knowledge in the future.

Directions: Use this worksheet to help you organize your thinking about the ways individuals apply the knowledge they have learned in the future. Applying knowledge is the seventh step in the workplace learning process. Answer the questions appearing below. There are no "right" or "wrong" answers in any absolute sense, though some answers might be more useful or insightful than others.

QUESTIONS

1	How do people in your organization apply the knowledge they learned in the future? Ask some people to find out.
2	What approaches to applying knowledge are most effective in your organization? Ask some people to find out.
3	How can your organization improve the capacity of individual workers to apply their knowledge in the future?

Exhibit 4-23: Reflecting on what was learned and applying that new knowledge to new situations in the words of a workplace learner.

A research associate at a university explained what it means to reflect on what she learned and apply that new knowledge to new situations: "You must reflect—always look at everything you do, no matter how small. See what you can learn from it."

---

ment interviews to fill a vacancy. You pull out your old notes from the training course, review them, and (as you review them) you discover some new ideas about the ways you want to carry out the employment interviewing process for the vacancy in your work unit. In this example, you are demonstrating the step in the workplace learning process known as "reflecting on what was learned and applying that new knowledge to new situations."

Step 9: Experiencing a Double-Loop Trigger and Evaluating the Learning Process

Experiencing a double-loop trigger and evaluating the learning process is perhaps the one step that is most rarely experienced by workplace learners. In this step, learners draw conclusions about *how they learned how to learn* in one situation and what that means for ways that they may improve their ability to learn how to learn. (See Exhibit 4-26 to read about what one workplace learner had to say about experiencing a double-loop trigger and evaluating the learning process.) Some key events or activities linked to this step in the workplace learning process model are listed in Exhibit 4-27. However, it may be argued that this step is only carried out when individuals make a self-conscious decision to consider it. Too rarely are they asked to reflect on their learning processes in work settings or in educational settings. Use the worksheet in Exhibit 4-28 to help you organize your thinking about ways to encourage a double-loop trigger and evaluate the learning process.

Imagine for a moment that you enroll in an employer-sponsored training program to prepare to take a test of the National Association of Security Dealers (NASD). After you take the course, you take and fail the

Exhibit 4-24: Reflecting on what was learned and applying that new knowledge.

- Think about what has been learned from other sources.

- Think about what has been learned from experience.

- Evaluate the usefulness of products/results.

- Apply all relevant knowledge to the issue or problem.

- Review outcomes or results of activities.

- Review the individual's performance on a daily basis.

- Get feedback from others about how well the learner has mastered the task or issue or solved the problem.

- Determine future needs.

- Find a new solution.

- Ponder how the application might work in other settings.

- Record an overview of the situation, issues, and solutions and link to names of helpful people.

- Evaluate whether outcomes matched intentions or goals.

- Evaluate whether outcomes solved a problem.

- Revise plans.

- Apply creative problem solving to reflect on new approaches to seeking information, solving problems, and/or meeting future challenges/opportunities.

- Ponder how other people were affected by the same experience.

- Make a mistake and reflect on it.

Exhibit 4-25: A worksheet to organize your thinking about reflecting on what was learned and applying that new knowledge to new situations.

Directions: Use this worksheet to help you organize your thinking about the ways individuals reflect on what they have learned and apply that new knowledge to new situations. Reflecting on what was learned and applying that new knowledge to new situations is the eighth step in the workplace learning process. Answer the questions appearing below. There are no "right" or "wrong" answers in any absolute sense, though some answers might be more useful or insightful than others.

QUESTIONS

1	How do people in your organization reflect on what they have learned and apply that new knowledge to new situations? Ask some people to find out.
2	What approaches to reflecting on what was learned and applying that new knowledge to new situations are most effective in your organization? Ask some people to find out.
3	How can your organization improve the ability of individual workers to reflect on what was learned and apply that knowledge to new situations?

Exhibit 4-26: Experiencing a double-loop trigger and evaluating the learning process in the words of a workplace learner.

A project director of a university program with a multimillion-dollar budget explained what it means to experience a double-loop trigger: "Finding out how you learn and why you learn that way. I believe your initial learning style is always going to be your major one, but you must learn how to learn in other ways."

Source: The direct quotation above is taken from an interview respondent in William J. Rothwell, "Models for the Workplace Learner." Unpublished research report. Copyright 2000 by William J. Rothwell, Ph.D. All rights reserved.

Exhibit 4-27: Double-loop trigger and evaluation.

- Assess how well the individual has carried out the learning process.

- Assess individual learning style in the context of the issue or problem that was investigated.

- Discuss how well a group is capable of innovating from the known to the unknown (focus on the group's process of learning).

- Reflect on what was learned about learning from the experience.

- Revise opinions about one's ability to learn based on the experience.

- Provide a summary of a group's or an individual's process of learning how to learn.

- Evaluate the payoff of the process.

---

test. At that point, you may go back to review what examination questions you missed. You might also reconsider how you studied in preparation for the test and resolve to try a new approach. If you did this, you would be demonstrating the step in the workplace learning process known as "experiencing a double-loop trigger and evaluating the learning process."

See Exhibit 4-29 for a summary of the stages in the workplace learning process. For additional information about the process, read about workplace learning in the learners' own words in Appendix C.

HOW CAN THE WORKPLACE LEARNING PROCESS MODEL BE USED BY LEARNERS AND WLP PRACTITIONERS?

The model of the workplace learning process has the potential for application by individual workplace learners and by WLP practitioners. This section briefly examines those possible applications.

Whenever workplace learners—which includes just about everyone—face a work challenge or a new situation that calls for real-time, on-

---

Exhibit 4-28: A worksheet to organize your thinking about experiencing a double-loop trigger and evaluating the learning process.

Directions: Use this worksheet to help you organize your thinking about the ways individuals experience a double loop trigger and evaluate their learning process. Experiencing a double-loop trigger and evaluating the learning process is the ninth step in the workplace learning process. Answer the questions appearing below. There are no "right" or "wrong" answers in any absolute sense, though some answers might be more useful or insightful than others.

QUESTIONS

1	How do people in your organization experience a double-loop trigger and evaluate their own learning process? Ask some people to find out.
2	What approaches to experiencing a double-loop trigger and evaluating the individual's learning process are most effective in your organization? Ask some people to find out.
3	How can your organization improve the ability of individual workers to experience a so-called double-loop trigger and evaluate the learning process?

the-job learning, they should consider planning for their learning by using the model of the workplace learning process. The model itself provides important clues about how to seize the advantage in managing learning situations. Give the worksheet in Exhibit 4-30 to learners for that purpose.

We shall have more to say in Chapter 6 about how WLP practitioners may apply the information found in this book about the workplace learning process model and workplace learning competencies, and Chapter 9 will have more to say about how to build a climate that encourages workplace learning. But, for now, realize that whenever WLP practitioners face a situation in which they are asked to design training or else facilitate the learning of an individual or a group, they should consider planning the effort in part through reference to the model of the workplace learning

(text continues on page 109)

Exhibit 4-29:　A summary of the steps in the workplace learning process.

	STAGE IN THE WORKPLACE LEARNING PROCESS**	WHAT HAPPENS IN THIS STAGE?	EXAMPLE
1	Triggering Circumstance	Work-related or life-related problems—or some other triggering circumstance, such as a significant emotional event—create an impetus for change in the workplace learner.	An individual is hired. That creates a "life change" that opens the individual up to new experience.
2	Recognition of Importance	The workplace learner recognizes the importance of the triggering circumstance and realizes that he or she needs to learn about something. The workplace learner also tries to envision what outcomes or results he or she is trying to achieve and seeks affirmation about the importance of the learning experience from himself or herself and/or from others.	An individual realizes that he or she must learn about the work, the organization, the people, the customers or users and others who affect what he or she does, how he or she does it, and how he or she is assessed about it.
3	Curiosity	The workplace learner grows curious about a work-related or life-related problem or the issues surrounding the triggering circumstance, and he or she begins a search for resources to help him or her solve the problem. (Resources may come from the workplace learner's experience and/or from external sources.) The workplace learner also tries to envision what outcomes or results that he or she is trying to achieve by learning more about the triggering circumstance. He or she also	Upon hiring, the individual wants to make a good impression on his or her new employer. That prompts curiosity about the work, the organization, the people and the customers.

(continues)

Exhibit 4-29: (Continued).

STAGE IN THE WORKPLACE LEARNING PROCESS**		WHAT HAPPENS IN THIS STAGE?	EXAMPLE
		seeks affirmation from self or others about the importance of the learning experience.	
4	Information	The workplace learner undertakes a search for information from other people or from other resources (written or media-based). The workplace learner also tries to envision what outcomes or results that he or she is trying to achieve and assesses the relative value of the importance of the information that he or she locates.	The individual seeks relevant information he or she can obtain about the organization and the work he or she is to do. He or she has some difficulty in assigning importance to the information and to assessing its relative validity.
5	Processing	The workplace learner sifts through the information that he or she has found, draws conclusions about what that information means, and develops questions to guide future investigation and to guide application of what he or she has discovered. The workplace learner also tries to envision what outcomes or results that he or she is trying to achieve by reviewing the information and seeking affirmation of the importance of the information from self or others.	The individual is overwhelmed with information. He or she asks many questions to seek resolution of conflicts inherent in that information. He or she processes the information, assigning it importance and assessing how valid (truthful) the information is.
6	Conversion/ Knowledge Transformation	The workplace learner converts the information he or she has acquired into useful knowledge that can be applied to his or her life situation, work and/or future decision-making. He or she also tries to envision what outcomes or results that he or she is trying to achieve and seeks affirmation of the importance of the knowledge from himself or herself or from others.	The individual converts the information he or she has acquired into useful knowledge suitable for workplace application.

7	Application	The workplace learner applies the knowledge he or she has acquired. If the knowledge is successfully applied, it leads to successful performance; if the knowledge is unsuccessfully applied, it prompts a return to an earlier step—such as stimulation, curiosity, information, or processing. The workplace learner also seeks affirmation of how well he or she has applied what he or she has learned both before and after application.	The individual applies what he or she has learned. Some knowledge proves useful; other knowledge must be modified based on experience, feedback or interaction from others, and real-world application.
8	Reflection	The workplace learner draws conclusions about *what* he or she has learned, thinking about what it means, what its implications are for future performance in current or future life/work settings. The workplace learner also seeks affirmation of the validity of his or her reflection from self or others.	The individual reflects on what he or she has learned through application (experience)—as well as from previous steps in the workplace learning process—and reaches new conclusions about the organization, the workplace, his or her work, and other people.
9	Double-Loop Trigger/Evaluation	The learner draws conclusions about *how* he or she learned. This, in turn, may prompt an evaluation of the learning process and/or an additional triggering circumstance. (*Evaluation of the learning process* means "an assessment or one or more conclusions about *how* the individual learns best.") The workplace learner also seeks affirmation of his or her evaluation of the learning process from self or from others.	The individual reflects on how he or she has learned and draws conclusions for the future about ways to approach similar learning situations.

The workplace learner may resequence steps or skip steps as situational and personal conditions warrant. That is why the process is depicted as a circle (see Exhibit 4-2). Each stage encompasses thinking, feeling, and doing (cognitive, affective, and psychomotor).

Exhibit 4-30: A worksheet to use with the workplace learning process model to guide real-time, on-the-job learning situations.

Directions: Use this worksheet as a guide to help you, as an individual, in real-time, on-the-job learning situations. Whenever you encounter a work-related problem, challenge, or opportunity, use this sheet to help you plan how to "attack" the problem and learn effectively. For each question appearing below, provide your own notes to help you plan your learning project or event.

QUESTIONS

1	What circumstances triggered your interest?
2	How did you recognize the importance of the problem, issue, or opportunity? What makes it important to you?
3	What has aroused your curiosity about this problem, issue, or opportunity? What do you want to learn more about—and why?
4	How will you go about seeking information related to the problem, issue, or opportunity? How well have you made use of the possible sources of information available through people? Online resources? Other sources of information?
5	How will you process information related to the problem, issue, or opportunity?
6	How will you convert that information into what is useful to you and thereby internalize it into short-term and/or long-term memory?

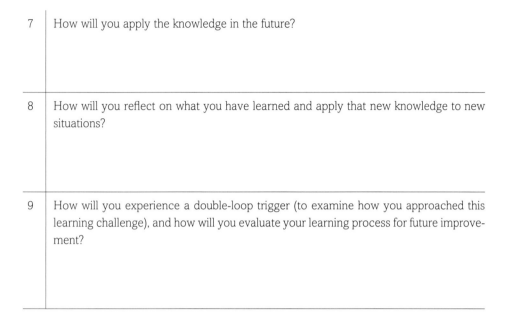

7	How will you apply the knowledge in the future?
8	How will you reflect on what you have learned and apply that new knowledge to new situations?
9	How will you experience a double-loop trigger (to examine how you approached this learning challenge), and how will you evaluate your learning process for future improvement?

process. The model itself provides important clues about how to facilitate learning situations effectively. Use the worksheet in Exhibit 4-31 for that purpose.

SUMMARY

This chapter explained why a model of workplace learning is important. It described a model of the workplace learning process and offered simple suggestions about how the model of the workplace learning process may be used by workplace learners and WLP practitioners.

This chapter listed nine key steps in the workplace learning process. The workplace learner:

1. Experiences a triggering circumstance.

2. Recognizes the importance of learning.

3. Experiences curiosity about the issue.

4. Seeks information.

5. Processes the information.

6. Converts that information into what is useful to the individual and thereby internalizes it into short-term and/or long-term memory.

Exhibit 4-31: A worksheet to use with the workplace learning process model to facilitate training or other planned learning events.

Directions: Use this worksheet as a guide to help you, as a WLP practitioner, to facilitate the real-time, on-the-job workplace learning of others. Whenever you are faced with the need to facilitate someone else's learning, use this sheet to help you plan how to "attack" the challenge of facilitating the workplace learning of others. For each question appearing below, provide your own notes to help you plan the learning project or event.

QUESTIONS

1	What circumstances will most effectively trigger the interest of individual learners, in your opinion?
2	How will you help others to recognize the importance of the problem, issue, or opportunity? What could make it important to them?
3	What could arouse their curiosity about this problem, issue, or opportunity? What could they be motivated to want to learn more about—and why?
4	How will you go about advising others to seek information related to the problem, issue, or opportunity?
5	How will you help individual workplace learners to process information related to the problem, issue, or opportunity?
6	How will you help individual workplace learners convert that information into what is useful to them and thereby internalize it into short-term and/or long-term memory?

7	How will you help individual workplace learners to apply the knowledge in the future?
8	How will you help individual workplace learners to reflect on what they have learned and apply that new knowledge to new situations?
9	How will you facilitate events so that individual workplace learners experience a double-loop trigger (to examine how they approached this learning challenge), and how will you facilitate a means by which individual workplace learners evaluate their own learning process for future improvement?

7. Applies the knowledge in the future.

8. Reflects on what was learned and may apply that new knowledge to new situations.

9. Experiences a double-loop trigger and evaluates the learning process.

This chapter also suggested that the model itself can be used as a means to help individuals plan their real-time workplace learning events and can offer valuable clues to WLP practitioners about what they should do when planning training or facilitating learning.

The next chapter turns to related issues. It defines the terms *role* and *competency* and explains why they are important. It also reviews the roles and competencies of workplace learners as revealed by my research.

Chapter 5

What Are the Roles, Competencies, and Outputs of the Workplace Learner?

What are competent workplace learners?

A reminder from Chapter 1: Competent workplace learners are individuals who are willing and able to seize initiative for identifying their own learning needs, finding the resources to meet those needs, organizing their own learning experiences, and evaluating the results. They are thus real-time, on-the-job learners who have mastered what it takes to "learn how to learn." To be fully effective, these learners carry out their efforts in organizations that encourage them to seize initiative for their own workplace learning.

This chapter describes the results of my original research on workplace learner competencies. The chapter addresses four important questions:

1. What are roles, and why are they important?

2. What are the workplace learner's roles in the workplace learning process model?

3. What are competencies, why are they important, and what competencies are associated with workplace learning?

4. What are outputs, and what outputs are associated with the competencies of workplace learners?

THE IMPORTANCE OF ROLES

People are hired into jobs or positions. Often, a *job description* outlines what they are expected to do, while a *job specification* describes the education, experience, or other requirements necessary to qualify for the job. Employee performance appraisals then measure, over some time, how well individuals are performing their assigned job duties.

Although job descriptions summarize what people do, they are not complete. They do not focus attention on results so much as on activities or responsibilities. How people approach their jobs is the other half of the equation. *Roles* are the parts played by an individual in an environmental, organizational, or work group context. Roles are thus associated with the ways by which individuals carry out their jobs. Role theory has long occupied a central place in competency modeling theory and practice, offering a useful way to address differences in competency application stemming from differences in corporate culture, organizational size, industry category, and other facts.[1]

RELATING THE WORKPLACE LEARNER'S ROLES AND THE WORKPLACE LEARNING PROCESS MODEL

Four key roles of the workplace learner can be derived from the steps in the workplace learning process model. The existence of these roles is also supported by my research based on interviews with workplace learners. The relationship of these roles to the workplace learning process model is shown in Exhibit 5-1. Each role is described more completely below.

Role 1: The Perceptivist

The perceptivist role remains sensitive to changing conditions in the workplace and the external environment surrounding it. Workplace learners

Exhibit 5-1: Relationships between the workplace learning process model and the roles of the workplace learner.

STEPS IN THE WORKPLACE LEARNING PROCESS MODEL		ROLES OF THE WORKPLACE LEARNER
Triggering Circumstance		The Perceptivist
Recognition of Importance		
Curiosity		
Information		The Information-Gatherer
Processing		The Analyst
Conversion/Knowledge Transformation		
Application		
Reflection		The Evaluator
Double Loop Trigger/Evaluation		

Source: William J. Rothwell, "Models for the Workplace Learner." Unpublished research report. Copyright 2000 by William J. Rothwell, Ph.D. All rights reserved.

who enact the perceptivist role undergo triggering circumstances, recognize their importance to their organizations and their work performance, and experience curiosity about the triggering circumstance and its implications for the organization, work performance, and themselves.

Role 2: The Information-Gatherer

The information-gatherer role seeks information from many sources to slake the thirst for knowledge. Workplace learners who enact the information-gatherer role are on a quest for useful information. They are patient enough to search out sources of information to satisfy an aroused curiosity. The aim of the information-gatherer is the pursuit of relevant information.

Role 3: The Analyst

The analyst role processes the information that has been gathered, converts it to useful information within the organizational context in which it is to be applied, tests it out, and experiments with it.

Role 4: The Evaluator

The evaluator role reflects on what has been learned from application and may also reflect on how well or how much has been learned in the situation. The results of this step may lead to other triggering circumstances that push the workplace learner to a quest for more knowledge and skills, and for new beliefs, values, and attitudes.

Awareness of these roles help WLP practitioners identify when, and how, people are enacting their roles. For instance, when people are encountering a problem for the first time, they are most likely functioning in the perceptivist role. Knowing this, WLP practitioners are better able to help learners carry out their role.

The Importance of Competencies

What are job competencies? What are organizational core competencies? How are they related? Why are competencies important? This section answers these questions.

Definition of Job Competency

A *job competency* is an "underlying characteristic of an employee (that is, a motive, trait, skill, aspects of one's self-image, social role, or a body of knowledge) that results in effective and/or superior performance in a job."[2] Many specific terms are associated with job competencies. Among them are:[3]

- **Competency Identification.** The process of identifying job competencies.

- **Competency Model.** The result of competency identification. A competency model is usually a narrative description of job competencies for an identifiable group, such as a job category, a department, or an occupation. It can describe key characteristics that distinguish exemplary (best-in-class) performers from fully successful performers.

- **Competency Modeling.** The process of writing out the results of competency identification by creating a narrative to describe the competencies.

- **Competency Assessment.** The process of comparing individuals in a job category, occupational group, department, industry, or organization to the competency model that has been developed for that targeted group.

- **Exemplary Performer.** Best-in-class or most productive workers.

- **Fully Successful Performer.** An experienced worker who is not best-in-class.

Competencies have emerged as important because they are properly linked to individuals rather than to jobs. As work changes more rapidly, competencies become more useful because they are more effective than job descriptions in clarifying what characteristics effective performers share in common. They are also more effective than job descriptions in identifying the so-called emotional intelligence needed by effective performers as well as the values, feelings, and beliefs of effective workplace learners/performers.

What Are Organizational Core Competencies?

Job competencies should not be confused with *organizational core competencies*,[4] which can be understood as the essential characteristic that makes one organization competitive. An organizational core competency is akin to a strategic strength, something that sets one organization apart from others.

Why Is Competency Modeling Important?

Competencies can provide the basis for all elements of an integrated human resources management (HRM) system. Competencies may be used instead of job descriptions as the foundation for employee recruitment, selection, orientation, training, performance management, compensation, benefits, safety, and any other HR function. And, of course, competencies can be used to assess what people must know, do, or feel to perform effectively. In the future, competency-based HRM may replace job-based HRM as mainstream practice.

COMPETENCIES ASSOCIATED WITH WORKPLACE LEARNING

As individuals learn, they must apply competencies to that process. Competencies are "internal capabilities that people bring to their jobs. They may be expressed in a broad, even infinite, array of on-the-job behaviors."[5] Although they are often identified by comparing differences between exemplary and fully successful performers, they can also be identified through other approaches.[6] One such approach is to analyze the thoughts, feelings, and actions of veteran performers.[7]

What follows is a list of competencies needed by those who learn in workplace settings. These are the results of my workplace learner competency study. These competencies are distilled from hundreds of interviews. (Examples of transcripts from three such interviews are presented in Exhibits 5-2 and 5-3 to give readers a flavor for the foundation of these distilled competencies.) Mastery of these competencies leads to workplace learning competence.

Core Competencies

Core competencies are shared by all the workplace learner roles. Some core competencies were identified by Smith and Senge.[8] They include:

FOUNDATIONAL COMPETENCIES

1. **Reading Skill:** Reads to a level of proficiency appropriate for learning in a workplace setting.

2. **Writing Skill:** Writes to a level of proficiency appropriate for learning in a workplace setting.

(text continues on page 129)

Exhibit 5-2: Sample behavioral interview event transcript #1.

Respondent: Personnel Manager, Fiscal Person, Operations Manager, and Education Coordinator. (Note: This is a very small business and the respondent performs a number of jobs.)

Question: What are your work requirements? Describe your work duties.

Includes a multitude of things, from financial management, personnel, doing bids and quotes, sales, as well as providing educational classes for individuals and groups of teachers.

Question: Think back to the *single most difficult learning situation* you have ever encountered in the workplace. This can involve *any* learning activity or effort—so long as it occurred while you were in the workplace. It could have occurred while you were in your present job or in another job. It could have occurred while you were with your present employer or with another employer. However, it is important that you describe the situation in detail. First, provide an overview of the situation. What was the learning challenge you faced? Then answer some background questions: When did this occur (approximate dates)? Who was involved (give job titles but not names)? Where did this occur (give approximate location)?

Coming from a place I had been really comfortable with for 12 years, I had a good knowledge base, I understood the workings of my former work situation. People came to me for the answers or I helped them in their decision making process. When I first started with the organization I was no longer in a position where I had answers. I was now in a position where I needed to get answers. It was a very different, uncomfortable position for me to be in. I knew the people (owners) involved and I felt confident I could work with them and they would help me through those changes.

I was learning everything. Specifically putting together a quote for a customer was reflective of the challenge at the time.

When did this occur? September 1997.

Who was involved? The owner, the sales person, and myself.

Where did this occur? Northampton, Massachusetts.

Question: Tell us *how you learned* in this situation. Be as specific as possible, describing what happened in the sequence that it happened. Be sure to explain what was happening, what you were doing, what you were thinking, and what you were feeling as events unfolded.

	WHAT WAS HAPPENING?	WHAT WERE YOU THINKING?	WHAT WERE YOU FEELING?
1	I sat down with the customers to get a detailed description of what they wanted.	I hope I get this right. I hope I don't blow it.	Really nervous. I made them repeat it. They may have been able to tell on the other end of the phone that I was really new.
2	Asked questions from the owner and sales person.	That my lack of knowledge is shining through. I have to rely on other people and I hope I am not disappointing them in the fact that I don't have this vast knowledge base.	Scary. Because I don't have the knowledge base.
3	Searched catalogs and on-line resources.	Beginning to sense it was coming together.	A little more confident.
4	Reviewed the information collected with the owner and sales person.	I had met that part of the challenge. I thought that it was well portrayed and I hoped that it met with approval.	Not cocky, but a little happy that I met that first piece of it. It felt good. It felt successful.
5	Put the quote together and forwarded it on to the customer.	I was hoping the customers would be happy with the quote they were getting and in fact place the order. That would have been the ultimate point of success.	I felt good about it. I felt much more successful about it than I originally did when I started. I may be conquering this.

Question: What did you *learn about how you learn* from this situation? If you faced the same situation again, how would you handle it—and why would you handle it that way?

Generally I take a positive approach. Saying I can do this. I take each step and break it down into small components that are successful. I break them down into pieces that feel good, they don't feel overwhelming. If you can get that little bit of success you are apt to move to the next piece of it. It's hard to get around obstacles and still feel successful, to learn and go forward. I have always tried to attack things with a positive attitude. I may take a little longer to do it, but I'd rather approach it from that angle.

If you faced the same situation again how would you handle it?

Pretty much the same way. Basically determine what it is that I need to do, figure out the sequence of steps which I need to do it in. Maybe break it down into smaller steps in order to move it forward.

(continues)

Exhibit 5-2: (Continued).

If you faced the same situation again, why would you handle it the way you said you would?

Taking a positive approach works for me. The minute you have a defeatist attitude you stop moving forward.

Question: Think about the *most common or typical learning situation* you encounter in the workplace. This can involve *any* learning activity or effort—so long as it occurs while you are in the workplace. First, provide an overview of the situation. What is the typical learning challenge you face? Then answer some background questions: When does this occur? Who is involved? How often does it occur? Why do you think it occurs?

Everyday there is a different challenge, it depends on the activity of that day. I have been called upon to train people in software I am not familiar with in a few hours. It can be typical, but not everyday. For example, someone was coming in for training on some software, I was familiar with a different version than the customer showed up with. I was on the spot with the person, learning it and teaching it at the same time. On a daily basis new things are learned, in this industry (Communications/Computer) things change on a daily basis.

What is the typical learning challenge?	Learning something new and teaching it to someone else.
When does this occur?	At any time during the workday.
Who is involved?	The customer and myself usually.
How often does it occur?	It can occur a couple of times per week. Things like this happen on a regular basis.
Why do you think it occurs?	Something that was state of the art yesterday is no longer state of the art today.

Question: Tell us *how you learn* in this situation. Be as specific as possible, describing what happens in the sequence that it happens. Be sure to explain what is happening, what you are doing, what you are thinking, and what you are feeling as events unfolded.

	WHAT WAS HAPPENING?	WHAT WERE YOU THINKING?	WHAT WERE YOU FEELING?
1	I quickly did an overview of the product to find out where the differences were.	Let's not mess it up. I did not have an opportunity to review this.	Felt very nervous.
2	Focused on the interest of the customer. The payroll module was the focus in this case.	Let's get the customer up and running. Do appropriately. Thanked God my background was accounting.	I felt good.
3	Looked more closely at the area the customer needed.		It was working the way it was supposed [to]. I was getting into a comfort zone.
4	Took mental notes on the differences.	I needed to take charge of the situation.	It felt good.

Question: What have you *learned about how you learn* in this most common or typical workplace learning situation? If you were advising others how to approach the situation, what advice would you give them and why?

I have learned that under pressure I can learn anything. That as long as my mind is open I am willing to embrace what is there. That it is not normally a problem, I can usually work my way through it.

If you were advising others how to approach this situation, what advice would you give them?

It is not a fun situation to be in the first place. Keep an open mind, most important and have a positive attitude. That will help you get over the first obstacle. Plug through it.

Why would you give others the advice that you would give them?

I have found that you have to break the negative attitude to get to at least an ok level platform before you can even begin to focus. It is important to get over the defeatist attitude first.

Question: What is your opinion about *what it takes to be successful in learning in the workplace*? Reflect on your own experience and describe what you believe to be essential to workplace learning in your occupation and in your organization.

Having a good attitude, keeping an open mind an a willingness to succeed. A want to move forward. With these pieces in place people will be able to work through. Take some calculated risks, put the benchmark a little higher than you were used to. To strive for something higher to prevent you from becoming complacent. People get real happy where they are at and they are not willing to move that next step forward. I always try to put myself a step higher than where I should be, because it gives me something to work toward. Otherwise life is not a challenge and you do not move forward. You stop your lifelong learning process when you become very complacent with what you are doing and you don't move forward any more, you don't learn any more, you don't gain knowledge and you don't become valuable to your company and yourself. You kind of spend your time, instead of being valuable.

Note: All respondents to this study were promised anonymity and confidentiality. Company and product names have been changed to disguise them.
Source: William J. Rothwell, "Models for the Workplace Learner." Unpublished research report. Copyright 2000 by William J. Rothwell, Ph.D. All rights reserved.

Exhibit 5-3: Sample behavioral interview event transcript #2.

Respondent: General Construction—Contractor

Question: What are your work requirements? Describe your work duties.

Responsibilities include planning the jobs, performing the work on the job, it covers a broad base. I do cost analysis and estimates, take offs, deal with potential clients, deal with sub-contractors. When we did bigger jobs, dealt with government agencies, zoning and everyone who would be involved with that.

Question: Think back to the *single most difficult learning situation* you have ever encountered in the workplace. This can involve *any* learning activity or effort—so long as it occurred while you were in the workplace. It could have occurred while you were in your present job or in another job. It could have occurred while you were with your present employer or with another employer. However, it is important that you describe the situation in detail. First, provide an overview of the situation. What was the learning challenge you faced? Then answer some background questions: When did this occur (approximate dates)? Who was involved (give job titles but not names)? Where did this occur (give approximate location)?

The largest job I had was about a $112 million project. I found out that I wasn't going to get the last $30,000. We had to hire attorneys on both ends and nothing ever came of it. Being a small business man losing $30,000 was quite a blow. The last payment is profit or how you pay yourself and I never got it. It involved a firm in town—a realtor that had hired a builder to build a series of townhouses for a third individual. The third individual was funding a project. The realtor was going to gain the potential to sell the four "pits." The builder in between went out of business and they needed someone to finish and take on the project. What I didn't know was that we should have had all of the contracts done up in my name rather than on good faith. Had to deal with the realtor because we were business partners and couldn't sue the other guy because didn't have a contract with him.

When did this occur?	The project began in 1989 and completed 1 year later, but the resolution of the matter wasn't until 1991.
Who was involved?	Self, a third individual who was financing, the realtor, and the builder who went out of business.
Where did this occur?	Pennsylvania.

Question: Tell us *how you learned* in this situation. Be as specific as possible, describing what happened in the sequence that it happened. Be sure to explain what was happening, what you were doing, what you were thinking, and what you were feeling as events unfolded.

Step 1. On the job, everything went smoothly, met with all individuals involved and felt very comfortable with them.

What was happening?

During the construction phase, met with all the individuals involved. Everything went very smoothly.

What were you thinking?

Thinking about the next project, and what that was going to be, could see work for months and years worth of work may be ahead.

What were you feeling?

Felt very comfortable with everyone and confident there was an upside to this.

Step 2. House was built.

What was happening?

Kept getting the run around, have to fix this and that. I did get $5,000 or $10,000 out of $40,000 that was owed to him.

What were you thinking?

At that point I didn't want to go back and said that I wasn't until I got the moncy. I didn't want my wife to know that there was a potential that I wasn't going to get paid.

What were you feeling?

Comfortable to leery, I was mildly uncomfortable, couldn't figure out why I wasn't getting paid.

Step 3. Picked up check.

What was happening?

Paid us enough to keep us going, like a mouse with a piece of cheese. We were done with the job and were working at another house and went back to take care of these little things. After a while, a year or so, maybe six months we thought the job was done.

What were you thinking?

I was still thinking I was getting the run around. Thought that this wasn't right and I may have to get *my* attorneys involved if something doesn't happen here quick. I may not have any choice but to get the attorneys involved.

What were you feeling?

Still felt I was getting the run-around. I had to wait and felt this is not right.

(continues)

Exhibit 5-3: (Continued).

Step 4. Got the wife of the realtor involved.

What was happening?

I got her involved because we were good friends and wanted to see if she could intervene on behalf of both parties to get some of the money freed up.

What were you thinking?

Thought she could make it work, cause she had the ability to make things happen, this would end up very quickly.

What were you feeling?

That it would end quickly.

Step 5. Next step, got the attorney involved.

What was happening?

About one year, had to get to the legal battle, first her attorney, and she found out he owed her money and that my beef was with her not with him, so I had to sue her if I wanted to get the money.

What were you thinking?

Again, it was going to be settled relatively soon, it will be over.

What were you feeling?

Felt confident this would be settled because there was an attorney involved. I was stuck in the middle, because they sued each other and [I] had to testify for both of them.

Step 6. Went on for another year with the attorneys and no one got anything.

What was happening?

Sent letters back and forth, between attorneys, no one got anything.

What were you thinking?

Starting to get angry because I was being dragged into a battle I didn't want to be in.

What were you feeling?

Feeling angry not at her but at the third party.

Question: What did you *learn about how you learn* from this situation? If you faced the same situation again, how would you handle it—and why would you handle it that way?

A lot of this I should have known. I took law courses. I had been in business for five years and never did anything without a contract. This time we did. I learned not to cut corners, not in building, but in contracts and legal stuff because that all costs money, but in the long run if I would have spent five hundred dollars in the beginning I probably would have saved the loss in the end. It's easy to say you learn not to trust anybody, but maybe that is not a fair assessment. Sometimes the ones you do on a handshake turn out better. Certainly on anything this size, I try to cross all the t's and dot all the i's.

If you faced the same situation again, how would you handle it?

Having faced that *again,* my wife says I'm not real persistent. I should get a contract. It has to be that way. I would be more tactful at the beginning and more persistent [if] I was sure that something was in writing.

If you faced the same situation again, why would you handle it the way you said you would handle it?

It was up and down for two years, it was an emotional roller coaster. I had to work with this on my mind and know what we would do with it up and down. Don't think we should have had to go through that emotional and financial middle.

Question: Think about the *most common or typical learning situation* you encounter in the workplace. This can involve *any* learning activity or effort—so long as it occurs while you are in the workplace. First, provide an overview of the situation. What is the typical learning challenge you face? Then answer some background questions: When does this occur? Who is involved? How often does it occur? Why do you think it occurs?

Learning new techniques and products, in the physical end of the business, mainly things change weekly and monthly. People are always looking for something new and innovative. It is not always easy to keep up with anything.

When does this occur? On the job or a regular basis? Who is involved?

The customer, new products, and myself. I self-taught new techniques, and watched someone who had been on the job for years and years.

How often does it occur?

Not necessarily daily, since I am always learning.

Why do you think it occurs?

Customers watch shows on TV and buy magazines and find new products.

Question: What have you *learned about how you learn* in this most common or typical workplace learning situation? If you were advising others how to approach the situation, what advice would you give them and why?

(continues)

Exhibit 5-3: (Continued).

Step 1. Used the example of laminate floors when they came out as a new product.

What was happening?	This product was new to the American market. I found out about it about five years ago. I found out about this from a guy who had a flooring business in town and I was invited to a seminar in Philly, if I was interested to teach people how to learn to install it.
What were you thinking?	I was thinking more work, and the product sounded pretty neat, and that this would take off.
What were you feeling?	Feeling like I am going to be the only guy that is an authorized installer, and how much business would I get the next six months, kind of being greedy.

Step 2. Attended the seminar, it was six hours, and there was about twelve of us from the same city.

What was happening?	The seminar lasted about six hours, showed a film how the product was made and showed us the product from Sweden, and did a small floor.
What were you thinking?	Thinking this looks easy, what can I charge for a square foot, how much is the public willing to pay me for this.
What were you feeling?	I was feeling pretty good, I was a bit leery, but when I saw it I thought a floor that floats, people are not going to buy it, maybe it was a wasted trip.

Step 3. Came back and talked to Jill, and thought was it worth the trip or not worth the trip, until I got the first job.

What was happening?	Talked to my wife to determine whether it was worth the trip or not.
What were you thinking?	Whether this is going to be worthwhile or not.
What were you feeling?	Pretty happy I went.

Step 4. Got the first job.

What was happening?	Got the first job about three months later in December. I had to put a floor down for the first time.
What were you thinking?	That I didn't want to screw up the first job.
What were you feeling?	Scared and worried since this was the first time, about the consequences if it didn't work out.

Step 5. Finished the job.

What was happening?	First day was slow, but gradually it got better each day. First sale the guy put down 1600 sq. feet.
What were you thinking?	Thought this was a good product and had a lot of potential. It's a simple product to put down, and the more widespread anyone could do it and you don't need an installer.
What were you feeling?	Felt pretty confident.

Step 6: Right after Christmas, guy's store burnt down, had more jobs lined up.

What was happening?	Store burned down, and did get more in to complete the other five or six jobs I had lined up.
What were you thinking?	What about the work, could not believe this.
What were you feeling?	Felt it was an omen.

Question: What have you *learned about how you learn* in this most common or typical workplace learning situation? If you were advising others how to approach the situation, what advice would you give them and why?

Found myself paying more attention to what is out there, keep in touch with salespersons. I subscribe to magazines and watch the shows for different things. I don't have a lot of time to log onto the internet, so in bidding, trying to get paid and trying to get paid for jobs I don't have a lot of time to find new things to introduce to the public, so I leave it to the customer and I figure out how it works.

If you were advising others how to approach the situation, what advice would you give them?

In the broader sense, so many people think having a business for yourself is a great way to go because you have control over your own hours. This is more easily said than done. The

(continues)

Exhibit 5-3: (Continued).

---

learning experience, I could tell someone everything we talked about here and they would not want to go into business for themselves. There are upsides to it, can control your own hours, if I had the opportunity to go work for someone else with less pay, with no structure, you can take advantage of the situation you are in and are your own boss. Sometimes it is better to have a supervisor that you can work with. You have to explore all your options and don't think the grass is greener. The failure rate in this business is high.

Why would you give others the advice that you would give them?

Past experience, had as many ups as downs. The downs can be hard. Financial stability is tied to success, if the checks aren't coming in then you really start to notice.

Question: What is your opinion about *what it takes to be successful in learning in the workplace*? Reflect on your own experience and describe what you believe to be essential to workplace learning in your occupation and in your organization.

- Have to have an open mind, the industry is always changing or certain products are changing, customers should get what they want.

- Never take short cuts, as they will come back to haunt you (I've rarely had callbacks).

- Make sure what legally you are doing, don't do anything without a change order or contract.

- Document everything.

- Can never learn enough, there is always someone who can do it better/cheaper. You have to keep up with the learning curve.

Source: William J. Rothwell, "Models for the Workplace Learner." Unpublished research report. Copyright 2000 by William J. Rothwell, Ph.D. All rights reserved.

3. **Computation Skill:** Applies mathematics to a level of proficiency appropriate for learning in a workplace setting.

4. **Listening Skill:** Listens effectively, and to a level of proficiency appropriate, for learning in a workplace setting.

5. **Questioning Skill:** Poses appropriate questions to others and to obtain meaningful and unambiguous answers to those questions.

6. **Speaking Skill:** Speaks to individuals, or presents to groups, with a level of proficiency appropriate for learning in a workplace setting.

7. **Cognitive Skills:** Thinks, draws conclusions, thinks creatively, makes decisions, and solves problems.

8. **Individual Skills:** Demonstrates a willingness to accept responsibility and display self-esteem.

9. **Resource Skills:** Allocates such resources as time, money, people, and information appropriately to learn in the workplace.

10. **Interpersonal Skill:** Works cooperatively with others, carries out formal or informal training or mentoring of others, and maintains effective interpersonal relations with customers.

11. **Informational and Technological Skill:** Acquires and analyzes data from various sources.

INTERMEDIATE COMPETENCIES

12. **Systems Thinking:** Views organizations and work from a systems perspective.[9]

13. **Personal Mastery:** Shows willingness to learn and takes pride in learning.

14. **Mental Modeling:** Creates, communicates, and critiques ingrained (and otherwise taken-for-granted) assumptions, beliefs, or values.[10]

15. **Shared Visioning:** Formulates, communicates, and builds enthusiasm about shared views of the future.[11]

16. **Team Learning Skill:** Participates effectively and actively in workplace groups and uses dialogue and other approaches to formulate, communicate, and test ideas generated by self or others.[12]

17. **Self-Knowledge:** Demonstrates "awareness and understanding of self as learner."[13]

18. **Short-Term Memory Skill:** Remembers facts, people, and situations for short time spans, usually about forty-eight hours or less.

19. **Long-Term Memory Skill:** Remembers facts, people and situations for longer time spans, usually exceeding forty-eight hours.

20. **Subject Matter Knowledge:** Possesses a solid foundation of background knowledge on the issue or subject that he or she sets out to learn about in the workplace.

21. **Enjoyment of Learning and Work:** Displays joy in the learning process itself and in the work that he or she performs.

22. **Flexibility:** Shows a willingness to apply what he or she knows in new ways as conditions warrant their application.

23. **Persistence and Confidence:** Shows determination to pursue new knowledge or skill even when finding it or mastering it proves more difficult than expected.

24. **Sense of Urgency:** Displays sensitivity to the importance of time to self and others.

25. **Honesty:** Gives information in a straightforward manner, free of deception, and elicits similar behavior from others.

26. **Giving Respect to Others:** Defers to others with more experience or knowledge.

COMPETENCIES ASSOCIATED WITH THE WORKPLACE LEARNER'S ROLES

Specific competencies are also associated with each workplace learner role. They are listed next:

The Perceptivist Role calls for the workplace learner to demonstrate:

27. **Work Environment Analytical Skills:** "Examines work environments for issues or characteristics affecting human performance."[14]

28. **Sensory Awareness:** Shows sensitivity to stimuli received from the outside world based on the use of any one or all of the five senses.

29. **Open-Mindedness:** Demonstrates a willingness to see, to observe, and to internalize what the world presents and reinterprets it afresh.

30. **Humility:** Displays modesty about what one does or does not know, a willingness to listen to fresh perspectives without pretending to know when one does not know.

31. **Analytical Skill (synthesis):** "Applies breaking down the components of a larger whole and reassembling them to achieve improved human performance."[15]

32. **Intuition:** Shows sensitivity to stimuli generated by self from memory or from the application of nonverbal logic.

The Information-Gatherer Role calls for the workplace learner to demonstrate:

33. **Information-Sourcing Skill:** Identifies the kind of information needed to satisfy curiosity and shows an ability to locate such information from credible sources.

34. **Information-Gathering Skill:** Collects information by talking to others, asking questions of others, facilitating groups to answer questions, and finding information from other sources.

35. **Information-Organizing Skill:** Organizes or structures information obtained from one or many sources and categorizes it into schemes that permit recall, comparison, or creative reexamination.

36. **Feedback Solicitation Skill:** Displays an ability to solicit feedback on what he or she has learned from others.

The Analyst Role calls for the workplace learner to demonstrate:

37. **Willingness to Experiment and Gain Experience:** Shows an openness to try out new ideas or approaches, even when they are untested or their results are unknown.

38. **Internalization Skill:** Translates general knowledge or information into specific information that can be immediately applied or tested.

39. **Application of New Knowledge Skill:** Uses new knowledge or skill in harmony with the way it was described or characterized from the original source(s).

40. **Ability to Adapt Knowledge to New Situations or Events:** Uses new knowledge or skill in creative, unusual, or novel ways.

The Evaluator Role calls for the workplace learner to demonstrate:

41. **Critical Examination of Information Skill:** Reflects on what was learned critically, offering follow-up questions or new ideas based on the information.

42. **Learning How to Learn Skill:** Reflects on how he or she acquired new information or knowledge and finds ways to improve the acquisition and application of new knowledge or skill in the future.

43. **Self-Directedness Skill:** Displays a willingness to be proactive about his or her own learning, to take action without needing to be directed to learn or to act by other people.

By knowing the outputs associated with the competencies, learners can assess how well their learning outcomes compare to the organization's performance expectations for their work. WLP practitioners can use it for the same purpose. It can be immensely useful to showing the link between learning and performance in the organization.

It is important to emphasize that competencies of this kind are focused on *how* people learn, not on *what* they learn. Nor do these competencies focus attention on the outputs of the learning process, a topic that will be covered next.

THE IMPORTANCE OF OUTPUTS

An *output* is "a product or service that an individual or group delivers to others, especially to colleagues, customers, or clients."[16] The workplace learning process model, like the HPI process model,[17] implies specific outputs. Outputs can be linked to competencies, though the exact nature of outputs may vary across different corporate cultures. Use the worksheet in Exhibit 5-4 to identify outputs associated with the core competencies and the role-specific competencies in your corporate culture.

SUMMARY

This chapter reviewed the roles, competencies, and outputs of the workplace learner. For the first time, the focus of attention has been on how learners carry out the learning process. By knowing how learners enact their roles, WLP practitioners are positioned to help them behave in ways appropriate to each role as the role relates to the workplace learning process. Workplace learning competencies provide a way to talk about *how* people learn, not *what* they learn. Moreover, these competencies provide a basis by which to assess individuals for their learning competence and thereby pinpoint areas for improvement in the learning process itself. Finally, outputs speak to results and to expectations for results. Awareness of outputs helps learners and WLP practitioners alike to think about the destination for a learning process.

Exhibit 5-4: A worksheet to identify the outputs associated with workplace learning competencies in your organization.

Directions: Use this worksheet to organize your thinking. For each competency listed in the left column below, identify under the right column the possible outputs for each competency in your organization's corporate culture.

CORE COMPETENCIES		OUTPUTS
FOUNDATIONAL COMPETENCIES		
1	*Reading skill:* Reads to a level of proficiency appropriate for learning in a workplace setting.	
2	*Writing skill:* Writes to a level of proficiency appropriate for learning in a workplace setting.	
3	*Computation skill:* Applies mathematics to a level of proficiency appropriate for learning in a workplace setting.	
4	*Listening skill:* Listens effectively and to a level of proficiency appropriate for learning in a workplace setting.	
5	*Questioning skill:* Poses appropriate questions to others and to obtain meaningful and unambiguous answers to those questions.	
6	*Speaking skill:* Speaks to individuals or presents to groups with a level of proficiency appropriate for learning in a workplace setting.	
7	*Cognitive skills:* Thinks, draws conclusions, thinks creatively, makes decisions, and solves problems.	
8	*Individual skills:* Demonstrates a willingness to accept responsibility and display self-esteem.	
9	*Resource skills:* Allocates such resources as time, money, people, and information appropriately to learn in the workplace.	

10	*Interpersonal skill:* Works cooperatively with others, carries out formal or informal training or mentoring of others, and maintains effective interpersonal relations with customers.	
11	*Informational and technological skill:* Acquires and analyzes data from various sources.	

INTERMEDIATE COMPETENCIES

12	*Systems thinking:* Views organizations and work from a systems perspective (Senge, 1990).	
13	*Personal mastery:* Shows willingness to learn and takes pride in learning (Senge, 1990).	
14	*Mental modeling:* Creates, communicates, and critiques ingrained (and otherwise taken-for-granted) assumptions, beliefs, or values (Senge, 1990).	
15	*Shared visioning:* Formulates, communicates, and builds enthusiasm about shared views of the future (Senge, 1990).	
16	*Team learning skill:* Participates effectively and actively in workplace groups and uses dialogue and other approaches to formulate, communicate, and test ideas generated by self or others (Senge, 1990).	
17	*Self-knowledge:* Demonstrates "awareness and understanding of self as learner" (Smith, 1982, p. 21).	
18	*Short-term memory skill:* Remembers facts, people, and situations for short time spans, usually about 48 hours or less.	
19	*Long-term memory skill:* Remembers facts, people, and situations for longer time spans, usually exceeding 48 hours.	
20	*Subject matter knowledge:* Possesses a solid foundation of background knowledge on the issue or subject that he or she sets out to learn about in the workplace.	

(continues)

Exhibit 5-4: (Continued).

21	*Enjoyment of learning and work:* Displays joy in the learning process itself and in the work that he or she performs.	
22	*Flexibility:* Shows a willingness to apply what he or she knows in new ways as conditions warrant their application.	
23	*Persistence and confidence:* Shows determination to pursue new knowledge or skill even when finding it or mastering it proves more difficult than expected.	
24	*Sense of urgency:* Displays sensitivity to the importance of time to self and others.	
25	*Honesty:* Gives information in a straightforward manner, free of deception, and elicits similar behavior from others.	
26	*Giving respect to others:* Defers to others with more experience or knowledge.	

COMPETENCIES ASSOCIATED WITH THE WORKPLACE LEARNER'S ROLES

THE PERCEPTIVIST ROLE

27	*Work environment analytical skills:* "Examines work environments for issues or characteristics affecting human performance" (Rothwell, 1996).	
28	*Sensory awareness:* Shows sensitivity to stimuli received from the outside world based from the use of any one or all of the five senses.	
29	*Open-mindedness:* Demonstrates a willingness to see, to observe, and to internalize what the world presents and reinterprets it afresh.	
30	*Humility:* Displays modesty about what one does or does not know, a willingness to listen to fresh perspectives without pretending to know when one does not know.	
31	*Analytical skill (synthesis):* Applies "breaking down the components of a larger whole and reassembling them to achieve improved human performance" (Rothwell, 1996, p. 19).	

32	*Intuition:* Shows sensitivity to stimuli generated by self from memory or from the application of nonverbal logic.	

THE INFORMATION-GATHERER ROLE

33	*Information-sourcing skill:* Identifies the kind of information needed to satisfy curiosity and shows an ability to locate such information from credible sources.	
34	*Information-gathering skill:* Collects information by talking to others, asking questions of others, facilitating groups to answer questions, and finding information from other sources.	
35	*Information-organizing skill:* Organizes or structures information obtained from one or many sources and categorizes it into schemes that permit recall, comparison, or creative reexamination.	
36	*Feedback solicitation skill:* Displays an ability to solicit feedback on what he or she has learned from others.	

THE ANALYST ROLE

37	*Willingness to experiment and gain experience:* Shows an openness to try out new ideas or approaches, even when they are untested or their results are unknown.	
38	*Internalization skill:* Translates general knowledge or information into specific information that can be immediately applied or tested.	
39	*Application of new knowledge skill:* Uses new knowledge or skill in harmony with the way it was described or characterized from the original source(s).	
40	*Ability to adapt knowledge to new situations or events:* Uses new knowledge or skill in creative, unusual, or novel ways.	

(continues)

Exhibit 5-4: (Continued).

41	*Critical examination of information skill:* Reflects on what was learned critically, offering follow-up questions or new ideas based on the information.
42	*Learning how to learn skill:* Reflects on how he or she acquired new information or knowledge and finds ways to improve the acquisition and application of new knowledge or skill in the future.
43	*Self-directedness skill:* Displays a willingness to be proactive about his or her own learning, to take action without needing to be directed to learn or to act by other people.

Chapter 6

APPLYING THE WORKPLACE LEARNING

PROCESS, ROLES, AND COMPETENCIES

If workplace learners require specialized competencies to carry out their roles, then that means that WLP practitioners must be sensitive to the workplace learning process and to the roles, competencies, and outputs of the workplace learner if they are to be successful in facilitating WLP. There must thus be some relationship between what workplace learners do and what WLP practitioners should do to encourage learning-oriented interventions.

What are the roles of the WLP practitioner, and what are the implications of the workplace learning process model for the roles of WLP practitioners? What are some implications of the workplace learning process model for planning, conducting, and evaluating formal, informal, and incidental learning experiences? This chapter addresses these questions.

IMPLICATIONS OF THE WORKPLACE LEARNING PROCESS MODEL FOR THE ROLES AND COMPETENCIES OF WLP PRACTITIONERS

WLP practitioners necessarily serve their client organizations, the organization's stakeholders, and the learners within the organizations. While they strive for improved work performance and thus increased productivity, learning-oriented interventions are often key to their success. (Recall that *learning-oriented interventions* are any efforts that rely chiefly on learning as a means of changing people and that examples might include on-the-job training, off-the-job training, e-learning initiatives, job rotation programs, mentoring or coaching efforts, and many others.) There is thus a close, and sometimes symbiotic, relationship between what WLP practitioners do and the results they strive to attain and what workplace learners do. Indeed, to speak in figurative terms, if childbirth is akin to the learning process, then the workplace learner enacts a role akin to that of the mother and the WLP practitioner plays a role akin to that of the father. While much occurs in the process that is not directly attributable to the WLP practitioner—and informal and incidental learning can occur without much involvement from the WLP practitioner—the WLP practitioner has the ability to play the role of catalyst in every step of the workplace learning process model.

Recall from *ASTD Models for Workplace Learning and Performance* that WLP practitioners enact seven distinct roles, that some WLP practitioners will only perform certain roles in the context of their jobs, and that WLP practitioners will usually perform several roles at the same time.[1] WLP practitioners who enact these roles make use of the HPI process.[2] Consider for a moment the roles of the WLP practitioner as they may match up to the workplace learning process model.

The Workplace Learning Process Model and the WLP Practitioner's Role as Manager

The *manager* plans, organizes, schedules, monitors, and leads the work of individuals and groups to attain desired results.[3] She also facilitates the strategic plan, ensures that WLP is aligned with organizational needs and plans, and ensures accomplishment of the administrative requirements of the function. The *manager's role* is strategic in nature. WLP managers can—and should—have involvement in every step of the workplace learning process model for the organization and its stakeholder and worker groups. WLP managers establish a structure to guide formal learning experiences (such as a *curriculum*—that is, a set of planned learning requirements—for all job categories in the organization) encourage informal learning by mounting efforts to build a High Performance Workplace (HPW) or a learning organization, and draw attention to incidental learning as a tool or means by which individuals, groups, and the organization may be developed over time. As a chief learning officer, a manager is an orchestrator of learning who provides consulting to the organization's management about how to create the appropriate conditions in which workplace learning can flourish.

To apply the results of my research to the WLP practitioner's role as manager, the manager should ask such questions as:

- What can this organization do to help learners carry out their roles?

- How can learners be helped to build workplace learning competence?

- How can the organization stimulate learners to use each step of the workplace learning model?

- How can the organization establish conditions that will encourage individual learning while reducing barriers erected by the organization that discourage workplace learning?

The answers to these questions should provide clues about the subsequent actions that WLP practitioners should take.

The Workplace Learning Process Model and the WLP Practitioner's Role as Analyst

The *analyst* troubleshoots to isolate the causes of human performance gaps or identifies areas for improving human performance.[4] The *analyst's role* matches up particularly well to the first three steps in the workplace learning process model. Analysts create or intensify triggering circumstances for the organization, groups, or individuals by bombarding them with stimuli. For example, suppose you are trying to stimulate supervisors to learn about handling tough employee disciplinary problems. You might start by posing them with a series of situations, such as, "How would you handle an employee who punched you in the nose?" or "How would you handle a female employee who told an off-color joke in a mixed group, and it obviously upset everyone?" Through their troubleshooting and opportunity-finding efforts, analysts help learners recognize the importance of opportunities to learn for their benefit in solving problems or intensifying improvement opportunities. Through their own fact-finding, analysts attempt to pique the curiosity and interest of learners, thereby motivating them to take self-directed steps to learn. For instance, analysts may uncover a problem with a work process. They could pose questions about those problems to other people. As they do that, they are stimulating interest and curiosity.

To apply the results of my research to the WLP practitioner's role as analyst, the analyst should ask such questions as:

- What can the organization do to diagnose and troubleshoot workplace learning problems?

- What issues keep workplace learners from being more effective in their learning process, and how can those issues be addressed by individuals and by the organization?

The answers to these questions should provide clues about the subsequent actions that WLP practitioners should take.

The WLP Practitioner's Role as Intervention Selector and Intervention Designer and Developer

The *intervention selector* chooses appropriate interventions to address root causes of human performance gaps.[5] In contrast, the *intervention designer and developer* creates learning and other interventions that help to address the specific root causes of human performance gaps. Some examples of the work of the intervention designer and developer include serving as instructional designer, media specialist, materials developer, process engineer, ergonomics engineer, instructional writer, and compensation analyst. Both the *intervention selector role* and the *intervention designer and developer role* may share a focus on helping learners organize and pursue information that will help them to satisfy their curiosity—and improve performance for the individual and organization's benefit.

The *intervention selector,* by choosing appropriate interventions to address performance gaps, can thus facilitate learners who seek the best ways and sources of information by which to meet their needs. The *intervention designer and developer* is similarly engaged in activities that necessitate helping individuals to discover their own solutions to performance problems. Examples might include choosing a job rotation program as an intervention and then organizing how people are introduced to the job rotation, how planned learning activities are guided during the rotation, and how people are debriefed as rotations are brought to a close. Rotations give people exposure to new people, new work requirements, and even new supervisors—and each stimulus can prompt learning.

To put this into practice, intervention selectors should pose such questions as:

- How much does individual learning competence play a role in the choice of a strategy to solve a performance problem?

- What learning competencies and learning outputs will be essential for the success of an intervention, and how can such competence be built before, during, and after the intervention?

Intervention designers and developers should pose such questions as:

- How can individual workplace learning competence be built (or enhanced) during an intervention through materials, resources, or other support provided by the organization?

- What approaches to delivering materials will most likely be effective for the intervention?

The WLP Practitioner's Role as Intervention Implementor

The *intervention implementor* ensures the appropriate and effective implementation of desired interventions that address the specific root causes of human performance gaps.[6] Some examples of the work of the intervention implementor include serving as administrator, instructor, organization development practitioner, career development specialist, process redesign consultant, workspace designer, compensation specialist, and facilitator.

The *intervention implementor role* is, in part at least, linked to the processing and conversion/knowledge transformation steps in the workplace learning process model. During processing, the workplace learner makes sense of the information he has found. That information is only useful to the extent that it meets the needs of the workplace learner and addresses the root causes of human performance gaps. During conversion/knowledge transformation, the workplace learner reviews what information she has found and distills it into that which is most useful to her.

To put this into application, the intervention implementor should pose such questions as:

- How can the intervention implementation process be facilitated so that it aligns with the individual learning competence of the participants?

- How can individual learning competence be built in the context of the intervention's requirement(s)?

The WLP Practitioner's Role as Change Leader

The *change leader* inspires the workforce to embrace the change, creates a direction for the change effort, helps the organization's workforce to adapt to the change, and ensures that interventions are continuously monitored and guided in ways consistent with stakeholders' desired results.[7]

The *change leader's role* is linked to the application step of the workplace learning process model. The reason is that, during application, the learner must find ways to embrace change, create a direction for the change effort, and ensure that interventions are continuously monitored and guided. The WLP practitioner's role is thus to help learners do just that. One way to do that is to post a story on the company Web site about the successes achieved from a training course or other planned learning event that could inspire workers.

To put this into practice, change leaders should pose such questions as:

- How can participants in an intervention be inspired to learn in ways that encourage the success of the intervention?

- How can managers, supervisors, and other leaders be encouraged to serve as real-time change champions to help build the learning competence of participants during an intervention?

The WLP Practitioner's Role as Evaluator

The *evaluator* assesses the impact of interventions and provides participants and stakeholders with information about the effectiveness of the intervention implementation.[8] The *evaluator's role* is linked to the reflection and double-loop trigger of the workplace learning process model. WLP practitioners thus help learners make sense of what they learned and think of ways to improve their own learning processes.

To apply this in practice, evaluators should pose such questions as:

- How can the results of the intervention be evaluated in terms of how much it helped participants build their individual workplace learning competence?

- How can the outputs of learning be documented by the organization for future use as need arises?

Relationships between WLP practitioner roles and the workplace learning process model are helpful because they suggest ways in which WLP practitioners should focus their roles from the standpoint of the "learners" they serve. Exhibit 6-1 summarizes possible relationships between WLP practitioner roles and the workplace learning process model.

Exhibit 6-1: Relationships between the roles of the WLP practitioner and the workplace learning process model.

ROLE OF THE WLP PRACTITIONER	STEPS IN THE WORKPLACE LEARNING PROCESS MODEL								
	TRIGGERING CIRCUMSTANCE	RECOGNITION OF IMPORTANCE	CURIOSITY	INFORMATION	PROCESSING	CONVERSION/ KNOWLEDGE TRANSFORMATION	APPLICATION	REFLECTION	DOUBLE-LOOP TRIGGER/ EVALUATION
Manager	▓	▓			▓	▓	▓	▓	▓
Analyst	▓	▓	▓						
Intervention Selector				▓					
Intervention Designer & Developer				▓					
Intervention Implementor					▓	▓			
Change Leader							▓		
Evaluator								▓	▓

Source: William J. Rothwell, "Models for the Workplace Learner." Unpublished research report. Copyright 2000 by William J. Rothwell, Ph.D. All rights reserved.

IMPLICATIONS OF THE WORKPLACE LEARNING PROCESS MODEL FOR LEARNING EXPERIENCES

What are the implications of the workplace learning process model for planning, conducting, and evaluating formal, informal, and incidental learning experiences? The answer to that question is that, in a nutshell, the workplace learning process model creates a roadmap for WLP practitioners—or for workplace learners themselves—to design, develop, deliver, and evaluate learning experiences, which is linked to *how people learn* and *how people learn to learn*. That is quite different from one of the forty or so versions of the ISD model, which focuses primarily on what the instructional designer/trainer does.[9] It can also serve as a road map for any organizational change effort, because there is a high correlation between the learning process and the change process.[10] Using the workplace learning process model to guide a change effort is akin to using appreciative inquiry to guide a change effort. *Appreciative inquiry* (AI) is, after all, based on the assumption that organizations—and people—change in the direction of what they learn and study. Any change intervention using AI progresses through four distinct phases: (1) discovery, (2) dream, (3) design, and (4) delivery.[11]

For an overview of how the workplace learning process model creates a road map for WLP practitioners, see Exhibit 6-2. That exhibit relates the steps in the model to the steps that WLP practitioners should use to design formal or informal learning experiences, guide debriefings of incidental learning experiences, and conduct group change efforts. Applying it is akin to using the conditions of learning.[12] To use the model shown in Exhibit 6-2, note that the steps in the workplace learning process model are shown in the inner circle of the figure and that the actions to be taken by WLP practitioners are shown in the outer circle of the figure. So, for instance, for the step called "triggering circumstance" in the WLP model, WLP practitioners should take actions associated with capturing learner attention. Each step of the WLP model thus implies an action—or a series of possible actions—to be taken by WLP practitioners.

What follows is a description of how WLP practitioners may use the steps of the workplace learning process model to guide learning interventions and change efforts. As you read about these steps, remember that

Exhibit 6-2: Encouraging self-directed learning using the workplace learning process model.

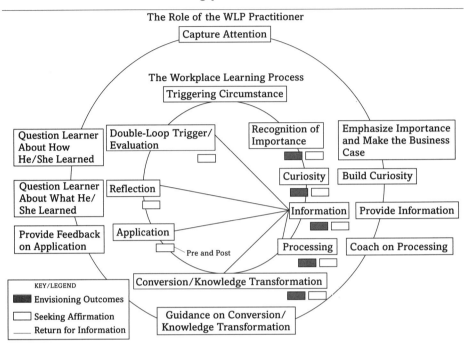

the workplace learning process model is divided into steps but that (1) the steps may be taken out of sequence; (2) the steps may be skipped by individuals during learning projects; and (3) each step includes a thinking, feeling, and doing component. Examine the model appearing in Exhibit 6-3 and then read the descriptions below.

Step 1: Capture Attention

To apply the model, the WLP practitioner must begin by capturing learner attention. That can be done by finding learners in a *teachable moment*— what I called in an earlier chapter a *learnable moment*—which is an instant when she is particularly susceptible to learning due to a life problem or a work problem, or due to the realization of a possible opportunity for improving herself or her organization. To do this, the WLP practitioner must monitor conditions in the external environment, in the organization, and

Exhibit 6-3: A model to illustrate what WLP practitioners should do to encourage the workplace learning process.

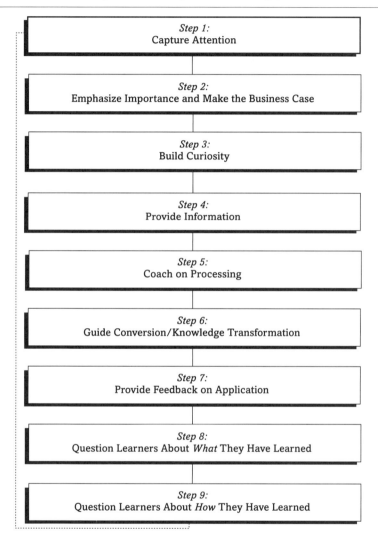

Step 1:
Capture Attention

Step 2:
Emphasize Importance and Make the Business Case

Step 3:
Build Curiosity

Step 4:
Provide Information

Step 5:
Coach on Processing

Step 6:
Guide Conversion/Knowledge Transformation

Step 7:
Provide Feedback on Application

Step 8:
Question Learners About *What* They Have Learned

Step 9:
Question Learners About *How* They Have Learned

Source: William J. Rothwell, "Models for the Workplace Learner." Unpublished research report. Copyright 2000 by William J. Rothwell, Ph.D. All rights reserved.

with individuals carefully to find them at a moment when conditions lend themselves to learning. As an example, if an accident occurs on the job, people are usually ready and eager to hear about safety methods to avoid such accidents in the future. WLP practitioners can provide instruction on those methods. Specific events linked to capturing attention are the same as those related to triggering circumstances.

Step 2: Emphasize Importance and Make the Business Case

People want to learn only when they see some value to it and believe they can be successful at it. Consequently, to emphasize value, the WLP practitioner should gather evidence about the importance of learning something new and thereby "make the business case." To do that, assemble any evidence that will be compelling to learners. Such compelling evidence may include information about the cost of a problem, the benefits associated with solving a problem, and more personally focused benefits that portray possible gains to the individual if he pursues a learning opportunity. For instance, if WLP practitioners are making the case for customer service training, they might collect examples from customers who were not served properly or courteously.

Step 3: Build Curiosity

Adult learners may see the importance of learning, but that does not necessarily mean that they are motivated enough to pursue it. To build that motivation, the WLP practitioner must pique their curiosity by asking questions about the problem or issue, benchmarking what others have done to solve the problem or address the issue, and feeding that information back to learners. The goal is to heighten the learners' desire to discover more on their own.

Step 4: Provide Information

Workplace learners may be aroused to learn, but that does not mean they know how to organize a plan to seek information to satisfy their need. They may not know whom to ask, what to ask, when to seek information, where to seek information, how to seek information, or other issues associated with "enabling" them to find the information they need to meet their need and solve their problem. The WLP practitioner's role, then, is to facilitate this process by helping learners locate the resources they need to enable their learning. WLP practitioners do that informally by saying such things as, "Why, you should talk to so and so" or "Have you read the article by so and so?" A good place to start is by facilitating a data collection plan so that learners know how to organize their own learning experience and are aware of some initial places to look for information. WLP practitioners do that by organizing a planned discussion with each learner. Learning plans, of course, can come in many forms. Some might be quite informal. Others might be written out to specify learning objectives, desired results, learning activities, and evaluation strategies.

Step 5: Coach on Processing

Once learners have found information, they do not always know what to do with it or how to organize it. Here the WLP practitioner can be helpful by facilitating the learner's information processing. That can be done by helping people develop a scheme for organizing the information they obtain through their own self-directed learning efforts. In effect, WLP practitioners function as learning counselors to encourage people as they learn. In group settings, this step can be facilitated, in part, by small group activities in which learners are tasked to organize information obtained from other sources.

Step 6: Guide Conversion/Knowledge Transformation

Once learners have organized information, they do not always know how to translate it into terms that relate to their own situations or see how it can be applied to their own situations. At this step of the workplace learning process model, the WLP practitioner can help learners make that leap from general to specific information that may be helpful to them. That can be done by asking questions, by forming small groups and tasking them with the goal of establishing useful information, or by forming task forces or action learning teams to attack problems in real-time workplace settings.[13]

Step 7: Provide Feedback on Application

To consolidate what learners have gleaned from new information, they must do something with it for it to be meaningful to them. In short, they must apply it or experiment with it. Here the WLP practitioner can be helpful by suggesting ways to experiment, offering advice on what is happening during an application, or by suggesting ideas and issues to experiment with and ways to carry out that experimentation and exploration. The feedback can be offered by e-mail, by threaded discussions, by interpersonal contact, and by other methods.

Step 8: Question Learners About *What* They Have Learned

Workplace learners do not naturally debrief themselves. That is an important role that a WLP practitioner can play. The WLP practitioner can evoke the reflection stage of the workplace learning process model by posing questions to learners about what they have learned, what that means, and how it may be applied or experimented with in the future.

Step 9: Question Learners About *How* They Have Learned

If workplace learners do not naturally reflect on *what* they have learned, they are even less likely to reflect on *how* they learned. Here again WLP practitioners can play a vital role in stimulating, consolidating, and advancing the workplace learning process by asking learners about what they have learned about how they learn in a situation. They can also ask learners what implications may be drawn about ways to improve how they learned how to learn and what they can do to improve that process in similar situations or in all situations.

Application

The worksheet in Exhibit 6-4 is meant to serve as a road map for WLP practitioners who wish to apply the workplace learning process model as an organizing device for structuring formal or informal learning or for debriefing learners about incidental learning situations they have experienced. It can also serve as a general guide for group change efforts.

SUMMARY

This chapter revisited the roles of the WLP practitioner based on the implications of the workplace learning process model. The chapter described

Exhibit 6-4: A worksheet to guide learning experiences.

Directions to WLP practitioners: Use this worksheet to guide your efforts to facilitate learning with individual learners or to guide change efforts with groups of learners. For each question appearing in the left column below, make some notes about what you can do to help learners. There are no "right" or "wrong" answers in any absolute sense, of course. However, this worksheet is meant to provide the foundation for a general "plan of attack" to guide an intervention based on the workplace learning process model.

	THE WLP PRACTITIONER SHOULD:	HOW COULD YOU DO THAT IN THIS SITUATION? (LIST WHAT TO DO):
1	Capture learner attention.	
2	Emphasize the importance of the learning situation and make the business case for taking action.	
3	Build the learner's curiosity.	
4	Provide information (offer advice on what to look for and where to find it).	
5	Coach learners on how to process information (offer advice on how to organize information).	
6	Provide guidance to learners on how to convert the information so that it is applicable to them in their situation now.	
7	Provide feedback on application before, during, and after learners "try out" the implications of new information and "experiment" with it in their situation(s).	

(continues)

Exhibit 6-4: (Continued).

8	Question learners about *what* they have learned.	
9	Question learners about *how* they learned and how they learn best or most effectively/ efficiently.	

the relationship between WLP roles and the steps in the workplace learning process model. It also briefly described some implications of the workplace learning process model for planning, conducting, and evaluating formal, informal, and incidental learning experiences.

The next chapter examines the organization's role in the workplace learning process. That is important because organizations create a context in which individuals enact their workplace learner roles, demonstrate their workplace learning competencies, and apply the steps in the workplace learning process model. Not all organizations are equally conducive to learning. For that reason, deliberate steps must be taken to establish a climate that encourages the workplace learning process.

UNDERSTANDING AND BUILDING AN ORGANIZATIONAL CLIMATE CONDUCIVE TO LEARNING

Part Three, which consists of Chapters 7 through 9, focuses on the organizational setting in which the workplace learning process is carried out. The organizational context can encourage or discourage workplace learners. Although much has been written in recent years about learning organizations and about organizational learning, WLP practitioners are often confused by the theories about those issues.

Part Three draws from the results of my second research study that focused on conditions established by organizations that encourage or discourage workplace learning. The chapters in Part Three:

- Define a *learning organization* and explain how it affects workplace learning.

- Define *organizational learning*, and explain how it is related to individual workplace learning.

- Define *workplace learning climate* and *workplace learning culture.*

- List, based on my research, the ways by which an organization establishes a workplace learning climate and culture that encourages or discourages the workplace learning process.

- Suggest ways to assess the organization's workplace learning climate.

- Recommend ways to change the workplace learning climate.

Chapter 7

WHAT IS THE ORGANIZATION'S ROLE IN

WORKPLACE LEARNING?

"The ability to learn faster than your competitors," observed Arie De Geus, head of planning for Royal Dutch/Shell, "may be the only sustainable competitive advantage."[1] And, in like vein and in response to a question posed in my study, one workplace learner—an office manager and service writer in an auto repair shop—noted that:[2]

> *Successful learning in the workplace is dependent on the employer-company relationship.* [Emphasis added.]
>
> *First, the company must screen employees when hired. Prospects should be told the importance, availability, and participation in com-*

pany training programs and policies. In larger companies another method is to blend your more experienced employees with new employees who have potential. My experience is to require some training and motivate employees to participate in additional training. Training or learning need not be career-specific. Learning skills such as assertiveness training, first aid, or CPR are not related to careers, but they benefit the company and the individual just as much as career-based training.

With the above quotation by way of introduction, we are prompted to ask several important questions:

- What is a *learning organization*, and how does it affect workplace learning?

- What is *organizational learning*, and how is it related to workplace learning?

- How do organizations *encourage* workplace learning?

- How do organizations *discourage* workplace learning?

By addressing these questions, this chapter begins to describe the climatic and cultural conditions that must exist to establish a learning organization and facilitate the organizational learning process. The next two chapters also focus on the related topics of measuring the workplace learning climate and changing that climate.

WHAT IS A *LEARNING ORGANIZATION*, AND HOW DOES IT AFFECT WORKPLACE LEARNING?*

Much has been written about learning organizations. Most authorities, however, believe interest in the learning organization has resulted from the growing volatility in business markets and from a growing awareness

*This section on the learning organization is indebted to the work done by Li Yan (Yan, L., "A Literature Review on the Learning Organization," unpublished master's paper, The Pennsylvania State University, 2000).

among business leaders that an organization's ability to adapt to change is a key to competitive success. A *learning organization* is thus, in one sense at least, an organization that ensures continuous adaptation to changing external conditions.[3] Indeed, the notion of the learning organization is bolstered by the state of continuous change in which many organizations find themselves.[4]

Joan Bennett linked the "learning organization" to the essential knowledge that organizations must possess to perform effectively.[5] Bennett examined twenty-five organizations that claimed to be learning organizations and that had actively pursued a deliberate effort to become such organizations. He concluded that several characteristics must be aligned for a learning organization to exist, and those characteristics are:[6]

- Strategy/vision

- Executive practices

- Managerial practices

- Climate

- Organization/job structure

- Information flow

- Work processes

- Performance goals/feedback

- Training/education

- Individual/team development

- Rewards/recognition

- Continuous dialogue

A learning organization is one that has aligned these characteristics with learning as a means of adapting to—or even anticipating—external environmental change. According to that view, then, individual workplace learning would thus be encouraged when the organization's leadership has effectively achieved continuing alignment among these characteristics.

WHAT IS *ORGANIZATIONAL LEARNING*, AND HOW IS IT RELATED TO WORKPLACE LEARNING?

Organizational learning, although related to the learning organization, is not synonymous with it. Organizational learning has a meaning of its own that should not be confused with the concept of a learning organization. As Hedberg writes:[7]

> *Although organizational learning occurs through individuals, it would be a mistake to conclude that organizational learning is nothing but the cumulative result of their members' learning. Organizations do not have brains, but they have cognitive systems and memories. As individuals develop their personalities, personal habits, and beliefs over time, organizations develop worldviews and ideologies. Members come and go, and leadership changes, but organizations' memories preserve certain behaviors, mental maps, norms, and values over time.*

Encouraging organizational learning, as well as individual learning, is a goal of the learning organization. *Organizational learning* refers to how organizations gain experience, reflect upon it, and even anticipate new experience as a means of gaining competitive advantage. It means "learning at the system rather than individual level."[8] Although organizations do not learn in the same way that individuals do because they are not living organisms, they do experience the steps of the workplace learning process.

But how can organizational learning be conceptualized? What levels typify organizational learning? How can organizational learning be linked to organizational performance? How is organizational learning related to individual workplace learning? The next sections address these questions and issues.

How Can Organizational Learning Be Conceptualized?

In a classic treatment, Argyris and Schön described many ways to conceptualize organizational learning.[9] Each way that they articulated is worthy of brief review, because each perspective sheds light on the nature of organizational learning:

> First, the organization can be viewed as a group of people. In that sense, learning occurs in a group context. When individuals interact to achieve results and share in tasks, the group itself can be said to learn. That can be understood to mean group or team learning.

> Second, the organization can be regarded as a vehicle by which to achieve social objectives. Organizational learning in that sense, then, means improvements that result from organizational experience and lead to the general betterment of the human condition.

> Third, the organization can be regarded as a social structure. Learning is thus linked to changes in organizational structure as manifested by changes made to the organization chart or in the allocation of work duties and responsibilities. When organizations are reorganized to cope with external change, they are adapting—and thus can also be said to be learning.

> Fourth, the organization can be regarded as a system. In that sense, then, organizations learn as changes occur in the processes by which decisions are made or work processes are carried out. The goal is the correction—or even the prevention—of errors and the achievement of a high-quality standard, such as six sigma or better.

> Fifth, organizational learning can be viewed from the perspective of corporate culture. Issues linked to organizational learning include individual socialization into the corporate culture, efforts to change the culture, and organizational approaches to correct or prevent errors. Culture means a group's shared perceptions and social meanings, and organizational learning occurs as individuals flow into that corporate culture, strive to interact in it, or even try to change it.

> Sixth, organizations can be viewed as political systems in which individuals form groups and then attempt to gain advantage or power through deliberative group action. "Organizational learning might include the competition of business firms for market, of government agencies for resources, and of nations for hegemony."[10]

Many other writers have, of course, written about organizational learning and offered important perspectives about it. For instance, Hedberg stated that "organizational learning includes both the processes by which organizations adjust themselves defensively to reality and the processes by which knowledge is used offensively to improve the fits between organizations and their environment."[11] Hedberg believed that organizations can learn, unlearn, and even relearn. To him, "learning thus encompasses the process whereby learners interactively map their environments and use their maps to alter their environments."[12] Learning results from feedback provided to the organization and its members from interactions with clients and the external environment. "Unlearning," writes Hedberg, "is a process through which learners discard knowledge. Unlearning makes way for new responses and mental maps."[13]

Shrivastava reviewed the extensive literature on organizational learning and concluded that several themes could be found.[14] First, organizational learning means adaptation. Second, organizational learning is about the sharing of assumptions. Third, organizational learning is associated with evolving knowledge about the relationships between what the organization does (action) and its results (outcomes). Fourth and finally, organizational learning is closely tied to the experiences of the organization—that is, successes, failures, and other key events that have shaped how organizational members perceive reality.

What Levels Typify Organizational Learning?

Authorities on organizational learning often distinguish between different types or categories of learning. It is important to be aware of them.

For instance, Argyris and Schön distinguish between single-loop and double-loop learning. *Single-loop learning* occurs when "members of the organization respond to changes in the internal and external environment of the organization by detecting errors which they then correct so as to maintain the central features of organizational theory-in-use."[15] In short, one feedback loop links action outcomes to organizational strategies or shared assumptions. Decision-makers keep the organization's performance in harmony with strategies and assumptions. Shared norms are not altered. But *double-loop learning* occurs when decision makers question or otherwise challenge shared assumptions or norms.

In a somewhat similar vein, Peter Senge, author of *The Fifth Discipline,* distinguishes between generative and adaptive learning. *Adaptive learning* is about coping with existing conditions and events. *Generative learning,* on the other hand, is associated with creativity, the process of coming up with new options or alternatives. "Generative learning," writes Senge, "[is] unlike adaptive learning [because it] requires new ways of looking at the world, whether in understanding customers or in understanding how to better manage a business."[16]

March also distinguished between two types of learning.[17] The first type he called *exploitation learning,* which he associated with the process of achieving regularity in systems and processes. It stands in stark contrast to what he called *exploration learning,* which he associated with experimentation, search, risk taking, discovery, and creativity. Clegg, when describing March's notion of exploration learning, emphasized that it "offers distant time horizons and uncertain benefits as its vision. While it offers the chance of increasing performance levels significantly beyond trend-lines there is also the risk that performance might be significantly lower if risky ventures fail."[18]

How Can Organizational Learning Be Linked to Organizational Performance?

Most authorities who have written about organizational learning regard it as a means to an end. The desired end is organizational performance, meaning competitive success. And yet specific links between organizational learning effectiveness and organizational performance have proven to be elusive to demonstrate. One reason is that it is not always clear what exactly is meant by organizational performance and how it is measured. Chang, for instance, listed seven variables that he believed could be measures of organizational performance:[19]

1. Sales in dollars per employee

2. Operating profit margin before depreciation as a percentage of sales

3. Return on investment

4. Finished goods inventory turnover

5. Raw materials inventory turnover and WIP inventory turnover

6. Quality

7. Flexibility

Traditional measures of organizational success are expressed by profit or client satisfaction measures.

Much recent attention has centered around attempting to show relationships between organizational learning and performance. One study relied on a written questionnaire that was mailed to 400 randomly selected CEOs in Denmark, France, Germany, and the United Kingdom.[20] The survey results revealed that, in the opinion of CEOs, creating an organizational climate that encourages employee creativity and learning is essential to success. Another study in a large U.S. government agency found from a survey that respondents perceived a link to exist between innovation as manifested by the number of ideas generated and the organization's climate.[21]

Richards and Goh devised an organizational learning survey.[22] After applying a factor analysis to 103 responses, the researchers reduced the survey from fifty-five to twenty-one questions, focused on such categories as clarity of organizational mission and purpose, leadership and facilitation, transfer of knowledge, and teamwork and group problem solving. In later use with the survey, the researchers found that the highest score was 4.6 out of a possible 7.0, and they concluded that organizations had just begun to explore the notion of organizational learning.

In yet another study that may be regarded as focused on the theme of organizational learning, Virany, Tushman, and Romanelli conducted longitudinal research to explore organizational learning ideas by directly investigating the relations between CEO succession and executive-team change on subsequent organizational performance in volatile competitive conditions.[23] They believed that, while CEO succession or executive-team change by themselves would be resisted by recalcitrant teams and conservative organizational traditions, the combination of CEO succession and executive-team change would alter team demographics and dynamics in a way that would enable the executive team to take decisive action. They also believed that CEOs promoted from within might be better able than externally recruited CEOs to harness the advantages of the organization's politics in implementing team change at the executive-team level.

But, contrary to the researchers' predictions, both CEO succession and executive-team change were significantly associated with subsequent organizational performance. There was no interaction effect of executive-team change and CEO succession on subsequent organizational performance. Evidently, new CEOs are not actively resisted by their executive teams, and revised executive teams are not blocked by incumbent CEOs. Rather, new CEOs and/or new executive teams seem to provide, on their own, sufficient diversity of expertise and a change in team-interaction processes to facilitate organizational learning in a volatile competitive environment. The results of the study emphasize the importance of executive succession as a means by which to improve organizational performance and for sustaining existing high-performance levels.

How Is Organizational Learning Related to
Individual Workplace Learning?

Experience is a source of stimulation to organizations and individuals alike. Individuals learn by trying out something new. That experience (in turn) leads to success, failure, or else mixed results. The memory of that experience is retained. The fruits of experience are thus linked to learning, and that is why experience is so prized.

The same basic principle also applies to organizations. Leaders formulate the strategic objectives (targets) for the organization and guide the organization toward achieving those objectives (strategy). As the strategy is pursued, the organization encounters challenges to be overcome. And, ultimately, the objectives are reached, are not reached, or else the strategy meets with mixed results. The memory of that experience is retained by veteran workers, is described in company documents, and so on. The fruits of experience are thus linked to learning, and the accumulated wisdom of "what works" and "what does not work" becomes the organizational culture, the web of meaning that is taken for granted by organization members. Stories often embody the organizational culture, and they also contain the fruits of organizational experience.

The culture that is established from organizational experience has an impact on individual learning. It creates conditions that encourage or discourage individual learning. Measuring how much the organization encourages or discourages individual learning means essentially measuring the organization's learning climate.

THE ORGANIZATION'S ROLE IN ENCOURAGING THE WORKPLACE LEARNING PROCESS

According to *Trends That Affect Learning and Performance,* three of ten important trends affecting the future workplace will be:[24] (1) "Integrated high performance work systems will proliferate"; (2) "companies will transform into learning organizations"; and (3) "organizational emphasis on human performance management will accelerate." These three trends are particularly noteworthy because they point the way toward a growing awareness that the managers bear responsibilities for creating a climate conducive to achieving strategic goals, maintaining competitiveness domestically and internationally, and establishing conditions that encourage individuals and groups to learn, innovate, and exceed customers' expectations.

The organization's role in supporting the workplace learner can be examined from the standpoint of the high-performance workplace (HPW), from the standpoint of the learning organization, or from a simpler approach. The results of my study later summarized in Exhibits 7-2 and 7-3 also provide additional evidence about what conditions must be provided by organizations to support workplace learning.

Clues from the HPW

Many clues to what decision makers should do to encourage individual workplace learning can be found in research on the HPW. In the HPW, of course, individuals find themselves performing in a work environment where their efforts are fully encouraged and supported. The organizational climate is fully supportive of optimal performance and productivity.[25]

Many of the same elements must also be present in a learning organization. The reason? According to Senge, "The organizations that will truly excel in the future will be the organizations that discover how to tap people's commitment and capacity to learn at *all* levels of the organization."[26] There is thus a close relationship between the organization that encourages learning and the HPW.

Research sponsored by the U.S. Department of Labor on the HPW is summarized in Exhibit 7-1. Review those criteria in light of how—and how much—you believe the identified criteria for an HPW might encourage workplace learners in the workplace learning process. If you wish, measure your organization against those criteria.[27]

Clues from the Learning Organization

A *learning organization*, according to Senge, "is an organization that is continually expanding its capacity to create its future."[28] A learning organization possesses five characteristics that encourage learning:

1. **Systems thinking** is the first discipline of the learning organization, according to Senge. It is the ability to see the whole as well as the parts. An effective systems thinker can identify *inputs* (what flows into a system), *processes* (how inputs are transformed), *outputs* (what flows out of the system), and *feedback loops* (how information about outputs helps to improve the reception of inputs, the transformation of them into outputs through processes, and the reception of outputs by users).

2. **Personal mastery** is the second discipline of the learning organization. Individuals possessing this characteristic "approach their life as an artist would approach a work of art. They do that by being committed to their own lifelong learning."[29] To practice this discipline, individuals must identify what they want out of life—and then vigorously pursue it. They do not become discouraged or neglect their own learning; rather, they pursue learning—like their lives—with vigor.

Exhibit 7-1: HPW practices criteria.

	CATEGORY		SUBCATEGORY		CRITERIA FOR THE HIGH PERFORMANCE WORKPLACE
I	**Skills and Information**	I.1	*Training and Continuous Learning*	I.1.1	Investments in training and employee development reflect a higher proportion of payroll than competitors.
				I.1.2	There are programs to support continuous learning (e.g., job rotation and cross-functional team training).
				I.1.3a	Training program effectiveness is measured.
				I.1.3b	Training programs are effective.
		I.2	*Information Sharing*	I.2.1	All workers receive information on operating results, financial goals, and organizational performance.
				I.2.2	Employees are appropriately trained to apply information on the organization's operating results, financial goals, and its organizational performance.
				I.2.3	There are multiple mechanisms by which internal communication occurs so that information flows up, down, and across the organization.
II	**Participation, Organization, and Partnership**	II.1	*Employee Participation*	II.1.1	Workers are actively involved in continuously improving their work process(es) and redefining their jobs.
				II.1.2	Workers can rapidly modify their work processes to correct quality, safety, or other problems.
				II.1.3	Workers are actively involved in problem-solving, selecting new technology, modifying the product or service provided, and meeting with customers.
				II.1.4	When individuals or teams make suggestions, they always receive feedback about their suggestions.

		II.2	*Organization Structure*	II.2.1	The organization has recently made one or more efforts to reduce layers of management.
				II.2.2	Most workers are organized into work teams with substantial autonomy.
				II.2.3	There are cross-functional teams or other mechanisms to share innovative ideas across organizational boundaries.
		II.3	*Worker-Management Partnerships*	II.3.1	Workers and their representatives are partners in decision making on a range of issues traditionally decided solely by managers (e.g., new technology, quality, and safety).
				II.3.2a	If the organization is unionized, the union-management relationship has moved toward joint participation and decision making.
				II.3.2b	If the organization is unionized, collective bargaining is based on interest-based techniques and cooperative problem solving.
				II.3.3	If the organization is unionized, the company and the union have engaged in innovative collective bargaining arrangements.
III	**Compensation, Security and Work Environment**	III.1	*Compensation Linked to Performance and Skills*	III.1.1	The organization's incentive system incorporates new ways of rewarding workers.
				III.1.2	Individual workers or work teams receive financial rewards when they improve the product, the work process, or make other improvements.
				III.1.3	Individual compensation is tied to both individual and corporate performance.
				III.1.4	Executive pay is tied to corporate (or business unit) performance.

(continues)

Exhibit 7-1: (Continued).

CATEGORY		SUBCATEGORY		CRITERIA FOR THE HIGH PERFORMANCE WORKPLACE
	III.2	*Employment Security*	III.2.1	Comprehensive organization employment planning strategies and policies exist in order to minimize or avoid laying off workers.
			III.2.2	If layoffs have occurred in recent years, the organization actively helped laid-off workers find new jobs.
			III.2.3	The organization has a stated policy that workers will not suffer adverse effects from suggestions that result in productivity gains.
	III.3	*Supportive Work Environment*	III.3.1	The company attracts and retains a talented work force. (*Issue to consider:* Why do people leave?)
			III.3.2	There are policies and programs in place to encourage better employee morale and greater workforce commitments. (*Issue to consider:* What practices are in place to ensure that all problems with morale are promptly and systematically addressed?)
			III.3.3	Employees are actively involved in designing and implementing health and safety policies and programs.
			III.3.4	Accident rates in this organization are below the industry average.
			III.3.5	Family-supportive policies (e.g., flexible work schedules, child care, and/or elder-care) are in place.
			III.3.6	The organization actively hires, trains, retrains, and promotes a diverse work force.

IV	Putting it All Together			IV.1	*The company fully integrates its human resource policies and workplace practices with other essential business strategies.*
				IV.2	*Quality and continuous improvement efforts are meshed with training, work organization, employee involvement, and alternative compensation programs.*
				IV.3a	*Workers are involved in the design and purchase of new technologies.*
				IV.3b	*Workers have the opportunity to regularly modify the technologies they use.*
				IV.3c	*Employees receive adequate training to use new technologies effectively.*

Source: William J. Rothwell, *Beyond Training and Development: State-of-the-Art Strategies for Enhancing Human Performance* (New York: AMACOM, 1996), pp. 14–17. Used by permission. Adapted from U.S. Department of Labor, *The Road to High Performance Workplaces* (Washington, D.C.: Superintendent of Public Documents, Office of the American Workplace, 1994).

3. **Mental models** are the third discipline of the learning organization. Mental models, as Senge defines the term, have to do with "deeply ingrained assumptions, generalizations, or even pictures or images that influence how we understand the world and how we take action."[30] Working with mental models means communicating—and receiving feedback—about assumptions, ideas, and approaches.

4. **Building shared vision** is the fourth discipline of the learning organization. Leaders are able to create a compelling vision that excites others to action and builds enthusiasm for the organization's goals and strategic objectives. Senge believes, however, that effective organizations are able to build and sustain a shared vision that motivates "people to excel and learn, not because they are told to, but because they want to."[31]

5. **Team learning** is the fifth and final discipline of the learning organization. It is linked to the ability of individuals to work, and learn, effectively together in groups. Senge believes team learning is important because "teams, not individuals, are the fundamental learning unit in modern organizations."[32]

According to Senge, all five disciplines must work together synergistically for a learning organization to function effectively.

A Simple Approach

One way to identify how much the organization supports workplace learning is to call together a group of workers from the organization and pose the following questions:

- What conditions in this organization most *encourage* learning?

- What conditions in this organization most *discourage* learning?

- What *actions* should be taken in this organization to more effectively *encourage learning and eliminate barriers to it*?

In posing these questions, you should stress that workplace learning can—and does—occur on the job, near the job, and off the job, and that it can be formal, informal, or incidental. If you wish, pose the same questions by electronic mail, electronic bulletin board, face-to-face interviews, or mail survey.

HOW DO ORGANIZATIONS *ENCOURAGE* WORKPLACE LEARNING?

My research involved about sixty interviews with individuals representing diverse industries and hierarchical levels.[33] The respondents were interviewed about conditions that encourage workplace learning, conditions that discourage their learning, and actions that they believe could be taken by the organization to create conditions that would encourage people to learn more effectively. More specifically, they were asked to respond to the following questions about supportive conditions:[34]

- Think back to a time when you were asked to do something new and different in the workplace and you felt *encouraged* by conditions in the organization that encouraged you to learn. This can be considered a *learning situation,* whether it occurred during your work or during training about your work. It should have occurred while you were in your present job and with your present employer. It is important that you describe the situation in detail and explain specifically what happened that made you feel encouraged in learning something new. First, provide an overview of the situation. What was the learning challenge you faced? Then answer some background questions: When did this occur (*give approximate dates*)? Who was involved (*give job titles but not names*). Where did this occur (*give approximate location*).

- Tell me *what happened in this situation that made you feel encouraged about learning something new.* Be as specific as possible, describing what happened in the sequence that it happened. Be sure to explain what was happening, what you were doing, what you were thinking, and what you were feeling as events unfolded.

- What do you believe were the conditions in the organization that *encouraged* your learning in this situation? Summarize or list those conditions in your own words.

The results of that research revealed that organizations encourage workplace learning when workers perceive certain conditions to be present. (See Appendix A.) Those conditions are summarized in Exhibit 7-2 and are described below.

Encouraging Condition 1: Sufficient Financial Resources Exist to Support Workplace Learning. Individuals are encouraged to learn in the workplace only when the organization supports such learning by providing adequate financial support. That support may include the purchase

---

Exhibit 7-2: Conditions that encourage the workplace learning process.

Workplace learning, according to the workers interviewed for the study on which this book is based, is encouraged to the extent that each of the following conditions is perceived to be met:

Sufficient financial resources exist to support workplace learning.

Realistic goals and expectations for learning have been established.

There is commitment by the organization to the learning process.

Sufficient trust exists in the organization.

Management shares a common understanding of vision and goals.

Sufficient time is provided to permit learning.

Good communication exists in the organization.

The organization fosters a means by which to collect and use feedback from customers.

Workplace learning is made a priority and is tied to performance expectations.

The leadership of the organization is perceived to support workplace learning.

Clear milestones have been established for the workplace learning process.

Managers, union leaders and learners exhibit buy-in and commitment to learning.

Individuals are matched to learning experiences for which they have the appropriate education and background.

The learning effort is closely tied to business needs.

Work standards are consistently applied within the organization.

The organization possesses clear methods by which to examine and measure work performance.

Learners are open-minded and possess an attitude that favors learning.

Measurement and accountability has been established and linked to the workplace learning process.

The workplace learning process is guided by a plan.

A clear sense exists about "next steps" following the workplace learning process.

The organization's union, if the organization is unionized, supports the workplace learning process/effort.

External environmental factors support the workplace learning process.

Fear has been reduced within the organization so that individuals are not afraid to take risks and learn.

Learners feel empowered.

Learners feel they have incentives and rewards sufficient to encourage them to pursue workplace learning and see "what's in it for them."

Responsibilities for who should do what in the workplace learning process have been clarified.

of materials, the use of staff time, or the purchase of other goods and services to support the workplace learning process.

Encouraging Condition 2: Realistic Goals and Expectations for Learning Have Been Established. Individuals expect their immediate supervisors or coworkers to help them establish realistic goals and expectations for their learning. Is it clear why they need to learn and what they should learn? Is it clear how the results of the learning process will contribute to achieving results of value to the organization? Only when these questions can be answered "yes" do workplace conditions encourage workplace learning.

Encouraging Condition 3: There Is Commitment by the Organization to the Learning Process. Organizational commitment takes many forms. Do top managers indicate that learning is important? Do they demonstrate that commitment by providing sufficient resources such as time, money, and people to encourage the learning process? Do individuals see this commitment expressed in both words and actions? When individuals need to learn something new, are they given sufficient time and help to do it? These questions relate to the perceived level of commitment by the organization to the learning process.

Encouraging Condition 4: Sufficient Trust Exists in the Organization. Trust is key to the workplace learning process.[35] Trust is necessary because individuals must feel that, as they learn, they will not be penalized for the mistakes they make during the learning process. Without trust, people will not feel the "psychologically comfortable" climate that is a well-documented requirement for successful adult learning.[36]

Encouraging Condition 5: Management Shares a Common Understanding of Vision and Goals. People cannot learn successfully if managers do not share a common understanding of vision and goals. In short, managers must know what they want, express that clearly, and not reveal conflict among themselves about the ideal future of the organization to be realized.

Encouraging Condition 6: Sufficient Time Is Provided to Permit Learning. Learning takes time. If people are sent to participate in off-the-job training, they need time to participate. They may also need time to catch up on their work when they return to the work setting from off-the-job learning experiences such as training or conferences. Time is also required if people are rotated to other jobs to learn them, are investigating practical solutions to workplace problems, are participating on organizational task forces to make change happen, or read books and articles to improve their knowledge.

Encouraging Condition 7: Good Communication Exists in the Organization. Good communication is important to encourage workplace learning because people must know where to find the information they need when they need it. That requires communication. Without it, individuals may not feel confident that they are getting reliable information in a timely fashion from trustworthy and reliable sources.

Encouraging Condition 8: The Organization Fosters a Means by Which to Collect and Use Feedback from Customers. Learning occurs through experience. Experience with customers on a daily basis is of key importance if individuals are to learn what delights customers, what distresses them, and what they do not care about. Feedback from customers can be a powerful source of information about what is worth knowing—and how well the organization (or the workplace learner) is meeting or exceeding customer needs. The organization must establish and maintain methods for acquiring that information from customers and make timely, specific, and useful feedback available to workers. That may be accomplished, of course, through such diverse means as customer surveys, focus groups, response cards, and many other means.

Encouraging Condition 9: Workplace Learning Is Made a Priority and Is Tied to Performance Expectations. Do individuals perceive that the organization's decision makers make learning a priority, or does it always seem to take second or third place to other activities? Do individuals perceive that they are expected to learn as they work, or are those performance expectations left unspoken and undercommunicated? For the organization to support workplace learning, individuals must perceive that learning is a high priority and that they are expected to be successful at it.

Encouraging Condition 10: The Leadership of the Organization Is Perceived to Support Workplace Learning. Do individuals perceive that the top managers of the organization support workplace learning? In short, how much commitment to workplace learning do individuals observe from the organization's leaders? Commitment may, of course, be shown in many ways. One way is for leaders to talk about it. Another way is for leaders to be seen participating in high-profile efforts that showcase their commitment, such as conducting training or actually showing themselves participating in the learning process.

Encouraging Condition 11: Clear Milestones Have Been Established for the Workplace Learning Process. People cannot be expected to learn everything at once. For instance, if a manager has been rotated into the job of another manager, complete mastery of the job will not be instantly achieved. Realistic, measurable, and clear milestones should be established to guide the learning process. A good time to do that is at the start of the learning process—to cite an example, the beginning of a job rotation. At that time it is desirable to formulate achievable learning goals and then establish milestones to determine how much or how well the goals have been achieved.

Encouraging Condition 12: Managers, Union Leaders, and Learners Exhibit Buy-In and Commitment to Learning. Individuals take cues from their leaders. Not only must top managers be supportive of the learning process, but so must other influential stakeholders. That includes managers and, when organizations are unionized, the union leaders. Of course, the learners themselves must also be given ways to provide input into the learning processes in which they are engaged. They must see "what's in it for them."

Encouraging Condition 13: Individuals Are Matched to Learning Experiences for Which They Have the Appropriate Education and Background. Putting people into "sink or swim" experiences is anxiety producing. That is particularly true when the organization's leaders treat learning as a "one-size-fits-all" experience. If, for example, all workers are required to attend the same training, then they may vary dramatically in their educational credentials and work backgrounds. Some people may not need that training. It is therefore important to match learning experiences to the individual's previous education and experience. When the organization is regarded as doing that on a regular basis, then individuals come to regard this condition as supportive of the workplace learning process.

Encouraging Condition 14: The Learning Effort Is Closely Tied to Business Needs. How clearly do individuals see the link between learning efforts and organizational needs? When individuals perceive that link to be strong, then conditions in the organization encourage workplace learning.

Encouraging Condition 15: Work Standards Are Consistently Applied Within the Organization. Learning is not carried out for its own sake; rather, it is carried out to achieve results. But does the organization have consistent work standards by which to measure results? If so, workplace conditions support continuous learning.

Encouraging Condition 16: The Organization Possesses Clear Methods by Which to Examine and Measure Work Performance. Does the organization have clearly understood methods by which to measure and assess individual and group performance? If so, then the workplace conditions are supportive of workplace learning because individuals feel that what they learn can be applied to their work and measured appropriately.

Encouraging Condition 17: Learners Are Open-Minded and Possess an Attitude That Favors Learning. Individuals have responsibilities in the workplace learning process. One such responsibility is that they keep an open mind and a positive attitude about the learning process. Many trainers have had experience with groups in which one or more persons were troublemakers. They have a negative attitude about the learning process. Often, they do not see why they should be participating ("why didn't you ask my boss to attend this instead of me?") or do not have an open mind about what they are learning ("what's this, another stupid idea given to us by the training department?"). But, for organizational conditions to support workplace learning, learners must keep open minds and positive attitudes.

Encouraging Condition 18: Measurement and Accountability Has Been Established and Linked to the Workplace Learning Process. Much has been written about the need to evaluate training and make trainers accountable for achieving returns on training investments. However, learners and their immediate supervisors should also be measured and held accountable for supporting the learning process. How have learners been measured and held accountable for their learning? Although their learning can be assessed by knowledge and performance tests, they should also be held accountable for their willingness to learn. Their immediate supervisors should be held accountable for facilitating the transfer of what they have learned to work applications.

Encouraging Condition 19: The Workplace Learning Process Is Guided by a Plan. Planning is necessary for most human efforts. The organization should establish a plan for learning to establish alignment between corporate strategic objectives and plans and planned learning initiatives.[37] Likewise, individual development plans (IDPs) should be established to provide guidance for individuals about what they should learn, how they should learn, over what time period they should learn, and how results should be measured.[38] When a plan exists to guide learning for individuals and for the organization, then organizational conditions support workplace learning.

Encouraging Condition 20: A Clear Sense Exists About "Next Steps" Following the Workplace Learning Process. A workplace that encourages learning facilitates the establishment of action plans to guide learning. These may take the form of action learning projects, task force assignments, and other capability building initiatives. At the end of each such experience, learners are guided by their supervisors, facilitators, or other means to think about "next steps" to practice, apply, reflect on, and learn more about what they have already learned.

Encouraging Condition 21: The Organization's Union, if the Organization Is Unionized, Supports the Workplace Learning Process/Effort. Obviously, unions can affect how much individuals seek to learn. Only if the union supports individual improvement efforts will individuals be encouraged to learn.

Encouraging Condition 22: External Environmental Factors Support the Workplace Learning Process. Competitive conditions and other factors in the external environment may exert influence on the willingness of individuals to learn. How supportive, in the perception of learners, are external environmental conditions to the learning process?

Encouraging Condition 23: Fear Has Been Reduced Within the Organization So That Individuals Are Not Afraid to Take Risks and Learn. Fear can reduce the willingness of individuals to take the risks that are so important in the workplace learning process. If individuals perceive that they will not be penalized for making efforts to learn, then they will learn. A psychological comfort level is essential to establishing a climate that is conducive to workplace learning. Of particular importance is the role of the immediate supervisor. Is the supervisor perceived to support the individual's efforts to learn? If so, the climate is conducive to workplace learning.

Encouraging Condition 24: Learners Feel Empowered. How much do learners feel able to control their own fate and to experiment with creative approaches to difficult workplace problems? Only when workers feel that they are empowered and "in control" of their own learning is the workplace conducive to learning.

Encouraging Condition 25: Learners Feel They Have Incentives and Rewards Sufficient to Encourage Them to Pursue Workplace Learning and See "What's in It for Them." Do workplace learners feel that they will be rewarded somehow for successful learning? Of course, if the organization has established a program, such as "pay for knowledge" or its related approaches,[39] workers will perceive that they will receive tangible payoffs for pursuing learning. Will learning lead to increased opportunities for advancements or other, less tangible, rewards? Will learners be recognized for their learning efforts?

Encouraging Condition 26: Responsibilities for Who Should Do What in the Workplace Learning Process Have Been Clarified. How clear are the responsibilities expected of various stakeholders in the workplace learning process? Are workers told that they are expected to learn? Are supervisors encouraged to facilitate the learning of their workers and rewarded accordingly? In short, has the organization gone on the record to clarify who should be responsible for what, avoiding the notion that the WLP department should be the source of all learning?

HOW DO ORGANIZATIONS *DISCOURAGE* WORKPLACE LEARNING?

Over the years, increasing attention has been focused on the barriers that prevent adults from participating in learning experiences. This issue takes many forms, of course. For instance, what are the deterrents that prevent adults from participating in off-the-job educational experiences? One summary of research findings on that topic is provided in Exhibit 7-3. Although many barriers stem from issues unique to individuals,[40] other barriers stem from organizationally related issues.[41]

As part of this study, some sixty individuals from diverse industries and hierarchical levels were interviewed about conditions impeding their learning. More specifically, they were asked to respond to the following questions:[42]

- Think back to a time when you were asked to do something new and different in the workplace and you felt *discouraged* by conditions in the organization that prevented you from learning. This can be considered a learning situation, whether it occurred during your work or during training about your work. It should have occurred while you were in your present job and with your present employer. It is important that you describe the situation in detail and explain specifically what happened that made you feel discouraged in learning something new. First, provide an overview of the situation. What was the learning challenge you faced? Then answer some background questions: When did this occur (*give approximate dates*)? Who was involved (*give job titles but not names*)? Where did this occur (*give approximate location*)?

- Tell me *what happened in this situation that made you feel discouraged about learning something new.* Be as specific as possible, describing what happened in the sequence that it happened. Be sure to explain what was happening, what you were doing, what you were thinking, and what you were feeling as events unfolded.

- What do you believe were the conditions in the organization that *discouraged* your learning in this situation? Summarize or list those conditions in your own words.

The results of this research revealed that organizations discourage workplace learning when workers perceive certain conditions to be present. Those conditions are listed in Exhibit 7-4 and are described next:

Exhibit 7-3: Deterrents to participation in off-duty adult education programs.*

Didn't have the time for studying.

Course scheduled at inconvenient time.

Would take away from time with family.

Didn't think I could attend regularly.

Course at an inconvenient location.

Time required to finish course.

Couldn't afford miscellaneous expenses.

Wasn't willing to give up leisure.

Couldn't afford registration fees.

Don't enjoy studying.

Didn't think I would finish.

Courses did not seem interesting.

Felt unprepared for the course.

Trouble arranging for child care.

Family problems.

Courses not useful, practical.

Wanted something specific.

Course not on right level for me.

Didn't think course would meet needs.

Transportation problem.

Not confident of my learning ability.

(continues)

Exhibit 7-3: (Continued).

Didn't meet course requirements.

Not that interested in taking courses.

Courses available were poor quality.

Employer wouldn't give financial aid.

Prefer to learn on my own.

Education wouldn't help me in my job.

Family didn't encourage.

Didn't know about available courses.

Course was in an unsafe area.

Couldn't compete with young students.

Personal health problems.

Felt too old to take the course.

Friends didn't encourage.

*Ranked in order of importance from most to least important.
Source: C. Martindale and J. Drake, "Factor Structure of Deterrents to Participation in Off-Duty Adult Education Programs," *Adult Education Quarterly, 39, 2* (1989): 67. Used by permission of *Adult Education Quarterly.*

Discouraging Condition 1: Insufficient Financial Resources Exist to Support Workplace Learning. People are discouraged to learn when they perceive resources are lacking. If they are unable to purchase books, periodicals, or other resources to support their learning process, then conditions in the organization do not support workplace learning. Of course, as in all these conditions, it remains a matter of perceptions. However, perceptions can shape reality.

Discouraging Condition 2: The Organization Does Not Establish Realistic Learning Goals and Expectations. Workers complained that they are sometimes asked to learn new things too quickly—or without goals and expectations being clearly established at all. Sometimes their im-

---

Exhibit 7-4: Conditions that discourage the workplace learning process.

Workplace learning, according to the workers interviewed for the study on which this book is based, is discouraged to the extent that each of the following conditions exists:

Insufficient financial resources exist to support workplace learning.

The organization does not establish realistic learning goals and expectations.

No commitment exists to support the learning process.

The organization is characterized by a general lack of trust.

The organization is torn by the strife of factions in the organization that are pursuing competing goals.

The time constraints placed on the workplace learning process are unrealistic or unclear.

The learning lacks focus, goals and objectives.

Communication in the organization is perceived to be poor.

The organization has placed limitations on the feedback that customers may provide to workers.

Workers are subjected to multiple, conflicting, or unreasonable demands.

The organization experiences a lack of leadership.

There are no plans or milestones for workplace learning.

There is a lack of buy-in and commitment to learning by different stakeholders such as top managers, supervisors, workers, or other groups.

The learners have an inadequate education or background to take advantage of the learning opportunities provided to them.

The organization applies double standards to the learning.

(continues)

Exhibit 7-4: (Continued).

The organization does not possess a clear process for examining and measuring work performance.

Individuals experience a lack of motivation to learn.

Individuals demonstrate a poor attitude toward learning.

The organization has not established ways to measure learning and hold stakeholders accountable for playing their parts in it.

No long-term plan exists to guide workplace learning for the organization.

Once individuals learn, they are not guided to see "next steps."

The union, if the organization is unionized, does not support the workplace learning effort.

External environmental factors do not support the workplace learning process.

Fear exists within the organization.

Workers do not feel empowered.

The incentives and reward system of the organization does not support learning or its results.

Source: William J. Rothwell, "Models for the Workplace Learner." Unpublished research report. Copyright 2000 by William J. Rothwell, Ph.D. All rights reserved.

---

mediate supervisors expect them to do one thing, while their trainers or coworkers expect something else. These conditions obviously do not encourage workplace learning.

Discouraging Condition 3: No Commitment Exists to Support the Learning Process. Commitment is a complex issue that takes many forms. However, workers expect managers to demonstrate commitment to the workplace learning process. If managers at all levels are not seen as participating in what they have asked others to do, then they are not perceived as demonstrating genuine commitment. That sometimes occurs when workers have been asked to learn new approaches, new technologies, new work methods, or other challenges.

Discouraging Condition 4: The Organization Is Characterized by a General Lack of Trust. If learners are concerned that they will be penalized for the mistakes they make while learning something new, then they do not perceive the organization to have established conditions that support workplace learning.

Discouraging Condition 5: The Organization Is Torn by the Strife of Factions in the Organization That Are Pursuing Competing Goals. If workers perceive that divisions, departments, or teams of an organization are torn by strife—such as "turf battles" or concerns over whose responsibility it is to do what—then they do not perceive the organizational conditions to be supportive of workplace learning.

Discouraging Condition 6: The Time Constraints Placed on the Workplace Learning Process Are Unrealistic or Unclear. When managers do not make clear how much time can be afforded to workers to master something new, then workers do not perceive the organization's conditions to be supportive of workplace learning.

Discouraging Condition 7: The Learning Lacks Focus, Goals, and Objectives. When workers do not perceive that the learning experience has a clear focus, goals, and objectives, then they do not believe that the organization has encouraged workplace learning.

Discouraging Condition 8: Communication in the Organization Is Perceived to Be Poor. One way that learning occurs in organizations is by information that is spread rapidly. However, when the organization has not established clear communication or communication channels to spread new information—or the results of experience—then workers perceive the organizational conditions to be discouraging for workplace learning.

Discouraging Condition 9: The Organization Has Placed Limitations on the Feedback That Customers May Provide to Workers. Feedback is an important means by which people learn. It allows individuals to self-correct, to improve on what they are doing. If the organization places limitations or filters on the feedback that customers may provide to workers, then the workers regard organizational conditions to be discouraging for learning.

Discouraging Condition 10: Workers Are Subjected to Multiple, Conflicting, or Unreasonable Demands. If workers are asked to carry out multiple tasks at the same time, then they are torn with conflict by the differing demands. If, for example, they are told to serve the customer but their immediate supervisors order them to save costs, then they do not know which directive to give priority. In those situations, they regard the organizational conditions to be discouraging for workplace learning.

Discouraging Condition 11: The Organization Experiences a Lack of Leadership. An organization that experiences frequent turnover at the top or in the management ranks will often shift a business's focus based on the new leadership. Workers in such companies do not know what issues are to be given priority. After all, management sets priorities. If management is always shifting, or changing too quickly, then workers are confused about what priorities are most important. As a consequence, they regard organizational conditions to be discouraging for workplace learning.

Discouraging Condition 12: There Are No Plans or Milestones for Workplace Learning. If workers are asked to learn but are not helped to establish a plan for learning or a means by which to measure their accomplishments, then they consider organizational conditions to be discouraging for workplace learning.

Discouraging Condition 13: There Is a Lack of Buy-In and Commitment to Learning by Different Stakeholders Such as Top Managers, Supervisors, Workers, or Other Groups. If different hierarchical levels of management express different views about the value of learning something new, then workers become confused about it. On those occasions, they regard organizational conditions to be discouraging for workplace learning.

Discouraging Condition 14: The Learners Have an Inadequate Education or Background to Take Advantage of the Learning Opportunities Pro-

vided to Them. If workers must master new information, skills, or attitudes for which they are not equipped by education or experience, then they regard organizational conditions to be discouraging for workplace learning. For instance, organizational decision makers may mandate that workers participate in statistical process control (SPC) training when, in fact, workers do not possess sufficient knowledge of mathematics.

Discouraging Condition 15: The Organization Applies Double Standards to the Learning. If some workers are expected to master new ideas, information, or skills at one level and other workers are not given the same expectations, then workers see that as the application of a double standard. Alternatively, if some people are given the chance to participate in learning experiences, others are not, and no explanation for this difference is given, then workers regard the organizational conditions to be discouraging for workplace learning.

Discouraging Condition 16: The Organization Does Not Possess a Clear Process for Examining and Measuring Work Performance. Ultimately, workplace learning should lead to improved work performance. However, if the organization has not established a means by which to examine and measure work performance, it is not possible to discern how much or how well learning experiences contribute to improved work performance. As a result, workers view the organizational conditions to be discouraging for workplace learning.

Discouraging Condition 17: Individuals Experience a Lack of Motivation to Learn. Workers must see why it is important to learn. If they view participation in a learning event as punishment—or as a mandate without a reason—then they will not be motivated to learn.

Discouraging Condition 18: Individuals Demonstrate a Poor Attitude Toward Learning. If some workers are disruptive of the learning process or otherwise demonstrate a poor attitude through such means as complaints, and if the organization has not addressed either the cause of the complaint or of the workers' attitude, then the organization has not established conditions that encourage learning.

Discouraging Condition 19: The Organization Has Not Established Ways to Measure Learning and Hold Stakeholders Accountable for Playing Their Parts in It. Everyone has a stake in workplace learning. As a consequence, if the organization has not established straightforward ways to measure learning and has not established ways to hold people accountable for playing their part in encouraging or reinforcing learning, then organizational conditions discourage learning.

Discouraging Condition 20: No Long-Term Plan Exists to Guide Workplace Learning for the Organization. Although learning can certainly be done for its own sake, workers expect that the learning sponsored by the organization should be tied to business results. They want to know how learning contributes to achieving results. If there is no plan to guide the organization's learning process, then workers believe that organizational conditions discourage workplace learning.

Discouraging Condition 21: Once Individuals Learn, They Are Not Guided to See "Next Steps." The organization should establish routine ways by which to show individuals how to learn more, apply what they learn, and reinforce their learning. If they wish to progress further on their own, the organization should establish routine ways by which to encourage and facilitate it. When such ways have not been established, workers perceive organizational conditions to be discouraging for the learning process.

Discouraging Condition 22: The Union, if the Organization Is Unionized, Does Not Support the Workplace Learning Effort. The union, if the organization is unionized, plays an important role as mediator and arbitrator of what is really important. If the union opposes learning efforts, then workers do not see that the organization has established supportive conditions. They then believe that the organization discourages workplace learning.

Discouraging Condition 23: External Environmental Factors Do Not Support the Workplace Learning Process. The external environment is complex. It includes everything outside the organization, including economic conditions, competitive conditions, technological conditions, and many other factors that influence organizational conditions. Although management does not control that environment, management does serve as a focal point to provide workers with information about that environment. If external environmental factors are not considered to be supportive of learning for purposes of adaptation or change, then workers do not believe that external environmental factors encourage the workplace learning process.

Discouraging Condition 24: Fear Exists Within the Organization. If workers fear for their jobs or fear that they will be punished for taking risks or making mistakes—both of which are important in learning—then they will believe that organizational conditions discourage the workplace learning process.

Discouraging Condition 25: Workers Do Not Feel Empowered. If workers do not feel empowered and able to make decisions on their own to experiment and be creative in their approaches to serving customers or other key groups, then they will regard organizational conditions to be discouraging for the workplace learning process.

Discouraging Condition 26: The Incentives and Reward System of the Organization Does Not Support Learning or Its Results. Workers must see "what's in it for them" to learn. They must believe that they are encouraged or given incentives to learn and rewarded for obtaining better results when they do learn. When they do not perceive that to be true, they will regard organizational conditions to be discouraging for workplace learning.

See Exhibit 7-5 for samples of the actual questions and answers to the interviews in my original research study.

SUMMARY

This chapter focused on defining learning organizations and organizational learning to give you a better sense of how learning takes place in the organization. After reading this chapter, you should be able to identify the ways your organization successfully encourages learning as well as discourages learning. The next chapter helps you assess your organization even further by showing you how to measure the climate for learning in your organization.

Exhibit 7-5: Sample behavioral event interview: organizational conditions that encourage and discourage workplace learning.

Respondent: Lead Anesthesia Biomedical Equipment Technician

Q: What are your work requirements? Describe your work duties.

A: Responsible for the medical equipment (patient related) located in the surgical services departments. This includes repair, calibration, performance checks, and proper documentation of their services.

Q: Think back to a time when you were asked to do something new and different in the workplace and you felt *discouraged* by conditions in the organization that prevented you from learning. This can be considered a *learning situation*, whether it occurred during your work or during training about your work. It should have occurred while you were in your present job and with your present employer. It is important that you describe the situation in detail and explain specifically what happened that made you feel discouraged in learning something new. First, provide an overview of the situation. What was the learning challenge you faced? Then answer some background questions: When did this occur (*give approximate dates*)? Who was involved (*give job titles but not names*)? Where did this occur (*give approximate location*)?

Q: What was the learning challenge?

A: Ultrasound machines previously had been maintained by the manufacturer since the inception of the Biomedical Engineering (BME) department. I was asked to assume responsibility for this equipment.

(You may ask the respondent to be specific about exactly what it was that made him or her feel discouraged in the situation.)

Q: When did this occur?

A: About September of 1997.

Q: Who was involved?

A: Director of Biomedical Engineering.

Q: Where did this occur?

A: Hospital.

Q: Tell me what happened in this situation that made you feel *discouraged* about learning something new. Be as specific as possible, describing what happened in the sequence that it happened. Be sure to explain what was happening, what you were doing, what you were thinking, and what you were feeling as events unfolded. What was happening, and what were you doing?

A: These ultrasound machines had previously been maintained and serviced by the manufacturer. I was sent to school to learn about a specific model so that we could drop these service contracts.

Q: What were you thinking as this was happening and/or as you were doing what you were doing?

A: I had been to service schools before and had assumed responsibility for other types of equipment where we dropped the service contracts.

Q: What were you feeling as this was happening and/or as you were doing what you were doing?

A: I felt confident based upon previous experiences that I would be able to handle this task.

Q: What was happening, and what were you doing?

A: After being at school, we had about six months before the service contract expired. During this time, I worked with the units and their field personnel knowing that we had the tools and technical support of the service contract if needed.

Q: What were you thinking as this was happening and/or as you were doing what you were doing?

A: I learned a lot working with the manufacturer field personnel and knowing that the support was there.

Q: What were you feeling as this was happening and/or as you were doing what you were doing?

A: I felt confident with this particular model of ultrasound equipment.

Q: What was happening, and what were you doing?

A: Three months after the service contract was dropped, all of the service contracts for the other ultrasound equipment were dropped as they assumed that since I had been trained on one model, I could take care of all models.

Q: What were you thinking as this was happening and/or as you were doing what you were doing?

A: There was now no support for any of our ultrasound machines and the manufacturers removed any tools or calibration equipment that we had on site. Many of the units did not even have service or technical manuals, which made it difficult to quickly learn about the units that I had not been trained on.

(continues)

Exhibit 7-5: (Continued).

Q: What were you feeling as this was happening and/or as you were doing what you were doing?

A: While feeling confident with the model I had been trained on (repairs were timely and staff satisfaction was maintained), they (the staff) expected the same level of service for the models that I had not been trained on. This was frustrating as our manager assumed that I would be able to take care of all of our ultrasound equipment without proper resources and tools.

Q: What do you believe were the conditions in the organization that *discouraged* your learning in this situation? Summarize or list those conditions in your own words.

Q: What were the conditions?

A: A lack of understanding on the part of management and a lack of resources to learn.

Q: What is your summary of the conditions that discouraged your learning? List them:

A:
- Belief of the BME director that all models are similar
- Lack of money for proper training
- Staffing conditions that allow for proper training—either at the manufacturer school or sitting down at work with the manual to learn myself

Q: Think back to a time when you were asked to do something new and different in the workplace and you felt *encouraged* by conditions in the organization that encouraged you to learn. This can be considered a *learning situation,* whether it occurred during your work or during training about your work. It should have occurred while you were in your present job and with your present employer. It is important that you describe the situation in detail and explain specifically what happened that made you feel encouraged about learning something new. First, provide an overview of the situation. What was the learning challenge you faced? Then answer some background questions: When did this occur (*approximate dates*)? Who was involved (*give job titles but not names*)? Where did this occur (*give approximate location*)?

Q: What was the learning challenge?

A: In this situation, I was learning myself as well as being involved with training others. Training for users on the surgical laser equipment was needed in the operating rooms.

(You may ask the respondent to be specific about exactly what it was that made him or her feel encouraged in the situation.)

Q: When did this occur?

A: 1997.

Q: Who was involved?

A: Operating room staff, laser coordinator, and operating room nursing educator.

Q: Where did this occur?

A: Operating room.

Q: Tell me what happened in this situation that made you feel *encouraged* about learning something new. Be as specific as possible, describing what happened in the sequence that it happened. Be sure to explain what was happening, what you were doing, what you were thinking, and what you were feeling as events unfold. What was happening, and what were you doing?

A: There were several indicators that we needed training. Our department was getting many simple operation calls, the laser coordinator in the operating room was frustrated with the improper setup and operation during cases, and many of the staff indicated that they did not feel comfortable setting up and operating the equipment. In fact, many of the staff avoided cases where the laser was used.

Q: What were you thinking as this was happening and/or as you were doing what you were doing?

A: After attending many service schools and working on the surgical lasers, I had become a resource to the operating room (OR) staff for laser operation and general questions.

Q: What were you feeling as this was happening and/or as you were doing what you were doing?

A: This was encouraging as the staff saw me as a resource and actually wanted to learn and receive training so that they felt more comfortable in their roles. I was willing to offer all the resources that we could to be involved in this training effort.

Q: What was happening, and what were you doing?

A: I sat down with the nursing educator and the laser coordinator to work on specific training issues for the equipment. We identified specific needs for each type of laser, developed competency levels and checks, created and gathered information for resource guides, and began to plan and implement in-services.

Q: What were you thinking as this was happening and/or as you were doing what you were doing?

A: We did a lot of work to implement this training initiative, but felt that the end result would be a significant improvement. Our immediate result was a reduction of "nuisance calls" to the BME department for operator error issues.

(continues)

Exhibit 7-5: (Continued).

Q: What were you feeling as this was happening and/or as you were doing what you were doing?

A: I felt positive about the experience because fellow staff members would be helped in performing their job better, and the staff would be satisfied that they would not be "afraid" of using the equipment as they would know and understand the operation. It was not only satisfying in helping others learn, but I learned a lot about the training process and how it can impact the work we do.

Q: What do you believe were the conditions in the organization that *encouraged* your learning in this situation? Summarize or list those conditions in your own words.

Q: What were the conditions?

A: The environment was positive in that we were working together and had the support and understanding of management.

Q: What is your summary of the conditions that encouraged your learning? List them:

A:
- Staff was willing to learn.
- Staff assisted in the project.
- Management recognized the problem and provided resources to meet the identified needs.

Q: What actions do you believe could be taken by the management of your organization to create conditions that would encourage people to learn more effectively in the workplace? Make a list of those actions.

Q: What are the actions that could be taken by company management:

A:
- Management needs to sit down on a regular basis with staff and listen to their concerns, frustrations, and suggestions for improvement.
- Management then needs to report back on these suggestions what actions can be taken (or not) and allow staff to assist with the changes.

Q: What is your opinion about the *most important changes* that are occurring in your work setting that require you to learn and to master new ways of doing things?

Q: Make a list of the trends or changes that require you to change and to learn new things at work.

A:
- The realization that the health-care field is changing. Technology is increasing and the available financial resources are diminishing.
- Increasing need to use second-source parts.
- Use of manufacturer technical support as opposed to actual service calls.

Chapter 8

ASSESSING THE ORGANIZATIONAL CLIMATE AND CULTURE FOR WORKPLACE LEARNING

Chapter 7 focused on answering four key questions: (1) What is a learning organization, and how is it related to workplace learning? (2) What is organizational learning, and how is it related to workplace learning? (3) How do organizations encourage workplace learning? and (4) How do organizations discourage workplace learning? This chapter builds on the answers to these questions and therefore addresses two key questions: (1) What is the climate for workplace learning? and (2) How is the climate for workplace learning assessed?

WHAT IS THE CLIMATE FOR WORKPLACE LEARNING?

What is meant by the term *climate*? How is corporate culture related to climate? This section addresses these questions.

What Is Organizational Climate?

As Rob Altmann explains:[1]

> *At its most basic level,* organizational climate *refers to employee perceptions of the work environment. Generally, these perceptions are descriptively based rather than value based. For example, the phrase "I have more work to do than I can possibly finish" is a description of a person's workload, while the phrase "I like my job" is a positive evaluation of one's job. Thus, organizational climate is more than simply a summary of employee likes and dislikes. The assessment of organizational climate typically occurs via an off-the-shelf or customized survey containing questions about the work environment. Although administration procedures used when conducting a survey can vary, ideally employees are asked to report to a designated work-site at a scheduled time to complete the survey, and employee participation is voluntary.*

Examinations of organizational climate have tended to focus on issues of efficiency (doing things right) and effectiveness (doing the right things).

What Is the Climate for Workplace Learning?

The *climate for workplace learning* refers to how much individuals feel that the organization encourages or discourages workplace learning. Since "organizational climate helps to set the tone of the organization,"[2] notes Altmann, it is therefore key to creating an environment that encourages individual workplace learning. Without a supportive climate, there can be no learning organization, and organizational learning is probably not as effective as it could otherwise be.

What Is Corporate Culture?

Corporate culture is related to climate. It refers to the taken-for-granted assumptions, based on the organization's experience, about what to do, what not to do, what is worth doing, and how people should interact.[3]

Shadur, Kienzle, and Rodwell have pointed out the relationships between corporate climate and culture. They define *organizational climate* as "shared perceptions of organizational policies, practices, and procedures, both formal and informal"[4] and *culture* as "deeper, unconsciously held assumptions that help to guide organizational members."[5] They point out that "climate can best be characterized as a manifestation of culture,"[6] that "climate is an individual construct that reflects an orientation based on personal values," and that "culture is a shared phenomenon within a group or community."[7] Both climate and culture are key to understanding how much the organizational environment encourages or discourages workplace learning.

What Is the Culture for Workplace Learning?

Since the corporate culture is relatively enduring, then that suggests that the *culture for workplace learning* means the relatively enduring shared perceptions among organizational members about the organization's level of encouragement for workplace learning.

HOW IS THE CLIMATE FOR WORKPLACE LEARNING ASSESSED?

How can the climate for workplace learning be assessed? This section answers the question.

Assessing the Climate for Workplace Learning

Climate is assessed by asking individuals what they feel and how they feel about the organization's level of support for workplace learning.[8] Climate is, after all, a function of individual perception. It must therefore be measured by what individuals feel.

There are many ways to assess individual workplace perceptions. Decision makers who set out to determine individual perceptions of workplace conditions frequently use such methods as attitude surveys, focus groups, interviews, and observations. Each can be applied to assessing the climate for workplace learning.

For instance, consider the attitude survey presented in Exhibit 8-1. You may use this survey to assess the climate for workplace learning in your organization. Note that the survey is based directly on my research about conditions that encourage or discourage workplace learning, described in the previous chapter. This survey may be administered by group administration, direct mail, online, or before, during or after off-the-job training sessions. If group administration is used, then workers are called together as a group—such as at lunchtime or after hours—and asked to complete the survey. If direct mail is used, the survey is sent to the homes of workers and they are asked to complete and return it. If the survey is offered online, workers may be asked to visit a Web site established for this purpose and asked to complete the survey. A similar survey may be administered to a department, work group, or team to assess its unique learning climate.

However the survey is administered, individuals should not be asked to submit their names. The survey should be administered anonymously and confidentially, and workers should be assured that their names will not be matched up to the results. That is more likely to ensure an honest response even when the trust level in the organization is low.

It is important to understand that the survey results should be aggregated—that is, viewed as a group. As the old saying goes, "*perception is reality*." So it is with shared perceptions about the organization's levels of support for workplace learning. The survey should be helpful in pinpointing specific areas for improvement. That assumes that the organization's decision makers desire to improve those conditions, having been convinced that there is a relationship between organizational performance and productivity and workplace learning. Consequently, the organization's perceived support for workplace learning can be directly related to the organization's more general climate to support high performance and productivity. Of course, individual perceptions can be measured in ways other than by the survey shown in Exhibit 8-1. For instance, individuals may be

(text continues on page 209)

Exhibit 8-1: An instrument to assess the organization's learning climate.

Directions: Use this instrument to measure the workplace learning climate of your organization. For each condition listed in the left column in both Parts I and II, indicate in the right column how much you perceive that condition to exist at present in your organization. Use the following scale:

1 = This condition is *not applicable* to this organization.
2 = This condition is *never true* in this organization.
3 = This condition is *sometimes true* in this organization.
4 = This condition is *usually true* in this organization.
5 = This condition is *always true* in this organization.

There are no "right" or "wrong" answers to these questions in any absolute sense. Answer as you perceive the conditions to exist in your organization.

PART I

CONDITIONS		IN THIS ORGANIZATION AT THIS TIME, THIS CONDITION IS . . .				
		NOT APPLICABLE	NEVER TRUE	SOMETIMES TRUE	USUALLY TRUE	ALWAYS TRUE
		1	2	3	4	5
1	Sufficient financial resources exist to support workplace learning.	1	2	3	4	5
2	Realistic goals and expectations for learning have been established.	1	2	3	4	5
3	There is commitment by the organization to the learning process.	1	2	3	4	5
4	Sufficient trust exists in the organization.	1	2	3	4	5
5	Management shares a common understanding of vision and goals.	1	2	3	4	5
6	Sufficient time is provided to permit learning.	1	2	3	4	5

(continues)

Exhibit 8-1: (Continued).

7	Good communication exists in the organization.	1	2	3	4	5
8	The organization fosters a means by which to collect and use feedback from customers.	1	2	3	4	5
9	Workplace learning is made a priority and is tied to performance expectations.	1	2	3	4	5
10	The leadership of the organization is perceived to support workplace learning.	1	2	3	4	5
11	Clear milestones have been established for the workplace learning process.	1	2	3	4	5
12	Managers, union leaders and learners exhibit buy-in and commitment to learning.	1	2	3	4	5
13	Individuals are matched to learning experiences for which they have the appropriate education and background.	1	2	3	4	5
14	The learning effort is closely tied to business needs.	1	2	3	4	5

15	Work standards are consistently applied within the organization.	1	2	3	4	5
16	The organization possesses clear methods by which to examine and measure work performance.	1	2	3	4	5
17	Learners are open-minded and possess an attitude that favors learning.	1	2	3	4	5
18	Measurement and accountability has been established and linked to the workplace learning process.	1	2	3	4	5
19	The workplace learning process is guided by a plan.	1	2	3	4	5
20	A clear sense exists about "next steps" following the workplace learning process.	1	2	3	4	5
21	The organization's union, if the organization is unionized, supports the workplace learning process/effort.	1	2	3	4	5
22	External environmental factors support the workplace learning process.	1	2	3	4	5

(continues)

Exhibit 8-1: (Continued).

23	Fear has been reduced within the organization so that individuals are not afraid to take risks and learn.	1	2	3	4	5
24	Learners feel empowered.	1	2	3	4	5
25	Learners feel they have incentives and rewards sufficient to encourage them to pursue workplace learning and see "what's in it for them."	1	2	3	4	5
26	Responsibilities for who should do what in the workplace learning process have been clarified.	1	2	3	4	5
Total all the scores from items 1–26 above and place the sum in the box at right →						

PART II

CONDITIONS		IN THIS ORGANIZATION AT THIS TIME, THIS CONDITION IS . . .				
		NOT APPLICABLE	NEVER TRUE	SOMETIMES TRUE	USUALLY TRUE	ALWAYS TRUE
		1	2	3	4	5
1	Insufficient financial resources exist to support workplace learning.	1	2	3	4	5
2	The organization does not establish realistic learning goals and expectations.	1	2	3	4	5

3	No commitment exists to support the learning process.	1	2	3	4	5
4	The organization is characterized by a general lack of trust.	1	2	3	4	5
5	The organization is torn by the strife of factions in the organization that are pursuing competing goals.	1	2	3	4	5
6	The time constraints placed on the workplace learning process are unrealistic or unclear.	1	2	3	4	5
7	The learning lacks focus, goals and objectives.	1	2	3	4	5
8	Communication in the organization is perceived to be poor.	1	2	3	4	5
9	The organization has placed limitations on the feedback that customers may provide to workers.	1	2	3	4	5
10	Workers are subjected to multiple, conflicting, or unreasonable demands.	1	2	3	4	5
11	The organization experiences a lack of leadership	1	2	3	4	5
12	There are no plans or milestones for workplace learning.	1	2	3	4	5

(continues)

Exhibit 8-1: (Continued).

13	There is a lack of buy-in and commitment to learning by different stakeholders such as top managers, supervisors, workers, or other groups.	1	2	3	4	5
14	The learners have an inadequate education or background to take advantage of the learning opportunities provided to them.	1	2	3	4	5
15	The organization applies double standards to the learning.	1	2	3	4	5
16	The organization does not possess a clear process for examining and measuring work performance.	1	2	3	4	5
17	Individuals experience a lack of motivation to learn.	1	2	3	4	5
18	Individuals demonstrate a poor attitude toward learning.	1	2	3	4	5
19	The organization has not established ways to measure learning and hold stakeholders accountable for playing their parts in it.	1	2	3	4	5

20	No long-term plan exists to guide work-place learning for the organization.	1	2	3	4	5
21	Once individuals learn, they are not guided to see "next steps."	1	2	3	4	5
22	The union, if the organization is unionized, does not support the workplace learning effort.	1	2	3	4	5
23	External environmental factors do not support the workplace learning process.	1	2	3	4	5
24	Fear exists within the organization.	1	2	3	4	5
25	Workers do not feel empowered.	1	2	3	4	5
26	The incentives and reward system of the organization does not support learning or its results.	1	2	3	4	5
Total all the scores from items 1–26 above and place the sum in the box at right →						

(continues)

Exhibit 8-1: (Continued).

SCORING

First review your score for Part I and read the interpretation of it below:

Conditions That Encourage Workplace Learning

IF YOUR SCORE WAS BETWEEN:	THEN:
130 and 105	Grade the organization's learning climate an "A." The conditions in your organization are most supportive of workplace learning. While some improvements can still be made in the spirit of continuous improvement, your workplace learning climate is exemplary.
104 and 79	Grade the organization's learning climate between a "B" and "C." The conditions in your organization *usually* support workplace learning. Examine carefully those items on which you scored your organization below a 5. Pinpoint 2–3 specific areas for improvement and take action to improve them.
78 and 53	Grade the organization's learning climate a "D." The conditions in your organization *sometimes* support workplace learning. Examine carefully those items on which you scored your organization below a 5. Pinpoint specific areas for improvement and take action to improve them.
52 and 0	Grade the organization's learning climate an "F." The conditions in your organization never support workplace learning. Examine carefully those items on which you scored your organization below a 5. Pinpoint specific areas for improvement and take action to improve them.

Then review your score for Part II and read the interpretation of it below:

Conditions That Discourage Workplace Learning

IF YOUR SCORE WAS BETWEEN:	THEN:
130 and 105	Grade the organization's learning climate an "F." Many conditions discourage individuals from pursuing workplace learning or discourage the organization from supporting it. Pinpoint specific areas for improvement and take action to improve them.
104 and 79	Grade the organization's learning climate a "D." Some conditions discourage individuals from pursuing workplace learning or discourage the organization from supporting it. Pinpoint specific areas for improvement and take action to improve them.
78 and 53	Grade the organization's learning climate between a "C" and a "B." A few conditions discourage individuals from pursuing workplace learning or else discourage the organization from supporting it. Pinpoint 2–3 specific areas for improvement and take action to improve them.

| 32 and 0 | Grade the organization's learning climate an "A." Your organization does not place many barriers in the way of workplace learning. Your organization should be congratulated. |

Note: It is possible that an organization can score high on both conditions that encourage workplace learning and conditions that discourage it. When that happens, examine carefully why that apparent discrepancy exists. Ask whether some parts of the organization are more supportive than others—and why that is so. Plan to take steps for improvement in areas of the organization that are less supportive of workplace learning than others.

interviewed at time of hire about their desired workplace learning climate. (See the interview guide in Exhibit 8-2.) Individuals may also be given an exit interview at time of termination about the workplace learning climate that they perceived to exist in the organization—and they can also be asked whether discouragers to workplace learning contributed, in whole or part, to a decision to leave the organization. (See the interview guide in Exhibit 8-3.)

Focus groups may also be used to assess perceptions about the climate for workplace learning.[9] A *focus group* is, of course, akin to a group interview. A group of people from the organization are gathered together in a room, usually for sixty to ninety minutes. They are usually asked only a few specific questions—usually not more than three—and then are prompted to respond to those questions. For instance, workers may be asked such questions as these:

1. How much support do you perceive that this organization provides for *workplace learning*, defined as practical learning that is tied to the work you do and the results you seek to achieve to be productive or to satisfy the organization's clients or customers?

2. What conditions in this organization do you believe tend to *encourage* workplace learning? What conditions *discourage* workplace learning?

3. What actions should management take to improve the climate for workplace learning? What other groups should take action to improve the climate for workplace learning, and what should those groups do?

Group responses can then be placed on a flipchart and summarized. The results can be fed back to group participants, decision makers, and WLP professionals to inform areas for continuous improvement.

Exhibit 8-2: An interview guide for use in selecting workers for preferences in the workplace learning climate.

Directions: Use this interview guide during the employee selection process. Ask new hires about their preferred learning climate. If you wish, you may also ask their opinions about how they learn best and related questions. For each question appearing in the left column below, take notes on what the interviewee says during the selection interview. Add paper as necessary.

Interviewer's Name	Interviewee's Name	Today's Date
QUESTIONS FOR THE INTERVIEWEE	NOTES ON THE INTERVIEWEE'S RESPONSES	
1 Learning on the job is an important expectation in this organization. Could you tell me about the conditions that you believe should exist in an ideal learning climate for you to learn on the job? Please describe what that climate would be like.		
2 Tell me a story about a time when you had to learn something new on the job or when you faced a work challenge that required you to learn in real time. What did you do? Please be detailed in your response.		
3 How much responsibility do you believe that workers should take for their own learning? Explain why you think so.		

It should not be assumed that all parts of the organization are equally supportive of workplace learning efforts any more than individual perceptions of the organization's climate will be uniformly shared. Indeed, differences in perceptions may exist across departments, divisions, work groups, teams, geographical locations, product lines, projects, or other distinctions in how the work is organized or in how people are grouped together to do it. The climate for workplace learning can thus vary across

---

Exhibit 8-3: An exit interview guide to gather information on the workplace learning climate.

Directions: Use this exit interview guide with an employee who is leaving the organization voluntarily. Ask him or her each question appearing in the left column below. Then take notes on his or her responses in the right column. Add paper as necessary.

Interviewer's Name	Interviewee's Name	Today's Date
QUESTIONS FOR THE INTERVIEWEE	**NOTES ON THE INTERVIEWEE'S RESPONSES**	
1 Learning on the job is important in this organization. Could you tell me about how much you believe this organization encourages real-time learning on the job to meet work challenges?		
2 Tell me a story about a time in this organization when you had to learn something new on the job or when you faced a work challenge that required you to learn in real time. What did you do? Please be detailed in your response.		
3 How much responsibility do you believe that workers should take for their own learning? Explain why you think so.		
4 Could you elaborate on your reasons for leaving this organization? Would it be fair to say that there was something having to do with the organization's climate for learning or individual development that contributed to your decision to leave? Please explain whether that it is true or not true.		

an organization, and some groups may need to focus on improvement efforts that are not necessary for other groups.

Individual interviews may also be conducted to assess perceptions of the climate for workplace learning. Although that is a more time-consuming (and expensive) approach, it also tends to yield more in-depth, and sometimes more valuable, information. After all, individual perceptions may be probed in a way that cannot happen through written surveys or through focus groups where a few people may dominate the discussion.

Interviews may be conducted in person or by phone.[10] Structured interviews rely on a structured survey, like the example shown in Exhibit 8-1. Unstructured interviews rely on a few questions, like those posed for focus groups, but permit deeper follow-up questioning.

HOW IS THE CORPORATE CULTURE'S SUPPORT FOR WORKPLACE LEARNING EVALUATED?

Culture differs from climate in that it is taken for granted and is a shared perception of many individuals. Much has been written about evaluating culture and changing culture.[11] Generally speaking, however, most authorities believe that *storytelling* is the appropriate way to collect information about corporate culture.[12] Interpreting the stories is a way of analyzing culture to discover shared perceptions and common themes. Doing that requires the application of thematic analysis or other, related approaches to analyzing qualitative information.[13]

But if stories are to be used to transmit information about, and evaluate, the corporate culture for workplace learning, it makes sense to ask who should tell those stories, what stories should be requested, why they are worth hearing, how they should be interpreted, and how corporate culture can be changed.

Clearly, *who* should be asked to tell those stories is a function of experience. Experienced performers have been around the organization awhile. They have been part of the organizational experience that shaped the culture, and so they are well positioned to relate anecdotes about it.

What stories should be requested is a more challenging issue. However, if experience is the best teacher—and represents the past experience on which the culture is grounded—then it makes sense to ask experienced people in the organization for stories about workplace learning experiences. But a word of caution is in order here. If you ask people for stories about workplace learning, they will tend to think of *planned* learning experiences—such as off-the-job training efforts mounted by the organization, retreats organized by the training department, or similar situations. Although such experiences *are* part of the workplace learning culture of the organization, they are not all of it.

Consequently, ask questions like the following ones to elicit stories about the workplace learning culture of the organization:

Could you tell me a story about a time when:

1. You had to learn something new to do your work in this organization? What happened? How did you go about the process, and what did you find out about the way learning occurs in this corporate culture?

2. The organization needed to introduce some major change, such as the introduction of new software or a new product or service line? How was that handled? What does that situation show, in your opinion, about how well the organization's decision makers are able to manage the practical learning needed by people to do their jobs?

3. Some effort of the organization was stymied by lack of learning? For instance, suppose the organization introduced a new product or service line but workers were not trained on the product or service before it was launched. (Has that ever happened?) What could you tell me about how a failure of this kind demonstrates assumptions made by decision makers of this organization about the way people learn, or about the role of learning in helping the organization succeed?

It may be helpful to use the interview guide in Exhibit 8-4 to help you keep track of those stories.

Why are such stories worth hearing? The answer to that question is that whereas one story is insufficient by which to draw conclusions about

---

Exhibit 8-4: An interview guide to collect stories about the organization's workplace learning culture.

Directions: Use this interview guide to help you collect and analyze stories about the organization's workplace learning culture. For each question appearing in the left column below, write notes in the right column. Add paper as necessary. If the respondent is willing, ask him or her if the session can be tape recorded so that his or her exact words can be captured for future reference.

QUESTIONS	NOTES
Could you tell me a story about a time when:	
1 You had to learn something new to do your work in this organization? What happened? How did you go about the process, and what did you find out about the way learning occurs in this corporate culture?	
2 The organization needed to introduce some major change, such as the introduction of new software or a new product or service line? How was that handled? What does that situation show, in your opinion, about how well the organization's decision makers are able to manage the practical learning needed by people to do their jobs?	
3 Some effort of the organization was stymied by lack of learning? For instance, suppose the organization introduced a new product or service line but workers were not trained on the product or service before it was launched. (Has that ever happened?) What could you tell me about how a failure of this kind demonstrates assumptions made by decision makers of this organization about the way people learn? About the role of learning in helping the organization succeed?	

workplace learning in the corporate culture, a pattern of such stories does point toward shared understandings. That is worth knowing about, because a corporate culture that does not encourage workplace learning will most likely not reward, appreciate, or cherish innovation, creativity, and quantum-leap improvements in productivity, customer service, profitability, or anything else.

How should these stories be interpreted? Again, the answer is to look for shared themes. If the same issue is repeated many times by different people, then it is properly regarded as a shared perception. That is, of course, an indicator of a cultural issue. Once an analysis has been completed by counting the number of times the same issue is repeated across multiple stories, then it can be verified by feeding back the analysis to the storyteller he believes and asking whether it is true.

Once you have collected this information, you should use it to pinpoint the factors in your organization that encourage or discourage workplace learning. That can be the start of an effort to enhance the organizational climate and culture to encourage workplace learning, a topic treated in the next chapter. You may also use it as a starting point to benchmark with other organizations in which a similar assessment has been conducted. Use information collected from Exhibits 8-2 and 8-3 as starting points to address these issues.

Summary

This chapter addressed two key questions: (1) What is the climate for workplace learning? and (2) How is the climate for workplace learning assessed? *Climate* was defined as the psychological feel of the organization, and the climate for workplace learning has to do with how people in the organization feel about workplace learning. Many methods may be used to assess individual perceptions about the workplace learning climate, and these methods include attitude surveys, focus groups, interviews, and observations. *Corporate culture* refers to the shared views of a group about the "right" and "wrong" ways to behave in a given setting. The corporate culture for workplace learning can be assessed through storytelling.

The next chapter turns to the topic of changing the corporate climate and culture for workplace learning.

Chapter 9

Building an Organizational Climate and Culture That Encourages Workplace Learning

C hapter 8 focused on answering two major questions: (1) What is the climate for workplace learning? and (2) How is the climate for workplace learning assessed? This chapter goes one step beyond that to pose two additional but related questions: (1) How can organizations build a climate that encourages workplace learning? and (2) What issues other than workplace learning can influence individual and organizational performance?

How Can Organizations Build a Climate That Encourages Workplace Learning?

To build a climate that encourages workplace learning, WLP practitioners should be willing to assume a leadership role. Often, they may be given a title such as Chief Learning Officer (CLO) or chief knowledge officer (CKO).[1] In that capacity their role is to build a climate that encourages workplace learning and thereby encourages organizational innovation, creativity, productivity, performance, and other desirable climatic conditions that promote competitiveness.

But, the question is: How is that done?

There are no foolproof schemes that will work in every corporate culture. No step-by-step scheme can be offered here. After all, every corporate culture will probably have some conditions that discourage workplace learning. Their influence should be periodically measured, and efforts should be focused on reducing their influence at the same time that the conditions encouraging workplace learning should be intensified. The goal should therefore be to work on improving the organizational climate at the same time that work progresses to build individual learning competence. Some change strategies can—and will—work in this process. They are drawn from the fields of organizational change and organization development.[2]

What follows are some general guidelines for how to build a climate that encourages workplace learning while reducing the influence of conditions that discourage that learning.

Guideline 1: Think Strategically, but Act Operationally

This guideline is, of course, a creative paraphrase of the old saying, "think globally but act locally." The idea here is to ensure that efforts to build a climate that encourages continuous workplace learning, and therefore continuous improvement for the organization and its members, are aligned with the organization's strategic goals, objectives, and direction.

One suggestion is to encourage decision makers to discuss the desirable workplace learning climate that should be sought to facilitate achievement of organizational results. That can be done in the venues of strategic planning retreats, executive staff meetings, or periodic strategy review meetings.

A second suggestion is to cascade that approach downward.[3] Managers and supervisors at each level should be encouraged to discuss the workplace learning climate in their areas. They can also be asked to suggest improvement plans to make that climate better so that it will facilitate individual, team, and organizational improvement.

Guideline 2: Create a Vision and Work to Realize It

It is difficult to move toward any goal if that goal cannot be clearly envisioned.[4] For that reason, then, workers and decision makers alike should be asked to describe, in terms as clear and as specific as they can make them, what the ideal workplace learning climate should be like and what a competent workplace learner should be like. That positive vision should help to create excitement, energizing efforts to make the dream more of a reality.

Use the worksheet in Exhibit 9-1 to help decision makers and workers alike come up with a vision of workplace learning climate and workplace learning competence.

Guideline 3: Build Awareness of the Workplace Learning Process and the Workplace Learning Climate

WLP practitioners have their work cut out for them here. Too many people probably think of schools or training sessions when they think of a learning climate, and too many people probably think of what they did in school or how they behaved in training when they think about the learning process. Unfortunately, such recollections are not always positive ones. People need to be made aware that learning can—and usually does—occur in real time as individuals cope to solve problems, grapple with work-related issues, realize dreams, or achieve goals.

Building awareness requires more than a one-time effort. It requires continuous communication to build a sense that learning is as natural as breathing. It happens all the time. The question is how people can do better with it and how the organization can establish a climate that encourages useful learning to address organizational needs. That may require articles in organizational publications, such as company newsletters, briefing sessions, white papers, and other awareness-building approaches.

Exhibit 9-1: A worksheet to create a vision for the organization's workplace learning climate.

Directions: Use this worksheet as a way to organize your thinking—and the thinking of managers, employees, and other key stakeholders—about the desired vision for a workplace learning climate in your organization. Pose each question appearing below. Then take notes about what you, and others, say in response to these questions. Summarize them and then feed them back to everyone from whom you collected answers. Use the feedback you give them as a means to energize their thinking about what vision they share in common, or could be prompted to share in common, about the workplace learning climate of the organization.

QUESTIONS ABOUT THE MOST DESIRABLE WORKPLACE LEARNING CLIMATE

1	Think about the distinctive features of a workplace climate that encourages and even excites people to learn on the job and in real time so that they can be more productive in their work. What would be the distinctive features of that climate? List what you believe would be noticeable about that climate.
2	What would this organization look like if it gave everyone in it the distinctive impression that it encouraged practical learning to solve workplace problems? What would it need to be like for that to be true?
3	Think of a time in this organization when you felt most encouraged to learn to solve workplace problems or meet workplace challenges. When was that? Could you describe something about what was happening at that time and who was involved? What was special about that situation? How do you think we could get more of it?

Guideline 4: Measure Results, Provide Feedback, and Encourage Participative Action Planning

To ensure continuing credibility for efforts intended to build a workplace learning climate and workplace learner competence, WLP practitioners need to measure the results of what they do on an ongoing basis. Without that, decision makers and workers alike may regard such efforts as just new "flavors of the month" rather than strategic initiatives intended to get results. At a time when employee cynicism about change is growing, in part due to previous (and failed) change efforts, WLP practitioners should take steps to measure what happens as a result of what they do, feed that back so that people hear about the results, and ensure that change participants are involved in the important decisions of the change process.[5]

As one tool for this purpose, WLP practitioners may creatively adapt and use the worksheet in Exhibit 9-2.

Guideline 5: Institutionalize Efforts to Improve the Workplace Learning Climate and Workplace Learning Competence

An important way to emphasize—and give visibility to—organizational change efforts is to institutionalize them.[6] That means they should be integrated with other efforts. For this reason, then, WLP practitioners should strive to integrate a focus on learning climate and workplace learning competence with employee selection efforts (such as job interviews), orientation programs, training, employee performance management and appraisal systems, and incentive, recognition, and reward programs. That can be done simply by ensuring that workers at all levels are periodically asked what they think about the organization's workplace learning climate and their own workplace learning competence. As that happens, it will focus continuing attention on the issue, sending the message that it is important.

WHAT ISSUES OTHER THAN WORKPLACE LEARNING CAN INFLUENCE INDIVIDUAL AND ORGANIZATIONAL PERFORMANCE?

It would be unwise to give readers the impression from this book that workplace learning is the sole influence on individual or organizational performance. That is, of course, a fallacious viewpoint. Although learning can serve as a mediating factor, it is not the only factor in achieving improved productivity. Many other factors can, and do, influence performance.[7] To list but a few issues other than workplace learning that influence performance:

- **Organizational Design.** How are work responsibilities allocated in the organization, and how is work organized?

Exhibit 9-2: A worksheet to measure the results of a workplace learning climate and workplace learning competence.

Directions to WLP practitioners: Use this worksheet to collect information about situations or occasions when the workplace learning climate of the organization or else individual workplace learning competencies contributed to getting bottom-line results in cost savings for the organization, enhanced revenue or sales for the organization, or specific benefits for individuals. Distribute this worksheet in training sessions, by e-mail, or by other means (such as by mail or enclosed in paycheck stubs or other creative means). When you have collected this information, summarize it and then feed it back to decision makers and other stakeholders so that they may see how the organization gained from investing in efforts to improve the workplace learning climate or in efforts to improve individual workplace learning competencies.

Directions to workers: Use this worksheet to provide information about situations or occasions when the workplace learning climate of this organization or else your own individual workplace learning competencies contributed to getting bottom-line results in cost savings for the organization, enhanced revenue or sales for the organization, or specific benefits for individuals.

QUESTIONS

1	Describe a situation from your experience in this organization when the organization's avowed efforts to improve workplace learning climate or to build individual workplace learning competencies led to cost savings, revenue enhancement, or increased sales. Be as precise and clear as you can, describing the situation fully. Tell who was involved (but avoid using exact names and insert job titles instead). Tell what happened, step-by-step if possible, and when this event occurred. *What happened?* *Who was involved?* *When did this happen?*
2	What happened as a direct result of this situation? What benefits were realized by the organization and/or by individuals? *Results?*
3	What measurable cost savings, revenue enhancement, or increased sales can be documented and can be fairly attributed to the organization's efforts to improve the workplace learning climate or individual workplace learning competencies? Provide a specific dollar figure below and indicate how you computed it. *Dollar figure:* *How did you compute that?*

- **Job or Work Design.** How are job or task responsibilities allocated?

- **Feedback Systems.** How is the organization and its people given feedback on what they do, and on the consequences of what they do, from clients, customers, and other stakeholders?

- **Reward Systems.** How are people motivated and rewarded for performing in ways aligned with organizational goals, objectives, and strategy?

- **Selection Systems.** How are people hired, promoted, transferred, or moved?

- **Ergonomics and Sociotechnical Systems.** How is the performance of people tied to, and effectively integrated with, machines, tools, and technology?

- **Individual Abilities.** What are the capacities and talents of individuals—including their limitations on learning and performing?

- **External Environmental Conditions.** What is the competitive environment in which people are asked to perform?

WLP practitioners should bear in mind that many factors—and only a few of them are listed above—influence human performance. That point is worth emphasizing as WLP practitioners work to improve organizational conditions that encourage workplace learning and as they work to build individual learning competence. The approaches brought to the WLP field from HPI and human performance enhancement (HPE) should continue to be used to troubleshoot human performance problems and discover human performance improvement opportunities.[8] Often, that requires in-depth analysis of the root causes of problems, starting with *performance analysis* to distinguish problems that can be appropriately solved by training or other learning interventions from problems that require management action to change the work environment.[9] It then requires *cause analysis* to pinpoint the underlying cause or causes of performance problems so that appropriate performance improvement interventions may be selected, individually or collectively, to address those causes.[10]

The point, then, is that improving the workplace-learning climate and building workplace-learning competence will not solve every human performance problem. But they should help organizations and individuals alike more effectively adapt to future change. WLP practitioners should continue to use the tools of the performance consultant. They should add some new tools, however, to encourage the climate for workplace learning and build individual learning competence.

Summary

This chapter built on the theme begun in Chapter 7 and continued in Chapter 8. It focused on providing suggestions for building an organizational climate that encourages workplace learning. To that end, the chapter offered five guidelines for WLP practitioners. First, they should *think strategically, but act operationally.* The idea is to ensure that efforts to build a climate that encourages continuous workplace learning is aligned with the organization's strategic goals, objectives, and direction. Second, WLP practitioners should *facilitate the creation of an organizational vision of what an ideal learning climate would be like and what individual learning competence would be like.* Third, they should *build awareness of the workplace learning process and the workplace learning climate.* That is all the more difficult because too many people probably associate "learning" with "schooling" or "training." Fourth, they should *measure results, provide feedback, and encourage participative action planning.* Fifth and finally, they should *institutionalize efforts to improve the workplace learning climate and workplace learning competence.* That means integrating efforts to improve workplace learning climate and learning competence with other HR efforts.

Finally, the chapter concluded by emphasizing that efforts to encourage a climate conducive to workplace learning and build workplace learner competence should not be pursued as ends in themselves. WLP practitioners should continue to focus on improving organizational performance. They should therefore use the tools from HPI to help them do that.

THE ROLE OF THE WORKPLACE LEARNING AND PERFORMANCE PRACTITIONER

Many organizations employ individuals who assess learning needs, design and develop planned learning experiences, deliver those experiences, and evaluate results. They are given varying job titles, though they are often called WLP practitioners. The role of the WLP practitioner is the focus of this final section of the book, Part Four, which consists of Chapters 10 and 11.

More specifically, Chapter 10:

- Explains why it might be worthwhile to transform a training department into a learning department

- Offers suggestions about steps to transform a training department into a learning department

- Lists reasons trainers should become learning facilitators

- Describes how trainers may make the transition to learning facilitators

- Suggests ways that trainers can encourage others, such as supervisors or managers, to become learning facilitators

Chapter 11 concludes the body of the book. It offers final thoughts on using the workplace learning model, workplace learner roles, workplace learning competencies, and other information presented in this book. The chapter is organized around the uses of several possible audiences for this book—including mentors and WLP practitioners, supervisors, managers and other leaders, academicians, and workplace learners themselves.

Chapter 10

TRANSFORMING A TRAINING DEPARTMENT INTO A LEARNING DEPARTMENT

Those who work in training departments are often expected to orchestrate the planned learning processes of the organizations of which they are a part. To that end, they may carry out the roles identified through previous research, demonstrate the competencies necessary to enact those roles, and achieve the outputs expected of them by such stakeholders as individual learners, the learners' immediate organizational supervisors, top managers, customers, and other relevant groups. So-called trainers have experienced changing expectations about what they should do—and even who they should be—because the focus of their efforts has changed over the years as paradigm shifts have transformed the T&D field into HRD, HPI, and (most recently) WLP.

But the T&D department, sometimes charged with responsibilities for knowledge management and for cultivating the organization's intellectual assets, should undergo a change in focus and activities as it facilitates the efforts of self-directed or free agent workplace learners. Why is that worth doing? What steps can guide the transformation of a training department into a learning department? This chapter focuses on answering these questions.

WHY TRANSFORM A TRAINING DEPARTMENT INTO A LEARNING DEPARTMENT?

There are three key reasons why it is worthwhile to transform a training department into a learning department.

Reason 1: The Need for Learning Organizations

As earlier chapters have shown, a quiet revolution is under way. In a bid to increase competitiveness and cope with rapidly changing competitive conditions, organizational leaders are calling for strategies to transform their traditional—and sometimes bureaucratic and therefore slow—institutions into learning organizations that have the capacity to encourage individual learning and organizational adaptation. The key driver in this quiet revolution is a need for speed, since time has become an important strategic resource.[1] Organizations cannot remain competitive in the future if they cannot rapidly adapt to, and even anticipate, dynamic shifts in customer preferences, market conditions, technological change, and other volatile elements in the external environment.

Reason 2: The Need to Facilitate Organizational Learning and Performance-Oriented Innovation

At the same time that organizational leaders will be forced by dynamic external conditions to transform their institutions into learning organizations, they will also need to find betters ways of managing the collective knowledge of their organizations. Indeed, they must go beyond that to find new, innovative ways to contribute to the organization's competitiveness. To that end, they will need to tap into the awesome creative ability of their employees to find new ways to meet old as well as new challenges. One way to do that is to use traditional vehicles of learning—such as training, education, and such other learning interventions as job rotation programs, mentoring, coaching, online and face-to-face learning communities—as the means by which to explore new approaches, generate new ideas, and come up with creative solutions leading to new markets, new products, new services, and new approaches to meet client requirements. The old-style training department, which has traditionally served an important role in helping individuals become socialized into a new corporate culture and provide people with the distilled fruits of the organization's experiences, must add to that traditional role a new one—that of learning catalyst and learning facilitator. That should transform the old-style training department into sort of a research and development (R&D) effort. R&D has been much neglected in service firms and in other nonmanufacturing organizations, but that role must increasingly be served by those best equipped to help tap into the creative abilities of people. This new role thrusts traditional trainers into the new role of facilitators of learning, whose mission is, pure and simple, helping the organization come up with creative solutions to performance problems through the creation of new knowledge, new approaches, and new norms.

Reason 3: The Need to Facilitate Real-Time, On-the-Job Learning by Individuals

Finally, as e-learning revolutionizes approaches to transmitting information, "training" will fade in comparison to "workplace learning." Individuals will, by necessity, be forced to become proficient in learning how to learn and in skillful applications of informal and incidental learning. That will be part of the quiet revolution, since it will help individuals become more flexible in adapting to—and even anticipating—changes wrought by new work methods, new technologies, and rapidly shifting customer preferences. The old-style training department will be forced to do what schools do not do—that is, help individuals acquire better skills in how they learn in workplace settings.

For the reasons listed, training departments will need to shift their focus from "training" to "learning." That will, of necessity, call for leadership by WLP practitioners and creative applications of traditional approaches.

WHAT STEPS CAN GUIDE THE PROCESS OF TRANSFORMING A TRAINING DEPARTMENT INTO A LEARNING DEPARTMENT?

Chapter 1 described some key trends driving the quiet revolution toward workplace learning, and they were briefly summarized in the previous section. These trends are driving the need for corporate training departments to transition into learning departments. As I noted with my colleagues Carolyn Hohne and Steven King,[2] training professionals are moving away from training as the sole solution for all human performance problems or improvement opportunities. But a new trend is emerging to go beyond HPI to address, and tap into, the myriad ways that individuals can learn in workplace settings for the benefits that can be derived by individuals and their employers.

Transitioning from a training department—or even an HPI department—does not occur overnight. As in making any change in corporate culture, it requires skilled, persistent, and visionary WLP leadership. It also requires patience and dogged determination. No foolproof blueprint can be offered for how to go about leading this transformation. However, it is possible to list a few key steps that may be taken in this process. These steps are shown in Exhibit 10-1 and are described below. Use the worksheet in Exhibit 10-2 to help you organize your thinking and planning on how to apply these steps creatively.

Step 1: Demonstrate the Need

Perhaps the first step in transforming a traditional training department into a learning department is to demonstrate the need to key groups inside and outside the organization.

Exhibit 10-1: Steps to guide the process of transforming a training department into a learning department.

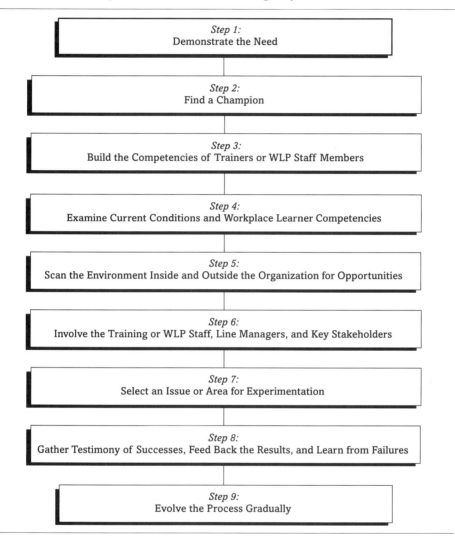

Step 1:
Demonstrate the Need

Step 2:
Find a Champion

Step 3:
Build the Competencies of Trainers or WLP Staff Members

Step 4:
Examine Current Conditions and Workplace Learner Competencies

Step 5:
Scan the Environment Inside and Outside the Organization for Opportunities

Step 6:
Involve the Training or WLP Staff, Line Managers, and Key Stakeholders

Step 7:
Select an Issue or Area for Experimentation

Step 8:
Gather Testimony of Successes, Feed Back the Results, and Learn from Failures

Step 9:
Evolve the Process Gradually

Exhibit 10-2: A worksheet to guide your thinking in transforming a training department into a learning department.

Directions: Use this worksheet to help guide your thinking in how to transform a training De-partment into a learning department. In the open block below, make any special notes to your-self about the project steps you might have to take to transform a training department into a learning department in your organization, since it has a unique corporate culture. Then, for each action step listed in the left column below, make notes to yourself in the right column about specific action steps you might need to take. There are no "right" or "wrong" answers in any absolute sense. Add paper as necessary.

Special Notes to Yourself About the Project Steps You Might Have to Take:

ACTION STEPS TO TRANSFORM YOUR TRAINING DEPARTMENT INTO A LEARNING DEPARTMENT		NOTES ABOUT WHAT TO DO
1	Demonstrate the need.	
2	Find a champion.	
3	Build the competencies of trainers or WLP staff members.	
4	Examine current conditions and work-place learner competencies.	
5	Scan the environment inside and out-side the organization for opportunities.	
6	Involve the training or WLP staff, line managers, and key stakeholders.	
7	Select an issue or area for experimen-tation.	
8	Gather testimony of successes, feed back the results, and learn from fail-ures.	
9	Evolve the process gradually.	

As an early step in this process, consider building awareness. Share with coworkers in the training department the issues described in this book. Do that by sharing "white papers" (summaries of the issue). Brief them in staff meetings or in staff development sessions. Then ask them what business challenges that the organization faces—or what special training challenges that the department faces—could be used to experiment with new approaches.

As one simple example, you might consider revising the company's orientation program to add a section for new hires on what responsibilities they bear in their own learning. Make a similar revision to supervisory or management development sessions to encourage management employees to discuss what responsibilities they bear in encouraging workplace learning and in helping individuals take more initiative for their own real-time, on-the-job learning. Use these opportunities to discuss with workers and with supervisors or managers what needs that the organization faces might benefit from increased individual initiative in the workplace learning process.

Step 2: Find a Champion

For any change in corporate culture to be successful, a champion is needed at the top. That person should be a visionary leader, one who is open to experimentation. Find such a champion to carry the banner to help transform the training department into a learning department. Start by briefing the person you choose for that role on the value of making this change and explaining the benefits that might be derived from making such a change.

Step 3: Build the Competencies of Trainers or WLP Staff Members

To serve as role models, trainers or WLP staff members should be willing—and motivated—early adopters of a focus on learning. Since many will be curious about helping people become better learners, tap into that curiosity by encouraging experimentation. Ask trainers or WLP staff members to participate in assessing the workplace learning climate of the organization—or their department. (For instance, ask them to complete the instrument provided in Exhibit 7-1.) Set priorities for ways to knock down the organizational barriers that they perceive discourage individual learning. Then encourage trainers or WLP staff members to assess their own individual workplace learning competencies using the assessment instrument supplied in Appendix E. Counsel them individually on how they might build those competencies and thereby become better workplace learners. Finally, debrief them individually and collectively on what they think about this process.

Step 4: Examine Current Conditions and
Workplace Learner Competencies

An early step in making the transition from a training to a learning department is assessing the current conditions in the organization. How much and how well does the organization presently encourage workplace learning? In what ways, and to what extent, is the organization perceived to discourage workplace learning? Measure the organization's present learning climate of the organization by using the instrument supplied in Exhibit 7-1. Then feed back results of that measurement to key decision makers and other stakeholders for their comments and their suggestions for action.

If a willing and supportive department manager or work group supervisor can be found, ask him to permit the assessment of employees for their workplace learning competencies. Use the instrument supplied in Appendix E for that purpose. Then work with that work group or department to counsel individuals on how they might build their capacity for learning. To that end, work with individuals to develop individual development plans (IDPs) or performance contracts to help them build their competence as learners.

Step 5: Scan the Environment Inside and Outside
the Organization for Opportunities

Like a good entrepreneur, you should be on the lookout for opportunities in which rapidly changing conditions inside or outside the organization might pose a challenge for people to become better learners.[3] For instance, if the organization pursues the implementation of an enterprise resource program, many people may be forced to learn new skills quickly. Organizational competitiveness may hinge on the outcomes. That opportunity, or similar ones, might be ideal times to propose focusing increased attention on *how people learn* rather than just on *what they need to learn*.

Step 6: Involve the Training or WLP Staff, Line Managers, and Key Stakeholders

As you experiment with transforming the training department into a learning department, be sure to make key stakeholders aware of it. Begin by building their awareness of what this means—and what business needs might make this transformation necessary. Network with colleagues to find out what other organizations might have been experimenting with new, unique, and innovative approaches to encourage real-time, on-the-job learning. Be prepared to gather information on what those organizations have attempted and what results they can document as a direct result of that experimentation.

Step 7: Select an Issue or Area for Experimentation

Do not try to revolutionize the organization or the training department all at once. To do so is to risk failure. Instead, pick an issue or area for experimentation and try out new approaches to generate knowledge (instead of just presenting it) and to increase individual capacity for real-time learning. Gather the perceptions of individuals who participate in these small-scale efforts.

One way to do that is to focus on an existing course or program already offered by the training or WLP department. Ask trainers or WLP practitioners how that course or program might be adapted to increase learners' responsibility for their own learning. Also ask how the course or program might be used as a venue to generate new knowledge; improve the organization's climate for workplace learning; or improve individual, group, or organizational performance.

Another way to do that is to create a new initiative, such as a new program to teach people how to learn better or how to take more responsibility for their own on-the-job learning. Use that opportunity to model the workplace learning process by organizing the program to facilitate learning rather than provide information or build skills.

Step 8: Gather Testimony of Successes, Feed Back the Results, and Learn from Failures

Neither organizations nor individuals will change if they do not hear reasons to do so. Often, those reasons must be stated in dramatic, compelling terms. If you are successful in pilot testing an effort to improve the climate for workplace learning and/or in building individual learning competencies, take steps to collect testimony from those who benefited from the effort. Then publicize it. Brief managers and supervisors about it, giving them feedback on what happened and what results were gained from it.

But when your efforts lead to missteps or failures, take note of them for future improvement. After all, failure can be an important source of learning for yourself. Of course, failures should usually not be as widely communicated as successes, since failures tend to put the brakes on change rather than accelerate it.

Step 9: Evolve the Process Gradually

Do not expect the quiet revolution from training department to learning department to happen rapidly. It might take years to achieve the switch-over. Be patient, but do show visionary leadership and confidence in the belief that trainers or WLP practitioners can make the switch from their traditional roles to learning facilitators. Also show confidence in the belief that the organization's employees can be transformed into more efficient, effective, and creative learners. That expectation of success should do much to create a self-fulfilling prophecy, particularly if you are the leader of the training or WLP department.

WHY SHOULD TRAINERS BECOME LEARNING FACILITATORS?

A facilitator is, quite literally, a helper.[4] A *learning facilitator* thus helps learners become more efficient and effective in their on-the-job, real-time workplace learning process.[5] Learning facilitators also direct attention to the workplace learning climate, helping the organization and its decision makers to assess and build a climate that is conducive to workplace learning and oriented to solving practical, work-related problems. The competencies required of learning facilitators are akin to those required of group facilitators.[6] Trainers should become learning facilitators for at least two reasons.

First, technological trends point toward increasing responsibility falling on the shoulders of learners to become self-directed in their orientation. E-learning removes teachers or trainers from the immediate proximity of learners, which means that the learners must be guided to become better at managing their own learning process. Some people will even become free agent learners, as Chapter 2 indicated. FALs are aggressive in their orientation to learning and highly impatient because of their extreme sense of urgency. They want immediate answers to the problems they face. They do not want to wade through books or sift through online or onsite courses to get answers.

Dealing with FALs is a fact of life. FALs have their good points. They do not require hand-holding. They have a strong sense of urgency, and that is a good thing. But, given that FALs may not know how to build their own learning competence—that is, their own ability to learn how to learn—their efforts may not be as effective as they could otherwise be. Moreover, their ability to apply their workplace learning competence can be limited by the workplace learning climate of the organizations in which they work. For that reason, FALs may need the assistance of WLP professionals to help them make the most of their abilities, and organizations may need WLP professionals to work on conditions that encourage workplace learning.

To cope with such learners and remain successful, trainers must become adept at serving as learning facilitators. They must guide learners to think through their problems, set objectives for their own learning projects, and get better at managing their own learning process. Trainers must also be enabling agents, helping learners find quick, effective answers to the problems they face.

Second, knowledge is turning over too quickly for teachers or trainers to continue to focus on supplying information. That should be relegated to online sources, which can more easily be kept current. But learners' abilities to interpret and store that information for real-time use cannot so easily be stored. For that reason, trainers must help learners become more adept at thinking through, and interpreting, what comes to them through their senses and is processed by their brains. To that end, learning—not training—becomes central to learner success. Successful trainers will thus be able to guide individuals, and groups, to think more creatively and filter or interpret the massive amounts of information to which they have easy access. That requires facilitation skills.

HOW CAN TRAINERS BECOME EFFECTIVE LEARNING FACILITATORS?

To encourage workplace learning, trainers should start by reflecting on their own role. Of necessity they should be prompted to undergo a paradigm shift in their viewpoint. They need to begin to see themselves, and their roles, differently from the ways they traditionally have. Rather than being purveyors of knowledge or distilled wisdom, they must become adept and agile at making learning happen on the job and in real time. They must also find ways to help people generate new knowledge and facilitate creative problem solving around performance-related issues.

For this paradigm shift to be made successfully, trainers need to change their mind-sets in five specific ways. Trainers should use the worksheet in Exhibit 10-3 to help them organize their thinking about each paradigm shift and how they can demonstrate effective behaviors linked to it.

Paradigm Shift 1: Expect Learners to Bear More Responsibility for Their Own Learning

First, to make the shift from trainer to learning facilitator, trainers need to expect individuals to bear greater responsibility for their own learning than they traditionally have done. Trainers should encourage learners to seize the initiative for learning. Learners are likely, in time, to be increasingly impatient about meeting their real-time work problems and needs, and so they will be more likely to seize the initiative.

Poll managers in your organizations to see if they see this trend emerging in the organization. Also ask if they see this trend emerging among their school-age children. If so, ask what the implications of this

---

Exhibit 10-3: A worksheet to guide reflection on making paradigm shifts from trainer to learning facilitators.

Directions: Use this worksheet to stimulate your thinking as a trainer about key changes in your point of view (paradigm) about the trainer's role. What will these changes mean in changed behaviors? Read each paradigm shift necessary for making the shift from trainer to learning facilitator in the left column below.

	REQUIRED PARADIGM SHIFT AND BRIEF EXPLANATION	WHAT WILL YOU, AS A TRAINER, HAVE TO DO IN ORDER TO MAKE THIS PARADIGM SHIFT? LIST THE SPECIFIC BEHAVIORS THAT YOU BELIEVE WILL BE NECESSARY.
1	*Paradigm Shift 1*: Expect learners to bear more responsibility for their own learning.	
2	*Paradigm Shift 2*: Become more proficient at real-time facilitation and serving as an enabling agent.	
3	*Paradigm Shift 3*: Abandon the notion that learning experiences must always be planned.	
4	*Paradigm Shift 4*: Build a repertoire of skills in identifying learning needs and devising learning strategies.	
5	*Paradigm Shift 5*: Draw on a list of approaches—and encourage others to do so.	

trend might mean for the organization's approach to managing training and learning.

Paradigm Shift 2: Become More Proficient at Real-Time Facilitation and Serving as an Enabling Agent

Trainers who wish to become learning facilitators should become more proficient in real-time facilitation and in serving as an enabling agent and broker for learning. They should first learn the key competencies of group facilitators.[7] They should then add skill building in facilitating technology-supported discussions, such as chat rooms, videoconferences, message boards, and listservs.[8]

Paradigm Shift 3: Abandon the Notion That Learning Experiences Must Always Be Planned

To make the transition from traditional trainers to learning facilitators, trainers need to abandon the notion that most learning must be planned or be organized for it to happen or for it to be useful. Learners can be trained to improve their skills in establishing their own learning objectives, finding their own resources to meet those objectives, and creating their own measures by which to evaluate what they learned.[9] Trainers, however, may have to become learning facilitators to show learners how to do that.

Paradigm Shift 4: Build a Repertoire of Skills in Identifying Learning Needs and Devising Learning Strategies

To make the transition from traditional trainers to learning facilitators, trainers should build their repertoire of skills in identifying learning (rather than training) needs and finding creative ways to address them. Improving their questioning skills is a powerful way to do that. Effective learning facilitators are particularly adept at questioning learners, stimulating them to find their own learning needs, and selecting appropriate strategies for meeting those needs.

Paradigm Shift 5: Draw on a List of Approaches— and Encourage Others to Do So

Finally, to make the transition from traditional trainers to learning facilitators, trainers should be willing to draw on a list of approaches—and encourage others, such as managers and workers—to use them as well. For instance, they will not assume that classroom-based training, on-the-job training, or e-learning is appropriate to meet learning needs. Instead, they will be more freewheeling and creative in their willingness to apply a range of methods to encourage learning. Use the worksheet appearing in Exhibit 10-4 to organize your thinking and devise a list of approaches to encourage workplace learning.

How Can Trainers Encourage Others to Become Learning Facilitators?

It is particularly important for supervisors and managers to function as learning facilitators as well, since on a daily basis they come into more frequent contact with workers than do trainers or WLP practitioners. Take five specific steps to encourage others to become facilitators and apply the skills of such a facilitator to real-time, on-the-job situations.

Step 1: Make Others Aware of the Need

Most change efforts begin by explaining the need for the change to others, building a convincing case that it is necessary. To encourage supervisors and managers that they should become learning facilitators, trainers should therefore make others aware of the need. They can do that by

---

Exhibit 10-4: A worksheet to organize your thinking on approaches to workplace learning.

Directions: Use this worksheet to organize your thinking. Think of all the ways that people may learn on the job and in real time. Be creative. Realize, for instance, that people can learn by the type of supervisor they are assigned to, the kind of work they do, the kind of deadlines they are given, and much more. In short, try to expand your thinking about what is workplace learning—and what approaches may be used to encourage it and stimulate it. List as many approaches to workplace learning as you can think of below. There are no "right" or "wrong" answers in any absolute sense, though some approaches may be better than others.

List as many ways as you can think of that people can learn in the workplace:

---

briefing supervisors and managers on the idea and emphasizing the importance of their role in the workplace learning process.

Step 2: Clarify What Learning Facilitators Do

The term *learning facilitator* may seem somewhat removed from daily
workplace practice to supervisors and managers. (Use another term if it
works better.) However, it is helpful to have a detailed sense of what learning facilitators do. Build a description of the activities of learning facilitators. An effective approach is to involve supervisors and managers in this
process, getting them to write a role description—akin to a job description—that makes clear what learning facilitators should do and why they
should do that. Use the worksheet in Exhibit 10-5 to help draft that role
description.

Step 3: Assess the Skills of Others to Enact
the Learning Facilitator Role

Once the role description of a learning facilitator has been prepared, create a means by which to assess how well each supervisor or manager is
presently enacting that role. Do that by creating an assessment instrument
for that purpose. Administer the instrument to individuals to collect their
perceptions, and then to their subordinates, peers, and immediate organizational supervisors. The assessment should serve to pinpoint gaps for
each supervisor or manager, and it may also reveal shared needs among
many of them.

Step 4: Build the Skills of Supervisors and Managers to
Serve as Learning Facilitators Through Training

Use training to help build the skills of supervisors and managers to serve
as learning facilitators. Meet shared needs through online, onsite, or
blended programs. A sample workshop outline to build learning facilitation skills for supervisors and managers is shown in Exhibit 10-6. Use that
as a starting point.

**Exhibit 10-5: A worksheet to develop a role description
of a learning facilitator.**

Directions: The role of the learning facilitator is not necessarily immediately obvious to everyone. To prepare a role description of the learning facilitator, call together a group of supervisors
and/or managers. Then invite them to participate in a brainstorming session. Begin by defining
a *learning facilitator* as anyone who helps others learn in real time and on the job. Then invite
the participants to brainstorm on the purpose and activities of the learning facilitator. Explain
that you are trying to prepare a role description, akin to a job description, that clarifies what a
learning facilitator does in your organization. Be sure to emphasize that everyone serves as a
learning facilitator or else has the potential to serve as one. Use a flipchart to record answers
to such specific questions as:

> What is the purpose of a learning facilitator in this organization?
> What does a learning facilitator do in this organization?
> What special qualifications, if any, should learning facilitators possess?

Summarize the participant comments on a flipchart. Then summarize the results in the space
below.

QUESTIONS

1	**Purpose:** *What is the purpose of a learning facilitator in this organization?*
2	**Activities:** *What does a learning facilitator do in this organization?*
3	**Qualifications:** *What special qualifications, if any, should learning facilitators possess?*

Step 5: Follow Up to Ensure That Others Are
Functioning as Learning Facilitators

To ensure supervisors and managers are enacting their role as learning
facilitators, periodically follow up with them. Use brief, informal meetings
for that purpose, if you wish. You may also administer written question-
naires, by paper or e-mail, to the supervisors' and managers' employees
to see if they perceive their immediate supervisors to be enacting the role
successfully. If corrective action is necessary—such as individual counseling or refresher training—be sure to supply it.

Exhibit 10-6: A workshop outline to build learning facilitation skills.

PURPOSE	The purpose of this brief workshop is to build the skills of anyone who is, or must serve as, a learning facilitator to encourage people in this organization to become more effective workplace learners in real-time, on-the-job situations.
OBJECTIVES	*Upon completion of this workshop, participants will:* ■ Define a learning facilitator. ■ Explain why the role is important to this organization. ■ Review the work activities of a learning facilitator. ■ Be able to demonstrate the skills associated with the learning facilitator role.
BRIEF OUTLINE	**I. Introduction** **II. What Is a Learning Facilitator?** A. Brief definition B. Explanation of why the role is important in this organization C. Description of how workers, supervisors, and managers serve as learning facilitators **III. How Do You Build the Skills of the Learning Facilitator?** A. Review the skills associated with the learning facilitator. B. Role play examples of each skill. C. Discuss and debrief each role play. **IV. Conclusion**

SUMMARY

This chapter focused on answering two key questions: Why should the training department be transformed into a learning department? and What steps can guide that transformation?

As the chapter noted, there are three key reasons to transform a training department into a learning department. First, there is a growing need to transform traditional institutions into learning organizations. Second, there is a growing need to find ways to facilitate organizational learning and performance-oriented knowledge creation. Third and finally, there is a growing need to facilitate the real-time, on-the-job learning of individuals.

Although there is no foolproof strategy that can be offered by which to transform a training department into a learning department, the chapter suggested a nine-step process that visionary leaders should follow. This chapter also explained why trainers and others should become learning facilitators and how they can do that. It defined a *learning facilitator* as someone who helps learners become more efficient and effective in their on-the-job, real-time workplace learning process. The chapter explained that, to encourage workplace learners, trainers should start by reflecting on their own role, and by making changes in their viewpoints about their role.

Trainers should also encourage supervisors and managers to serve as learning facilitators. After all, they have more daily contact with workers. To that end, trainers should make others aware of the need to become learning facilitators, clarify what learning facilitators do, assess and build the skills of supervisors and managers to serve as learning facilitators, and follow up to ensure that others are functioning as learning facilitators.

Chapter 11

AFTERWORD

The Afterword is meant to offer final thoughts on using the workplace learning model, workplace learner roles, workplace learning competencies, and other information presented in this book. The Afterword is organized around the uses of several possible audiences for this book, including mentors and WLP practitioners; supervisors, managers, and other leaders; academicians; and workplace learners.

USES FOR MENTORS AND WORKPLACE LEARNING AND PERFORMANCE PRACTITIONERS

Mentors are those who teach others.[1] As emphasized throughout this book, much learning occurs on the job, informally, and among peers. It also occurs by accident and by the consequence of individual experience. Mentors can thus be people with whom individual learners come in contact as they progress through their daily work or through planned learning experiences or learning projects. Mentors may include coworkers and WLP practitioners.

Mentors should be as sensitive to how people learn as they are to how they will teach or train. After all, the effectiveness of learning experiences depends on the learner, not on the trainer. Recognizing that, mentors and other learning facilitators may wish to revisit how they organize instruction so that it matches up to the workplace learning process model. They should thus track the workplace learning process model (described in Chapter 6) and take care to:

- **Supply a triggering circumstance.** Provide some form of sensory stimulus to learners.

- **Emphasize the importance.** Clarify "what's in it for the learners" and the short-term and long-term importance of the issue.

- **Evoke curiosity.** Ask questions of learners to stimulate their interest.

- **Supply information.** Permit learners to draw on the mentor for information to satisfy the learners' curiosity.

- **Encourage processing.** Ask questions to help learners reach a deeper level of understanding and make sense of the information with which they have been supplied.

- **Encourage conversion and knowledge transformation.** Ask learners how they may apply the new information to their immediate situations and to subsequent situations.

- **Encourage application.** Ask learners to experiment with new information in practical, hands-on ways and report back after they have done that.

- **Encourage reflection.** Invite learners to reflect on the hands-on experiences they have had and draw conclusions from them.

- **Encourage a double-loop trigger/evaluation.** Encourage learners to reflect on how they learned in the situation, how that learning process might be improved in the future, and how the learning situation may have differed from—or been similar to—previous learning situations they have encountered.

Mentors should also be aware of the three-dimensional nature of the learning process in that learners engage themselves through *thinking, feeling,* and *doing* in each step listed.

USES FOR SUPERVISORS, MANAGERS, AND OTHER LEADERS

The workplace learning process may well be a common denominator across many issues affecting individual learning, group learning, organizational learning, change, and even management.[2] If that is true even part of the time, then the workplace learning process model described in this book can become a common frame of reference by which to unite learning and change efforts for individuals, groups, and organizations. By briefing people on the model and using it as a road map by which to plan for individual, group, and organizational development, supervisors, managers, and other leaders can simultaneously create more self-directed—and thus more empowered—workers. At the same time, they may also reinforce the importance of the learning process as key to competitive success.

Just as mentors may rely on the workplace learning process model as a guide for their steps in encouraging individuals to learn, so too may supervisors, managers, and other leaders rely on the same model as a guide for their efforts to encourage change at the individual, group, and organizational levels. Consequently, to apply the model to change efforts, supervisors, managers, and leaders should track the workplace learning process model (described in Chapter 6) and thus:

- **Supply a triggering circumstance.** They should find ways to stimulate individual and group thinking around common issues.

- **Emphasize the importance.** They should emphasize the importance of an issue to individuals, the work group or team, and to the organization—or guide learners to assess this importance on their own.

- **Evoke curiosity.** Ask questions of workers to stimulate interest.

- **Supply information.** Serve as a resource and enabling agent for workers without mandating their action.

- **Encourage processing.** Encourage workers, individually and in teams, to explore information they find, discover, or intuit.

- **Encourage conversion and knowledge transformation.** Ask workers how they would apply new information to their immediate situations and to subsequent situations they may face.

- **Encourage application.** Ask workers to experiment with innovative approaches and then test out the information they find.

- **Encourage reflection.** Invite workers to reflect on the hands-on experiences they encounter and draw conclusions from them.

- **Encourage a double-loop trigger/evaluation.** Encourage workers to reflect on how they learn and change in specific situations, how they might improve that process in the future, and how each change or learning situation encountered by one worker or group of workers has taught lessons for future application about how the organization, group, or individual learned in the situation.

When supervisors, managers, and leaders use the workplace learning model as a guide, they are effectively emphasizing the importance of the learning process. They are also encouraging individuals to become more self-directed. Finally, they are building an expectation that learning is a key process for securing individual, group, and organizational performance success.

Uses for Academicians

It is a startling paradox of our time that, whereas much attention is devoted to teaching subject matter in academic institutions, very little time or attention has been devoted to helping students at any level learn how to become better learners. In most academic institutions, "learning" becomes a focal point for attention only when a student demonstrates some deficiency in "study skills" (such as below-average or even failing grades). And, yet, given the explosion of information with which students are bombarded and the escalation of advancing technology that places more information at their fingertips, interest should be growing in helping people become more efficient and effective learners and to increase their self-directedness and autonomy in the learning process.

To that end, this book may provide the starting point for helping academicians reexamine their programs from the user's—that is, the learner's—standpoint. Questions to consider might include the following:

- How are individuals in undergraduate, graduate, and/or certificate programs given the opportunity to assess their own needs, establish their own measurable objectives for study, identify their own resources for learning, take proactive steps to use those resources to meet their own identified learning needs, and evaluate their own results?

- What deliberate steps are taken by faculty to encourage learners to take independent action and mount independent, innovative investigations?

- How are faculty and administrators selected, rewarded, and evaluated for their ability to stimulate independence and self-directedness among learners? How can such self-directedness be identified, encouraged, and measured?

- What specific barriers exist in an academic institution that stand in the way of encouraging learner self-directedness? How can those barriers be removed or their influence minimized?

In many cases, promoting learner self-directedness will require academic institutions to reinvent their efforts. Helpful mechanisms to encourage such self-directedness might include:

- Using learning contracts both to guide programs and to guide student work in courses

- Applying specific teaching techniques that encourage self-directedness

- Using action learning groups in classes

- Providing students with career counseling and individualized advice about the value of taking independent action

- Encouraging students to formulate career goals and take proactive steps during their academic programs to realize those goals

- Stressing the importance of out-of-class informal or incidental learning experiences as well as formal class work in realizing individual career goals

- Encouraging students to develop individual portfolios or dossiers to show what they can do

- Appointing peer mentors to help individuals

USES FOR WORKPLACE LEARNERS

All who work should regard themselves—and those with whom they work—as workplace learners. Consequently, almost anyone can derive benefit from this book. To do that, individuals should use this book to reflect on how they may take more initiative in, and responsibility for, their learning and to marshal the resources they need to improve:

- With whom they learn

- What they learn

- When they learn

- Where they learn

- Why they learn

- How they learn

- How they measure and document the results of what they learn

- How they reflect and improve their ability to learn

- How they achieve optimal performance by applying, experimenting with, and reflecting on what they learn and how they learn

A PARTING WORD

This book was written to be provocative in the sense that it is intended to encourage you, the reader, to think about how people learn in the workplace and to find ways to focus more attention on that process. The goal should be to work toward making individuals more efficient and effective learners in real time and on the job. At the same time, organizational leaders should direct attention to establishing and maintaining conditions that encourage workplace learning while minimizing conditions that discourage workplace learning. The challenge we all face—whether we are mentors, WLP practitioners, supervisors, managers, other leaders, or academicians—is clear: We must find ways to build the competence of workplace learners while we build a supportive workplace learning climate. Good luck in your efforts toward that end.

A SUMMARY OF THE RESEARCH STUDY ON THE WORKPLACE LEARNER'S COMPETENCIES AND THE WORKPLACE LEARNING CLIMATE*

BACKGROUND

Much research has been done on the roles, competencies, and work outputs of trainers. But relatively little comparable research has been done on the roles, competencies, and work outputs of learners.

The purpose of the study was to investigate:

- Workplace learner roles, competencies, and work outputs

- Conditions that help or hinder workplace learning in the opinion of learners in selected industries and hierarchical levels

*Source: William J. Rothwell, "Models for the Workplace Learner." Unpublished research report. Copyright 2000 by William J. Rothwell, Ph.D. All rights reserved.

RESEARCH QUESTIONS

This study actually encompassed two related research studies. During the first study, the researcher focused on addressing the following questions:

- What model can describe the workplace learning process?

- What roles can be linked to the workplace learning model?

- What workplace learning competencies and outputs can be derived from an examination of the most difficult learning situations, the most common learning situations, and the perceived characteristics of successful workplace learners by individuals selected from a broad cross-section of industries and hierarchical levels?

During the second study, the researcher focused on addressing the following questions:

- What trends most affect workplace learning?

- What conditions must exist for the organizational environment to support workplace learning?

- What are the chief barriers to workplace learning?

- What action strategies are most effective in overcoming those barriers?

METHODOLOGY

The methodology of the two related studies was based, in part, on the SCANS study.[1] However, the SCANS study was used only as a starting point for the design of these studies. This section briefly describes the SCANS study and then provides a step-by-step description of how each of the author's two related studies was carried out.

The SCANS Study

In 1990, the U.S. Secretary of Labor appointed the Secretary's Commission on Achieving Necessary Skills (SCANS) to determine the skills needed by young people to succeed in the world of work. The commission's fundamental purpose was to encourage high-skill, high-wage employment. In conducting the research on which the SCANS study was based, the researchers reviewed workplace demands on young people. Focusing on five sectors of the U.S. economy—manufacturing, health services, retail trade, accommodations and food service, and office services—the SCANS researchers conducted behavioral event interviews (BEIs) with approximately five individuals in each of fifty occupations across these economic sectors.

The commission completed its work in 1992, and its findings and recommendations were printed in several final reports. The SCANS study has been influential in governmental efforts to ease the school-to-work transition and in welfare reform efforts. Its major impact has been felt most keenly in U.S. two-year community colleges. In those settings the SCANS study continues to be a focal point for curriculum development.

The results of the SCANS study pinpointed the following essential competencies for new hires:[2]

WORKPLACE COMPETENCIES

Effective workers can productively use:

- **Resources.** They know how to allocate time, money, materials, space, and staff.

- **Interpersonal Skills.** They can work on teams, teach others, serve customers, lead, negotiate, and work well with people from culturally diverse backgrounds.

- **Information.** They can acquire and evaluate data, organize and maintain files, interpret and communicate, and use computers to process information.

- **Systems.** They understand social, organizational, and technological systems; they can monitor and correct performance; and they can design or improve systems.

- **Technology.** They can select equipment and tools, apply technology to specific tasks, and maintain and troubleshoot equipment.

FOUNDATION SKILLS

Competent workers in the high-performance workplace need:

- **Basic Skills.** Reading, writing, arithmetic and mathematics, speaking and listening skills.

- **Thinking Skills.** The ability to learn, to reason, to think creatively, to make decisions, and to solve problems.

- **Personal Qualities.** Individual responsibility, self-esteem and self-management, sociability, and integrity.

Review of the Methodology of Study #1: Assessing Workplace Learning Competence

In the first study, I:

- Conducted a literature review on the topic of "learner competencies" focusing around the question "what competencies make for success in workplace learning situations?"

- Prepared a research précis.

- Drafted a structured interview guide for BEIs based on the research précis.

- Trained graduate students on BEI methods.

- Pretested the structured interview guide with graduate students enrolled in fall 1998.

- Refined the interview guide based on the pretest.

- Pilot tested the interview guide with ten individuals selected locally, based on their occupations and availability.

- Refined the interview guide based on the pilot test.

- Assigned occupations to students.

- Supervised the conduct of the BEIs.

- Began coding results to identify commonalities within and across occupational categories.

- Identified tentative competencies from the coded results.

Review of the Methodology of Study #2:
Assessing Workplace Learning Climate

In the second study, I:

- Conducted a literature review on the topic of trends affecting workplace learning, conditions favoring workplace learning, and conditions serving as barriers to workplace learning.

- Prepared a research précis.

- Drafted a structured interview guide.

- Trained graduate students on interviewing methods.

- Pretested the structured interview guide with graduate students enrolled in WFED 575, Current Policy and Practices in Training, in Spring 1999.

- Refined the interview guide based on the pretest.

- Pilot tested the interview guide with ten individuals selected locally, based on their hierarchical levels and availability.

- Refined the interview guide based on the pilot test.

- Assigned respondent categories to students.

- Invited participation.

- Supervised the conduct of the interviews.

- Began coding results to identify commonalities within and across industries and hierarchical levels.

Sample Selection

The sample selection for this study relied on exactly the same five industries as used in the SCANS study. However, instead of focusing on specific occupations, as did the SCANS study, I substituted the hierarchical levels used by the U.S. Equal Employment Opportunity Commission. In that way, the research directed attention to hierarchical levels rather than to occupations. The reason was that I wanted to examine learning competencies across the hierarchy. The sample was thus purposefully drawn according to the scheme shown in Exhibit A-1.

Analytical Methods

The results were subjected to thematic analysis. They were analyzed according to the scheme recommended by Lyle Spencer and Signe Spencer.[3]

Exhibit A-1: Targeted respondents by industry and hierarchical level.

HEALTH AND HUMAN SERVICES	OFFICE, FINANCIAL SERVICES, & GOVERNMENT	ACCOMMODATIONS SALES & PERSONAL SERVICES	MANUFACTURING, AGRI-BUSINESS, MINING, & CONSTRUCTION	TRADE, TRANSPORTATION, & COMMUNICATIONS
Officials and Managers	Officials and Managers	Officials and Managers	Officials and Managers	Officials and Managers
Professionals	Professionals	Professionals	Professionals	Professionals
Technicians	Technicians	Technicians	Technicians	Technicians
Sales workers	Sales workers	Sales workers	Sales workers	Sales workers
Office and clerical	Office and clerical	Office and clerical	Office and clerical	Office and clerical
Craft workers (Skilled)	Craft workers (Skilled)	Craft workers (Skilled)	Craft workers (Skilled)	Craft workers (Skilled)
Operatives (Semiskilled)	Operatives (Semiskilled)	Operatives (Semiskilled)	Operatives (Semiskilled)	Operatives (Semiskilled)
Laborers (Unskilled)	Laborers (Unskilled)	Laborers (Unskilled)	Laborers (Unskilled)	Laborers (Unskilled)
Service Workers	Service Workers	Service Workers	Service Workers	Service Workers

Source: Adapted, in part, from the U.S. Department of Labor, *What Work Requires of Schools: A SCANS Report for America 2000* (Washington, D.C.: Superintendent of Public Documents, 1991).

Conclusions and Recommendations

- There appears to be broad agreement among a cross-section of workers in different industry categories and at different hierarchical levels about the requirements for effective workplace learning.

- The organizational environment provides an important frame of reference for workplace learning, though efforts to measure the climate for workplace learning have so far been limited.

- Knowledge is not static. Increased attention should be devoted to the learning process ("how we learn") rather than to "static" knowledge, skill, and attitude requirements ("what we learn").

- Increasingly, success at work means success in learning.

- Workplace learning and work performance are closely related, and so the term *workplace learning and performance* is a fitting name for the field once called human resource development. However, WLP is not a widely known term yet in many work settings.

- Learning, as a metacompetency, deserves continued study and can become an important foundation for selecting, orienting, developing, appraising, rewarding, and providing feedback to workers/learners/performers.

- Organizational competitive success is influenced by individual workplace learning, in the opinion of the respondents to these studies.

BEHAVIORAL EVENT INTERVIEW GUIDE TO ASSESS WORKPLACE LEARNING COMPETENCE

Directions to Interviewers: Follow the directions on this guide explicitly. Ask individuals only the questions that you have been given to ask. Tape record the interview and have a signed release provided to you. When you finish, hand in this guide with any notes from the interview and your tape recordings.

Your Name	Name of Individual Interviewed

Respondent's Industry & Occupation Category *(Write in industry and occupation from the list given to you.)*	
Industry	Occupation

Today's Date	Job Title of Individual Interviewed

Employer of Individual Interviewed

BACKGROUND OF THIS STUDY

"Thank you for agreeing to participate in this study.

How people learn in the workplace may or may not be different from how they learn in other settings. The purpose of this study is to identify the competencies that workers need to learn most effectively. You will be asked about three major issues: (1) the most difficult learning situation you feel you have ever encountered in the workplace; (2) the most common or typical learning situation you feel you encounter in the workplace; and (3) your opinion about what it takes to be successful in workplace learning situations. Please be detailed in your answers to the questions."

Before participating in this interview, please read and sign the consent form provided to you.

RESPONDENTS' JOB REQUIREMENTS

QUESTION		NOTES ON THE ANSWER
1	What are your work requirements? Describe your work duties.	*List work requirements and duties.*

YOUR MOST DIFFICULT WORKPLACE LEARNING SITUATION

QUESTION		NOTES ON THE ANSWER
1	Think back to the *single most difficult learning situation* you have ever encountered in the workplace. This can involve *any* learning activity or effort—so long as it occurred while you were in the workplace. It could have occurred while you were in your present job or in another job. It could have occurred while you were with your present employer or with another employer. However, it is important that you describe the situation in detail. First, provide an overview of the situation. What was the learning challenge you faced? Then answer some background questions: When did this occur (*give approximate dates*)? Who was involved (*give job titles but not names*)? Where did this occur (*give approximate location*)?	*What was the learning challenge?*
		When did this occur?
		Who was involved?
		Where did this occur?

		STEP BY STEP	WHAT WAS HAPPENING, AND WHAT WERE YOU DOING?	WHAT WERE YOU THINKING AS THIS WAS HAPPENING AND/OR AS YOU WERE DOING WHAT YOU WERE DOING?	WHAT WERE YOU FEELING AS THIS WAS HAPPENING AND/OR AS YOU WERE DOING WHAT YOU WERE DOING?
2	Tell us *how you learned* in this situation. Be as specific as possible, describing what happened in the sequence that it happened. Be sure to explain what was happening, what you were doing, what you were thinking, and what you were feeling as events unfolded.	1	*Notes:*		
		2			
		3			
		4			
		5			
		6			

	7			
	8			

3	What did you *learn about how you learn* from this situation? If you faced the same situation again, how would you handle it—and why would you handle it that way?	*What did you learn about how you learn from this situation? Notes:*
		If you faced the same situation again, how would you handle it? Notes:
		If you faced the same situation again, why would you handle it the way you said you would handle it? Notes:

YOUR MOST COMMON OR TYPICAL WORKPLACE LEARNING SITUATION

QUESTION		NOTES ON THE ANSWER
1	Think about the *most common or typical learning situation* you encounter in the workplace. This can involve *any* learning activity or effort—so long as it occurs while you are in the workplace. First, provide an overview of the situation. What is the typical learning challenge you face? Then answer some background questions: When does this occur? Who is involved? How often does it occur? Why do you think it occurs?	*What is the typical learning challenge?*
		When does this occur?
		Who is involved?
		How often does it occur?

		STEP BY STEP	WHAT IS HAPPENING, AND WHAT ARE YOU DOING?	WHAT ARE YOU THINKING AS THIS IS HAPPENING AND/OR AS YOU ARE DOING WHAT YOU ARE DOING?	WHAT ARE YOU FEELING AS THIS IS HAPPENING AND/OR AS YOU ARE DOING WHAT YOU ARE DOING?
				Why do you think it occurs?	
2	Tell us *how you learn* in this situation. Be as specific as possible, describing what happens in the sequence that it happens. Be sure to explain what is happening, what you are doing, what you are thinking, and what you are feeling as the events unfold.	1	*Notes:*		
		2			
		3			
		4			
		5			
		6			

	7			
	8			

3	What have you *learned about how you learn* in this most common or typical workplace learning situation? If you were advising others how to approach the situation, what advice would you give them and why?	*What have you learned about how you learn in this most common or typical workplace learning situation?*
		If you were advising others how to approach the situation, what advice would you give them?
		Why would you give others the advice that you would give them?

YOUR OPINIONS ABOUT WORKPLACE LEARNING

	QUESTION	NOTES ON THE ANSWER
1	What is your opinion about *what it takes to be successful in learning in the workplace*? Reflect on your own experience and describe what you believe to be essential to workplace learning in your occupation and in your organization.	*What is your opinion?*

Thank You for Your Cooperation!

Learners' Perceptions of Workplace Learning in Their Own Words

Respondents were asked the following question: "What is your opinion about *what it takes to be successful in learning in the workplace*? Reflect on your own experience and describe what you believe to be essential to workplace learning at your level in the organization's hierarchy and in your organization." This Appendix is meant to give voice to what workplace learners had to say about that.

RESPONSES

The respondents' responses are given next, verbatim.

Officials and Managers/Health & Human Services

- **Director of Nursing, Association of Retarded Citizens**: "It takes repeated experience in asking questions and giving clear directions. It takes experience in recognizing drug-related side effects. The level of learning rests on communication among peers, assuring that communication is clearly understood and giving clear, accurate and detailed directions. It rests on trust of staff and past experience that they have good common sense in stressful situations."

- **Youth Consultant**: "Be motivated to learn. Have background information for information. Immediately applicable. You get paid to learn. Immediate gratification for successful learning."

- **Project Director, Family Planning Clinic**: "I think it is crucial to be willing to be honest and receive honesty back from your co-workers and colleagues in order to be successful at workplace learning. Also, I think it is crucial to make incremental steps to improve organizations systems/means of communication so that learning can be optimized without causing too much shock to the participants."

- **Office Manager**: "Need to be willing to admit when you make mistakes. Reflect on your day and think about how you can handle situations and what you could do better. Challenge yourself to continued improvement."

- **Laboratory Supervisor, Hospital**: "Have to be extremely diligent. You have to do a good job, have to enjoy learning the detail. Think about disease. Learning is a matter of mindset."

- **Executive Director, Special Project**: "Be open-minded. Listen to many. Be courageous and confident. Exercise maturity. Get experience. Show a willingness to learn."

- **Administrative Assistant to University President**: "Evaluate one's own behavior, post task, not just during the task. Autopsy the results."

Professionals/Health & Human Services

- **Assistant Professor, University Hospital Program**: "Requires support, employer patience for employees as they learn. It is 'our job' [as managers] to provide that support."

- **Dental Hygienist, Private Dentist's Office**: "Be open to new ideas. Be respectful to those who have more experience [and] training. Learn how to give suggestions in a calm tone of voice. Confront [people] in private, not in front of entire staff."

- **Registered Nurse, School District**: "Learn from several individuals. You must be willing to listen to what others have to say and, whether you agree or not, learn from what they say. [I] have found that some of my best 'trainers' are the students I teach. They usually tell it like it is, which is great for curriculum changes, classroom management, etc."

- **Surgical Resident, Metropolitan Hospital**: "This basically can apply to any kind of workplace. Basically, you must have a lot of knowledge in your field, and it doesn't matter [whether you are] an engineer, computer programmer, or in medicine. In order to obtain knowledge, you have to read widely and obviously. [My field is] always changing and I have to keep up with the changing pace. The best thing to do is just read."

- **Insurance Claims Adjuster**: "Know that you are a good worker and that you can do anything that you set your mind to (in spite of any obstacles)."

- **Dental Hygienist, Private Dentist's Office**: "Reflect on your own performance and how it can be improved. Take advantage of coworkers' experience, but don't become dependent on them."

- **Program Manager, Private Industry Council**: "Do what you ask of others. Be a diplomat with personnel problems, business interests. Try to maintain a management perspective. Maintain line between friend and supervisor. Make every employee feel respected. Be able to get your own work done. Be able to say no. Learn how your employees learn. Manage personalities. Learn from others."

- **Dental Hygienist, Private Dentist's Office**: "This is a career, not a job. I care about my patients. Be open-minded and well prepared. The positive reinforcement from my doctor gives me the confidence I need to be successful. He encourages me to discuss new products, and feedback helps me grow professionally. One good thing: School hygienist work at dental clinic hospital. On overcoming barriers: I had prior skill. Some things are difficult to coordinate. I would get discouraged and feel that maybe I was too old to do this. Paying for college was difficult. I worked two part-time jobs and borrowed the rest. I like to learn and needed a challenge. I wanted a better standard of living. I was the first in my family to go to college."

Technicians/Health & Human Services

- **Ultrasound Technician, Community Hospital**: "It takes patience. You're not going to learn everything at one time. There's a lot to remember. You'll get better the longer you do it, and the better you'll become. Practice."

- **Certified Respiratory Therapy Technician, Community Hospital**: "At a professional level it takes continuing education and participating more than just doing your work [and then] going home. It means things like participating on committees. For success with patients, it means being a good therapist and means it takes more compassion, patience, and a true understanding of what the patient is going through. Empathy. You will need to back it up with professional education. Patients look up to professionals and trust them. We have a responsibility to help them and not mislead them."

- **Dental Hygienist, Medical Clinic**: "I think you need to know what the employer expects of you as an employee. I think you need to know that even if we believe we are irreplaceable we truly are replaceable. To be successful you need education, drive to do the job well, be happy with what you are doing, and take one step at a time."

- **Nursing Assistant, Nursing Home**: "Successful learning in the workplace requires first a willingness to want to learn to do a job beyond satisfactory. When you learn you grow both personally and professionally."

Sales Workers/Health & Human Services

- **Service Representative, HMO**: "Be open-minded. Use new technology—can't do things the way they were done twenty years ago. Be accepting of all kinds of people. This is especially important here in Central Pennsylvania, where people seem to be more set in their ways. Have empathy for the customer. Be inspired."

- **Marketing Representative, Health Alliance**: "I have found it is important to find a mentor. Learn from every situation whether it is positive or negative. After completing an event, review all of the processes and activities to see what you can learn. It also helps if you learn the key players in your workplace and how to interact with them. In addition, learning the management style and how to work people in your organization also helps."

- **Self-Employed Food Sales**: "To be successful in learning in the workplace, the learner must have a good attitude, be willing to try new things and never assume that anything is impossible."

- **Special Events Coordinator, Community Health Care System**: "You need to be able to communicate your learning needs and try to understand others. Patience and tolerance are needed when dealing with peers."

- **Community Relations Coordinator, Community Medical Center**: "Open questions and open communication because it involves teamwork. Be considerate of other people's time."

Office and Clerical/Health & Human Services

- **Receptionist, Private Physician's Office**: "You should be yourself and ultimately pleasing and satisfying yourself is gratifying. Create success in life and in the workplace!"

- **Medical Records/Registration, Community Medical Center**: "There is nothing any worse than fear. When you fear something it's scary and it can tend to paralyze you. I don't learn to my full potential when I'm feeling like I'm not getting proper training. I learn best in one-on-one situations and from my peers."

- **Service Desk Attendant, Library**: "Learning content should be progressive from easy to difficult. It will help learning to understand. [The] patron is the most important aspect of this job."

- **Office Clerk, Hospital**: "People must have the ability to actually handle the task. They must also be able to grasp new challenges and understand new tasks."

- **Coordinator, Medical Staff Services, Hospital**: "Think before you leap. Plan ahead. Be aggressive in creating the best possible environment before starting anything—that is, training session, special project."

Craft Workers (Skilled)/Health & Human Services

- **Professional Baker, Restaurant**: "In this type of position, at this level, it takes a lot of flexibility in order to be successful. One must be willing to make plans, but also to change them often when things don't work, sometimes even in the middle of an activity. You must be patient and realize that acquiring technical skills takes time, and that your level of competence will increase. You must pay attention to details, especially when training with experts who may know tricks that can significantly increase efficiency. You must be flexible in your learning style as well—willing to watch and learn, learn by doing, learn by note-taking or reading, or by making mistakes."

- **Biomedical Technician, Health Care System**: "Good background from college. Real learning begins on the job. Read manuals. Ask for help from other techs to save time. Use repetition and trial and error. Communicate. Use common sense. Be confident."

- **Data Analyst, University Medical Center**: "Take training classes. Practice what you learned in class in real projects. Find a mentor for yourself."

- **Maintenance Worker, City Housing Department**: "First, it really helps to work with someone with experience before you go on your own. If you work with someone for awhile, you get the feel of things, you have training no matter how much of training [*sic*], you have to figure out things for yourself. A lot of the time, we have to call professional plumbers but we go as far as we can. Training is the way to know to do what you are doing and you have to work with someone who knows how the work is done. Training is the best. You have to think before you do. Make sure it is safe."

Operatives (Semi-Skilled)/Health & Human Services

- **Phlebotomist, Medical Clinic**: "Be confident. Don't let anyone put you down. Have good performance. Let customers ask for you. Pay attention to detail. Don't make mistakes. Ask questions."

- **Phlebotomist, Community Hospital**: "Communication is the big thing. There are different procedures or rules that change. Communication is important. Whether by memo, meetings, or just personnel [*sic*]."

- **Respiratory Care Assistant/Aide, Community Hospital**: "Be open-minded. Be open to suggestions. Be willing to learn, not stubborn, in medical and health care, because things change all the time. Ask when you don't know. Otherwise, it will end up hurting the patient."

Laborers (Unskilled)/Health & Human Services

- **Dietary Aide, Regional Medical Center**: "It is important to take time for yourself to think and get away to deal with stress. Your own personal time to let loose."

- **Maintenance Worker, Community Hospital**: "A good general understanding of what you're going to be working with or what you're going to be doing. The other thing is hands-on—a routine use of it. If you do anything daily, it becomes repetitious. To learn something, I relate it from one thing to another. An electrical layout is similar to a plumbing layout. Past experience—certain tools are good for one thing and not for another. The best way to learn is hands-on. You don't get bored that way."

- **Sterile Process Aide, Community Hospital**: "Observe with all your concentration. Take notes and refer back to them. Stay focused."

Service Workers/Health & Human Services

- **Career Development Counselor, Private Industry Council**: "Person needs to embrace change. Think out of the box. Can't wait—have to be proactive."

- **Nursing Assistant, Health Care System**: "Need enhanced (scheduled) educational programs; work neat, clean, and continuously (environmental issues); find work to do; good, consistent, concise communication among all levels."

- **Service Aide, Health Care System**: "Effort must be present. Low morale makes learning difficult. Easily influenced workers are not educated and have poor morale. Management must intervene for morale to improve and for improvements in attitude. Stress reduction in-service helps. Desire drives the effort. Improve communication (not just budgetary, overtime, etc.)."

- **Dental Assistant, Dentist's Office**: "It takes keeping an open mind and being flexible to be successful in learning in the workplace. Every day is a different set of circumstances. What may offend someone one day may make them laugh the next. The procedures, as routine as they are, change with every patient in some way. The challenge is learning the best way to adapt to each situation and keeping your temper."

- **Case Worker, Private Industry Council**: "You need to be: (1) prepared, (2) have skills, (3) receive training, (4) have prior knowledge. Helpful to have multiformat presentations during training in an organized fashion."

- **Office Case Manager, Private Industry Council**: "Not work-specific. Need to jump through the hoops to attain your goals based on persistence. ENDURE."

- **Night Shift Supervisor, University Physical Plant**: "On the job training is the best teacher. Need: patience, understanding, listening, not overreacting, showing compassion, role play by putting yourself in the other person's shoes."

- **Laundry and Dish Room Helper, University Food Service**: "Watch others perform. Experiment. Have a good attitude. Be patient. Attitude is the determining factor in learning something new."

Officers and Managers/Office, Financial Services, and Government

- **Office Manager, CPA Firm**: "I believe that it is essential to be able to learn in every situation and from every member of the organization. Listen to everyone's opinion—right or wrong—because sometimes they are right and you are wrong. Show due respect to every member of the organization. You have to go with new technology coming out whether you feel comfortable with the new electronic system. I just don't trust it completely."

- **Director, Continuing Education, Big Ten University**: "Need for a formal process to assess the skills and competencies of the organization—a competency profile. Know yourself. Understand your own strengths and weaknesses. Establish a formal learning plan. Take individual responsibility. Use learning experiences."

- **Superintendent of Schools, Rural School District**: "First you need a good background both experientially and in terms of formal classroom work. In order to learn to face new problems, you have to have a good theory base, but you also have to be able to learn from your time on the job. It's certainly very helpful in my field to have gone through a number of different positions. I know what it is to be a teacher, a coach, and a building administrator (principal). I've performed a number of different functions in the community. You put that together—things you get through formal training and things you gain through professional reading—and you try to merge those into some kind of viewpoint, world view, philosophy of how things ought to be and how you can accomplish them in a practical manner."

- **Business Owner/Entrepreneur, Technology Firm (Accounting Software)**: "Wanting to be in the workplace. Enthusiasm to be in the workplace. If it's not a healthy place, don't be there."

- **Director, University Program to Assist Migrant Workers**: "It's very important to be humble and to learn from your subordinates. You get a lot from them. If you keep the door to communication open and express yourself, staff will reciprocate. It's important to listen."

- **District Business Banker for Large Bank**: "To obtain and maintain good relationships with others should be the most important characteristic in learning in the workplace."

- **Minister of Protestant Church**: "So many facets to this particular job—I don't want to call it a 'job'—but I'll say 'job.' In one situation you're in counseling, sitting in a meeting, and you learn from that. You learn from studying. When you are handling conflict, you're learning from that. When you're leading a worship service, you're learning from that. It's just so many facets of what you do that it's hard to broadbrush it. You'd have to almost be specific in answering this question. Yeah, just be a well-rounded individual. In tune with the spiritual gifts because you need them all to operate in all these different settings."

- **Project Director, University Program with Multimillion Dollar Budget**: "Finding out how you learn and why you learn that way. I believe your initial learning style is always going to be your major one, but you must learn how to learn in other ways."

- **General Manager, Training Consulting Firm**: "Workplace learning is related to urgency and usage. If you want to use the knowledge, but you find you do not have it, it becomes urgent. To prevent this from happening, we should be pretty good at forecasting. In this way, we can prepare ourselves in advance for future challenges."

- **Supervisor, Family Employment Services, State Agency**: "The workers appreciate honesty and open communication. If they feel that management is hiding information from them, they will not cooperate with change."

Professionals/Office, Financial Services, & Government

- **Contract Compliance Officer, University**: "You have to take risks in order to accomplish your objectives. I didn't learn much [*sic*]. The only thing that I know is that I'm always going to try to do the right thing and let the chips fall where they may."

- **Instructor, University**: "In learning, your best resource is to learn and share with colleagues—it's the one thing that has helped me the most with my job. Even in the everyday, humdrum parts of work. If I'm unsure or shaky on something I really think you should talk to coworkers. My environment is very open and colleagues make themselves very available to each other, which helps; collaborate and share with other workers. *Star Trek: The Next Generation* is a good model for the ideal collaborative team where everyone consults with others constantly. This is the ideal."

- **Teacher, Small City School**: "Learning in the workplace requires background knowledge of what you do. It also requires flexibility. The ability to think quickly [*is important*] and usually occurs during stressful situations [*sic*]. You need to be able to not get too frustrated or stressed and think to a solution."

- **Second Teacher, Small City School**: "Open mind. Willingness to try. Willingness to listen and learn from the experiences of others. At first the new activity will be harder but will become easier with time."

- **Trainer, Diversity Office, University**: "A willingness to do a good job. Important to be flexible with your structure. Important to be approachable and willing to spend time helping others."

- **Student Teacher, Rural School District**: "Supportive peers and supervisors to allow you to take risks. Open communication between peers, students, and supervisors. Positive feedback/criticism. You must be willing to try different things. Respect."

- **Assistant Professor, Automotive Program, University**: "Understand the process. Understand how the equipment works. Understand how learning occurs. Understand how to make the process, equipment, and learning work together."

- **Research Associate, University**: "It is important not to be afraid to make mistakes and to try new things. Also, be able to rely on others."

- **Staff Attorney, State Supreme Court**: "Diligence, preparation, and patience [are] needed within the very specific framework of a court attorney. Have to follow through on your professional training and use it for on-the-job situations; not really specific differences in learning among attorneys in the entire profession, but in all cases you need to have specific training and education to fulfill job requirements."

- **Learning Facilitator, Vocational-Technical School**: "I learn through my own motivation, my drive to make good decisions based on well-researched information. I learn through reading, through conversation with various support persons, and by attending meetings and seminars dealing with special education populations."

- **Financial Officer, Corporate Headquarters**: "I assume at the outset that a person is capable of doing a job. From there, willingness to learn and try new approaches. Though necessary to have support from supervisor, that helps to expand potential."

- **Marriage and Family Therapist, High School**: "Must constantly stay on top of new techniques—continuing education is key to success-

ful learning. Don't stop learning after receiving professional credentials. Every therapist must have a therapist to learn how to
process [one's] own issues. Should work closely with supervisors
and colleagues to discuss alternatives and other opinions and to
receive help. Remain open to feedback and dialogue in order to
learn of other approaches to therapy."

- **Producer/Videographer, University**: "You need to have a positive attitude about learning. Learning is often fun and rewarding. Learning how to learn is one of the most important things you ever
learn. I wish I would have tried to learn this way when I was in
a course. Learning needs to be encouraged by supervisors and
coworkers as an ongoing activity."

Technicians/Office, Financial Services, & Government

- **Research Associate, University**: "You must be open-minded—be
able to look beyond your own ideas. You must reflect—always
look at everything you do, no matter how small. See what you can
learn from it."

- **Job Developer, Job Training Center**: "Collect information from others. Be flexible to change. Be open to learning. Be open to trial
and error. Be willing to change."

- **Supervisor, Payroll Department, Accounting Firm**: "Dedication. Need
to be able to meet deadlines. A good memory. Need to be able to
read and comprehend. Also need the hands-on application. Be a
self-learner."

Sales Workers/Office, Financial Services, & Government

- **Regional Sales Manager, Investment & Sales, Self-Employed**: "Commitment for studying and practicing. Discipline. Honesty. Knowledgeable about product. Keep informed through continuing
education. Practice the craft to stay sharp."

- **Personal Banking Representative, Branch of Large Bank**: "Don't be afraid of change. Ask lots of questions. Use the people around you. They might have ideas or answers that will help you in a snap. Be open to hands-on training. Teach yourself. Do not rely on others to teach you. At my level, using support people, my employees, reference manuals are essential to this position. The more I learn on my own, the better off I will be as an employee. Also listen to what is going on around you. Listen to answers given to others. Give answers when you can. You learn from others as much as you learn from yourself. If being able to help others if you know the answer will help yourself [*sic*]".

- **Personal Financial Analyst, Large Bank**: "It needs to directly relate to my work or future aspirations of work. Role playing is really effective. Successful learning takes place when people are excited to be there. When they see a direct benefit to them as the learner. Know the purpose of the learning situation. Personal experience is essential in successful transfer of knowledge."

Office and Clerical/Office, Financial Services, & Government

- **Office Manager and Superintendent, Large Apartment Complex**: "It takes motivation. It is all about attitude. You have to display the proper attitude, have some type of knowledge, be a team player for learning, be willing to do self-study and know your work and everything that pertains to it. A nice stress free work environment is essential."

- **Graduate Assistant, University**: "Important to know which persons are the holders of what information. Be aware of your own strengths and weaknesses. Know who can complement your weak areas."

- **Staff Assistant, University**: "In my opinion, what it takes to be successful: Go to work. Listen to others who may have been with the company longer. You can learn a lot by watching how others perform their jobs. You can learn the right way and sometimes you may even observe the wrong way. But the best part in both ways is both are a learning experience. Ask questions and, if needed, repeat the question until it is explained in a way that you understand. And if you happen to be doing a report and make a few mistakes, be thankful that someone pointed it out to you so you have a chance to correct it. Then re-do it and hand it back."

- **School Psychologist's Assistant, School District**: "Get along with co-workers. Don't be critical of others. Accept orders from supervisors. Learn to be confidential."

- **Marketing Research Assistant, University**: "Being able to communicate without getting personal. Being assertive."

- **Staff Assistant, University**: "Training and experience. Must know and understand what you are doing. Must be willing to go 'above and beyond.' Have support from supervisors."

- **Compensation & Employment Specialist, HR Dept., University**: "Your attitude is to be sensitive to people in other organizations. If they are doing better, you can analyze it and see whether you can apply it here. Be open to new ideas. Apply new ideas to current issues at your workplace."

- **Staff Assistant, Budget Clerk, University**: "Be real, real open to change. Be receptive to ideas. Keep up with training which goes along with change."

- **Office Receptionist, Urology Clinic**: "You need to be open to new ideas and try them. Seminars and in-services also provide insights to your job. A positive attitude aids in learning. With a merger in our practice last year, there was much frustration—organizational changes can cause this to occur. Your employer needs to be open to what you have to say and not use a top-down style of management as this makes you want to learn as you are a part of a team. I also get frustrated that sometimes we only learn the surface things such as on the computer to get the specific task completed. When something out of the ordinary happens, we only have the surface knowledge and cannot troubleshoot the system to fix the problem ourselves."

- **Keyboard Specialist, Correctional Facility (female)**: "It's tough to be friendly with the inmates. Because if you were these guys would give you love letters. If you were polite to the ones working in your area you could not do the same with those on the inside. It's very difficult to enter in the morning when you hear steel doors slam shut behind you as you entered the facility."

Craft Workers (Skilled)/Office, Financial Services, & Government

- **Groundskeeper, Assistant Union Steward, University Campus**: "Need to ask questions. Need to have the motivation to learn. I like to learn something every day. Take your time. Listen. Be safety conscious as much as possible."

- **Groundskeeper, Physical Plant, University Campus**: "Newer people can learn from the older people. The boss rarely stands before the group and teaches job techniques. To be successful, you must communicate well with others. Seek help and answers to questions from the most qualified sources. Don't be afraid to try new things. Don't be afraid to admit you don't understand something or have never done something. Pay attention. Try to get some hands-on time while help is nearby. Be confident in yourself, don't underestimate yourself. Tell yourself that if they can do it, so can you. In my job, so much of it is new that my learning has been non-stop. When there is nothing left to learn I will probably get bored and move on."

- **Carpenter, Rural School District**: "I've recently found the value of going to seminars and have been aggressive about seeking these opportunities. By going to these events and learning from the experts, you can learn simple things that significantly aid in your job. Some learning is by experience, but going to experts accelerates learning and also teaches you things you would not learn from experience."

Operatives (Semi-Skilled)/Office, Financial Services, & Government

- **Security Guard and Supervisor, Condominium Complex**: "Have to be happy with job. Have to be happy with coworkers. Have to be happy with the work environment."

- **Maintenance Supervisor, School District**: "You have to always be willing to learn. I'm always willing to learn anything. And you have to use common sense with it."

- **Maintenance Worker, University**: "Keep up training by working with more experienced people. Keep up with training from HR. In my opinion you learn more with experienced people through on-the-job training. The typical procedure of the Office of Physical Plant is to pair the experienced worker with inexperienced ones for one week."

- **Editorial Assistant, Journal**: "You have to be flexible about everything, because we are really in a very changing world, especially in technology. Be open to change. There will be new responsibility for you to come up with. Don't be afraid of new things and try to cope with them."

Laborers (Unskilled)/Office, Financial Services, & Government

- **Support Staff, Physical Plant**: "Observe people. Treat others the way you want to be treated. Do your day's work and be done with it."

- **Janitorial/Custodian, Vocational-Technical School**: "You have to pay attention and not goof off, especially if you are a person who already knows a lot. You are not going to learn anything if you are not paying attention. Also, keep your mouth shut and get along with people. Basically, do what you are asked to do and there would not be a problem. Enjoy what you are doing. If you don't enjoy what you are doing, there is no sense doing it. Working together helps get things done. Stay out of trouble."

- **Janitorial Worker, University**: "Attend as many training seminars as possible. Watch closely how your trainer does things during the first week when you are assigned a trainer to show you the work. Watch carefully all steps taken and do not eliminate a step."

- **Assistant Building Superintendent, University Union**: "Give and take. Be objective. Be open to constructive criticism. Have enough information about your job and yourself to sometimes go against the grain."

- **Head Building Custodian/Maintenance, Rural School District**: "Be open minded. Listen to others and sort it out. Have equipment maintenance manuals on hand."

- **Head Custodian, School District**: "You have to give and take to be happy and fair. Do your best. School is a good place to work. Kids are our future. Do the best for them."

Service Workers/Office, Financial Services, & Government

- **Personal Care Aide, Small City School District**: "Be personable. Don't be afraid. Liking what you do is the most important thing. It makes you more open to learning experience and possible upgrade of position. Take advantage of every learning situation."

Officials and Managers/Accommodations & Personal Services

- **Business Owner, Jewelry Store**: "Everything changes constantly. I've learned from a lot of different things. Biggest learning was from father. There were the ways things were done in the 1960s. But things have changed. If you don't change with them, you will not be successful. I learned that by watching my father. I've also learned that you can burn out. If you are tired, are burned out, get away from the business for awhile. You can't fake happiness."

- **Case Administrator, Insurance**: "Be good listener. Be patient. Deal with different people/personalities. Accommodate them regardless of their behaviors."

- **Owner/Caterer, Bakery Company**: "Keep an open mind. Realize that you never know it all. Recognize when you need help to learn.

When you need [help] go somewhere and get trained or find someone who can help you learn how to do that. Pray."

- **President and General Manager, Hotel**: "You have to be open to the aspects of competition and to new trends breaking in the industry. Be a curious observer so that always you can create a product people want at a price they want. If you are a manager, you should create a nonthreatening work environment so that people feel achievement from what they learn. To be effective learners, people should be attentive and interested and willing to trust others and be open to new ideas and new ways of doing things. They should be willing to take action to blast through the hierarchy and keep an aggressive, questioning mind both in researching industry trends and in observing what is gaining in the hotel industry in the USA."

Professionals/Accommodations & Personal Services

- **Associate Attorney, Law Firm**: "Be open to learning new things. Don't play it safe. Be willing to do whatever it takes and then just do it."

- **Owner, Beauty Shop**: "The successful learner in the workplace is willing to take risks, willing to risk rejection and pray a lot."

- **Proprietor, Small Business Consulting Firm**: "Be interested in what you are doing, and have the internal drive to not be too satisfied with oneself. Understand that, whatever you are doing, you can do it better with more information and knowledge."

Technicians/Accommodations & Personal Services

- **Maintenance Worker and Technician, Motel**: "Be attentive. Be willing to learn. Take the good with the bad. Try to make the situation better. Seek help from someone. Realize it's only a job."

- **Local Manager, Food Service Catering Firm Under Hospital Contract**: "To be successful in learning in the workplace, the company should give much more support to the structured learning process. Supervisors should be willing to help people learn. Also, people want to feel that supervisors are willing to spend the time they need to learn new tools for the job. Learning takes time and the company has to devote much more time to it."

- **Automobile Detailing Specialist, Auto Custom Shop**: "Be open-minded, because people come to you with new ideas. You can't get locked into your own way of doing things. Put pride on the back burner. Humbleness is very important. Appreciate your customers, give back . . . always give back."

- **Computer Interface Specialist, Consulting Firm**: "Patience. I encourage people to ask a question [about what] they don't know. Just continue reinforcing the way they learn."

- **Hair Stylist and Barber, Owner, Hair Design Shop**: "To be successful in learning in the workplace, you must be self-motivated and determined. You must be able to take on new challenges. You must constantly be thinking about what you are currently doing and try to find a better way of doing it. You must evolve with the environment you are working in. You must have some knowledge of what you are getting into and must remain flexible enough to learn new things. Never think that you know it all. Always strive to be better."

Sales Workers/Accommodations & Personal Services

- **Sales Manager, Hospitality Services, University Hotel**: "The individual is the key. The best learners find a way to make it happen. They have to be turned on and motivated to do this learning. Usually resources aren't readily available, and you have to find a way to do it, vary the schedule and get the resources. You may have to go outside the department and go to find others. Find out other departments' perspectives and take initiative. You need to make the time to learn."

- **Sales Director, Cosmetics Sales:** "In business, sales training and motivation, you have to learn from your experience, be honest with yourself, be willing to know when you need to change, be self-motivated and self-disciplined, manage time, be emotionally stable, have decent self-esteem, always be learning, listen more than talk, be open to listen to new ideas and try out the ones that might work."

- **Hair Stylist and Salesperson, Hair Design Shop**: "Be open-minded. Be a team player. Be self-motivated. Try to find new things to learn."

- **Associate Broker, Real Estate Firm:** "Training programs should be designed based upon trainees' abilities and needs. Facilitators should be familiar with both the tools (computer software) and the field (occupations, work). The interaction between trainer and trainee is an important factor of a training program."

- **Market Development Coordinator, Insurance Company**: "Listen to what has been successful. Value people with experience. Learn from others. Respect the opinions of others."

- **Sales Representative, Noodle Company, Hong Kong:** "Three points are very important. First, analyze your task or job. Second, learn while doing. Third, do while learning. I also believe that practice makes perfect."

- **Travel Consultant, Travel Agency:** "Be consistent and persistent. Never give up. Just because you make money today does not mean you will make it tomorrow. You never know the immediate future."

Office and Clerical/Accommodations & Personal Services

- **Administrative Assistant, University Department**: "Don't take on more than you can handle. Don't be afraid to say no. Be organized in your thoughts before conveying them to others. Listen intently to those giving you instructions."

- **Program Secretary, University Department:** "Learning to become organized is essential to success and to successful learning. Use all of the resources available to you (information, staff from other work units, etc.). Ask questions—lots of them. Don't reinvent the wheel. Concentrate on the task at hand. Try to make sense of it. Learning can be fun. Make a game of it. It can be like putting a puzzle together—with some of the pieces gone. When you find the missing pieces, you can see the big picture. Focus in on the big picture and try to see where you fit in. Learning to get organized and using the resources that are available can only streamline the process and lower the stress level of the project through to completion."

- **Front Desk Clerk, Hotel:** "First, be cordial to the people you come in contact with so they will have a good feeling. Stay focused. Remember that first impressions are most important."

- **Sales Secretary, Hotel:** "Be patient. Flexible. Open-minded. Use positive thinking. Smile—it relaxes people even over the phone. Be courteous and be willing to help others."

- **Front Desk Clerk, Hotel:** "Be open to new ideas. I have worked in many places, and it is inevitably done differently. You can't stick with 'well, this is the way it was done there' because you are not 'there' anymore. So you have to be open and receptive to a new way of doing things, and willing to learn, actively pursuing new knowledge."

- **Secretary, Photoshop:** "Be willing to change and adapt to new situations. Technology is changing all the time, so be ready at any moment. Be open to new possibilities. You never know what kind of person will walk through the door next."

Craft Workers (Skilled)/Accommodations & Personal Services

- **Self-Employed Cosmetologist**: "To be open to new ideas. Courtesy. Definitely be on time. Value the client's time. Cleanliness."

- **Maintenance Worker, Hotel:** "Learn their way. Think if this is the right or correct way or not in case something better comes along. Do the job right."

- **Automotive Mechanic, U.S. Postal Service**: "This is very subjective to the individual. Must be practical. Must have an application."

- **Front Desk Clerk, Hotel:** "You have to have an opportunity to reflect on what happened in order to be successful in the workplace. One should be able to detect where the problem is and be patient and be conscientious to make the right decision about your job."

- **Journeyman Painter, Painting Company:** "Must be open and willing to work hard. The rewards in this kind of business only come through painstaking work and perseverance. There is no easy money."

Operatives (Semi-Skilled)/Accommodations & Personal Services

- **Waitress, Restaurant**: "In order to be successful in the workplace you have to understand that you will work with good and bad people, that you will work with good and bad managers. You have to leave these things behind. It is essential that you look at the situation patiently. You have to be very open to accept how different the people (peers and customers) are. You have to be aware of it to survive difficult situations. Be patient and open-minded."

- **Switchboard Operator, Hotel**: "I could never learn anything out of a book. I always needed hands-on experience. I would learn the job fundamentals and then with the experience I could do the jobs very well. I have even done jobs that required a college degree and performed them very well. You have to become part of the organization and be part of the team and learn all you can."

- **Breakfast Bar Attendant, Hotel:** "Be open to suggestions, especially from the supervisor. Be willing to accept criticism—constructive criticism. Always think how you can improve what you're doing. Consider cost efficiency. Post job duties."

Laborers (Unskilled)/Accommodations & Personal Services

- **Delivery Person, Pizza Service**: "Be patient. Learn by trial and error. Succeeding takes persistence. Results are much more important than speed."

- **Unskilled Laborer, Home Cleaning Business:** "When in someone's home, be nice to people and talk to them. It's nice to know they like you and what you're doing and that you are doing a good job. Be honest. Expect to do hard work. Be friendly. Treat people with the same respect you expect to be treated with. Be motivated, energetic, fast, know what to keep confidential and learn to keep it to yourself."

- **Audiovisual Setup Worker, Hotel:** "You have to be open-minded. I enjoy learning so if there is a better way or an easier way don't wait to get stuck or in a rut. Share what you know with others so they don't get stuck in a rut. Everyone can and should contribute ideas."

- **Custodian, High Tech Firm:** "My opinion is you never stop learning no matter where you work or where you live. If you want to make yourself out to be someone on the top of your career ladder, you have to think, pay attention, and you must start at the bottom."

- **Custodian, Automotive Dealer:** "You need to be able to listen well and know who to listen to. You need to learn what operations include possibilities and interpret them."

Service Workers/Accommodations & Personal Services

- **Church Missionary**: "Desire. Because if you want a thing bad enough to go out and fight for it, to work day and night for it, to give up your sleep and your time for it. If only the desire of it makes your arm strong enough never to tire from it, if life seems all empty and useless without it, and all that you dream and scheme about is for it, then gladly you will sweat for it, plan for it, pray for all your strength for it. If you'll simply go after the thing that you want with all your capacity, strength, faith, hope, and confidence; if neither poverty nor cold, nourishment, nor sickness of your body or brain can turn you away from the aim that you want; if doggedly and grimly you bring your best to it, you'll get it."

- **Bodyguard for Religious Leader**: "You need to pay attention to details. Be observant. Keep high ethical standards. Don't compromise standards. Keep mentally and physically in shape. Keep abreast of the latest technology in surveillance equipment."

- **Child Care Aide, Daycare Service**: "You have to like children. You have to want to learn about children. They [teach] you many things and you teach [them] many things. Mostly to be there for them, because you are more of their parent and take care of six to ten children. Have a good time, especially with kids, or your life will be miserable. So will the kids."

- **Housekeeper (Self-Employed)**: "My opinion is that, to learn to be a good housekeeper, you need to clean well and work fast. You also need to speak with people and look at things and ask questions."

Officials and Managers/Manufacturing, Agri-Business, Mining, & Construction

- **Manufacturing Inspector, Rail Company**: "It takes . . . dedication, time, experience, development of contacts that can be helpful, cultivation of relationships, patience, being able to deal with people and learn from mistakes."

- **Facilities Manager, University Library**: "To be successful, you have to have effective listening skills. Not just hearing but understanding. Be able to ask questions. Get as much information as you can. In a corporate sense, employees dare not take [the] wrong question to the boss, because they are afraid to let [the] boss have a feeling that they are incompetent, managers need to create an open environment to welcome employees' questions."

- **Technical Director (R & D), Manufacturing Firm**: "Analytical skills and problem solving skills. Match computers, software, and its application; statistics; basic communication skills; responsibilities; accountabilities; have the high spirits to work everyday."

Professionals/Manufacturing, Agri-Business, Mining, & Construction

- **Industrial Engineer, Manufacturing Plant**: "Whether it's in the training seminars or on the job, learning occurs through asking questions, talking with others; fully participating in your work life is how you learn most successfully. You should always follow up with any issues needing clarification in order to best know how the company works and to be most fully involved in your own work."

- **Quality Engineer, Manufacturing Plant**: "A successful worker should want to learn, and he or she can find his reason for wanting to learn. A successful worker has the ability to listen with understanding. He or she can use all available resources. He or she has the ability to break complex tasks into manageable chops. Don't be afraid to ask questions. Don't become frustrated. Maybe you can talk with your peers. Be confident but not proud. Actually, being humble is good. Celebrate your success (psychology) to strengthen the motivation to learn future problems. Being proud is the biggest obstacle to learning."

- **Metallurgist, Manufacturing Plant**: "You need to have as a base the necessary educational background and work experience to understand your environment. You need specific information about your process and products. You need to be able to research, analyze, and compare to make educated directions. In many cases, you need to work with others and to communicate on various levels to be effective with those with whom you interact. You must be observant and willing to take on difficult tasks."

- **Construction Project Manager, Construction Firm**: "To be open-minded to new ideas/suggestions. Being able to apply what you have learned. Willingness to constantly learn and grow individually and in the organization. The company has provided us with the tools for effectiveness and the leadership and it is up to us as individuals as to how we apply those tools within our organizations."

- **Associate Buyer, Pharmaceutical Manufacturer**: "A person has to want to be in the workplace. A person should have enthusiasm to be in the workplace, and if it's not a healthy place, do not be there. Attend development sessions for learning to take place. Get hands-on experience. Get the right tools to the individuals and learn in a step-by-step manner."

- **Manufacturing Engineer, Manufacturing Plant**: "Try to pay attention to whatever problem you are undertaking. Ask questions if you do not understand something. Following the experienced workers can [help you] learn fast, especially when you get a new job. Learn by doing and redoing."

- **Production Scheduler, Manufacturing Plant**: "Learning is necessary for everyone while technology changes day by day. At most times, employers do not provide sufficient training due to budget problems, especially in small to medium-size companies. Employee has to spend his own money and time for self-study."

- **Product Marketing Engineer, Manufacturing Plant**: "Be aware of your goals relative to the company's and learn how to make them both work. Be humble in what you know and open-minded to others' ideas. There are a lot of knowledgeable people who can help you grow either with their expertise or related experience."

Technicians/Manufacturing, Agri-Business, Mining, & Construction

- **Product Analyzer, Manufacturing Plant (China)**: "If you really want to learn something, do not think the difficulties you met during the learning process were trouble. Think of them as challenges that would give you more valuable experience. Search the appropriate methods and tools to facilitate your learning process. Both skills and willingness to learn are important in the workplace."

- **Senior Chemical Technician, Chemical Manufacturing Plant**: "Listen very well. Be honest [about] the results, the coworkers, and the boss. Even when there are mistakes, just report them. Speak up when something is going wrong. Be on time to work. Care about your job. P. S. I'm special. I can master machines by nature."

- **Product Analyzer, Manufacturing Plant (China)**: "We should have a good schedule for workplace learning registration and attendance. We should know the other job arrangement and plan in advance. This will avoid the conflict between training assignment and job assignment. The supervisor should know the importance of workplace learning. We should think how we can improve our daily work through applying what we have learned in the training room."

Sales Workers/Manufacturing, Agri-Business, Mining, & Construction

- **Sales Representative, Equipment Manufacturing**: "Be open-minded and willing to accept the failures that will come. Draw one tidbit from someone. Don't assume anything. Be open-minded and sift through what you hear because you may not be able to use it. Pay attention."

- **Salesperson, Photoshop**: "You need to be flexible and open to change. The electronics business is changing too quickly and you can quickly be lost in the events if you don't make attempts to keep on top of things."

Office and Clerical/Manufacturing, Agri-Business, Mining, & Construction

- **Administrator, Manufacturing Plant (China)**: "Conducting face-to-face and step-by-step training is helpful for the learning process. Maintaining the training environment relaxed and in order is important to effective training. After conducting the training courses, the appropriate person should arrange site visit to track the training results and encourage the trainees to apply what they have learned to the daily job. The employee who has made improvements by applying what he or she has learned on-the-job should be rewarded in some way. This will help in setting up an environment that encourages practice in the company's culture."

- **Sales Coordinator, Manufacturing Firm**: "A good worker is a good team player with people with all kinds of personalities. A good worker should listen to other people/workers. You must have a positive attitude towards your job. You have to like what you are doing."

- **Automation Department Secretary, Manufacturing Firm (China)**: "It is helpful if you can expand your knowledge and skills through job transferring or job rotation. Although it may be difficult at the beginning, it will improve your ability, develop your potential. Most important of all, it will broaden your view. You are rewarded through the learning process."

- **Manufacturing Administrator, Manufacturing Plant (China)**: "Practicing what you learned is the best way to learn efficiently. You will understand thoroughly only after you do it! The training concept is feasible only after an appropriate amount of people have been trained and accepted the idea. The application of what you have learned in a training program needs an environment with consistent value."

Craft Workers (Skilled)/Manufacturing, Agri-Business, Mining, & Construction

- **Tool and Die Maker, Manufacturing Plant**: "Perseverance is important. Don't give up. Have the correct information. You have to apply your knowledge and practice it. You have to self-critique your results if no one else is around."

- **Maintenance Supervisor, Lumber Yard**: "Take things as they come. Communicate. Slow down. Look at the big picture. Get along with employees or that causes extra problems. Logically think through things."

- **Final Assembler, Utility Machinist, Manufacturing Plant**: "Have your wherewithal about you [*sic*]. A lot of things you have to figure out on your own. You need to have a sense of logic."

Operatives (Semi-Skilled)/Manufacturing, Agri-Business, Mining, & Construction

- **Weaver, Manufacturing Plant**: "Learn every step. Learn to read patterns. Learn fixing. Use common sense. Pay attention to details. Have a good perception of problems. Keep an eye on quality. Learn where to put what. Know reading, basic math, counting ends. Know the science of humidity and temperature. Use problem solving."

- **Customer Serviceperson, Gas Company**: "[You] must enjoy the job, like what you're doing, and enjoy the challenge of a new situation every day on every service call. Have to be dedicated to one thing you do very well. You have to know the natural gas business very well. Working out in the field, in emergency situations, there's no time to think. You have to already know what to do. Taking time to ponder or worry could mean lives lost. Have to decide quickly and decision has to be right! Can only be done by knowing the job through experience. Learn to take life very seriously, don't take life for granted because of constant danger."

- **Maintenance Supervisor, Manufacturing Plant**: "Take time. Try not to hurry. Don't see what is wrong and get frustrated. Don't play know-it-all. Don't hurry. Dot your i's and cross your t's."

- **Laborer, Lumber Company**: "Pay particular attention, close attention. Don't take anything for granted. Don't be a know-it-all."

- **Lead Operator, Manufacturing Firm**: "To learn everything you possibly can. You should have the ability to learn and then teach the skills to other workers later in life. Learn from other people's mistakes. A good worker should not make the same mistakes repeatedly, including mistakes that are made by others. A good worker should finish the job completely. A good worker should get along with others smoothly. When facing a difference, a good worker should accept the facts that can't be changed and think in a spirit of a compromise."

Laborers (Unskilled)/Manufacturing, Agri-Business, Mining, & Construction

- **Bi-Level Leader/Loader, Manufacturing Plant**: "Perseverance. You can't give up."

- **Machine Operator, Manufacturing Plant**: "There should be written instructions. Videos of people doing the job helps. People should be interested in the work and motivated to learn. People should be respectful so they can learn from others. They should also treat equipment well and take care of it."

- **Production Worker, Manufacturing Plant**: "Work hard, offer help all the time, watch, listen to everything others say and get along with everybody. Ask questions and display a good attitude."

- **Laborer and Sewing Machine Operator, Garment Factory**: "Be determined to do the job. Be flexible and adaptable. Speed is essential. Accuracy is essential. Lay work out properly for the next worker. Must be able to get along with other people. That is very important."

Service Workers/Manufacturing, Agri-Business, Mining, & Construction

- **Produce Worker, Grocery Store**: "In order to be successful in learning in the workplace, a worker must be attentive, very disciplined, and organized. He or she should have very good communication skills. He or she should be able to adapt to changing situations and have the ability to learn rapidly."

- **Self-Employed Building Contractor**: "To be successful in learning in the workplace, one must be dedicated, willing to listen to people who have more experience."

- **Grower, Flower Shop**: "You have to be patient, even in stressful situations. I'm at a point where I know my routine. My learning comes from teaching others. I take time to instruct new people, 'This is what works for me.' It would have been easier if there was a school around here that teaches this. But the pay that you get doesn't compensate for the knowledge."

- **Safety Inspector, Manufacturing Plant**: "Be open and willing to learn. Don't feel you know everything. Variations occur daily. "

Officials and Managers/Trade, Transportation, & Communications

- **Manager, Media Services Company**: "Need an adequate amount of time. Chart a course, get the end result in mind, then go back and learn in steps. Get plenty of rest so you can concentrate. Don't get stressed so you can limit some frustration. Be realistic."

- **President, Information Technology Company**: "Ask for help and learn from each other. Even though you know better, you may have to learn from others. To learn from others you should listen and observe. We will be smart if we humble ourselves."

- **Vice President, Sales, Toy Company:** "First, regardless of your experience, don't have a closed mind to new ideas. You can always learn something new from a fresh or different perspective. Don't be shortsighted and react impulsively, but take the time to analyze a situation and look at it from your perspective and the other side. Draw from all resources within your organization. Understand others' strengths and liabilities. Encourage subordinates to take responsibility and make decisions so they can learn and grow. Don't think you have all the answers. Working in toy sales, I am in a constantly changing environment and need to keep abreast of retailers' financial conditions, mergers and acquisitions, buyer changes, competition, product knock-offs, rates of sale, fashion and entertainment trends. I gather information from my rep network and/or buyers on a regular basis. One might consider it gossip from the industry grapevine. 'Did you hear ABC Company is introducing Product X,' but it is the latest information in the business. Through store visits and reading trade publications, I'm also exposed to what is new in the industry. This information is then used to direct the company's product development process and make appropriate sales recommendations to buyers."

- **Deputy Director, National Accounts, Fortune 100 Multinational**: "Learn while you do it. Start your career from an ordinary employee. Make sure to do the right things from the beginning. Find good ways to interpret the work to your colleagues. Learn in all these stages."

- **Interface Design Manager, Web Company:** "Mastery of content. Learn about how things work. Learn how to apply what I know in the right context. Know and recognize my teaching role to others. I believe in situated learning."

Professionals/Trade, Transportation, & Communications

- **Electrician, Self-Employed**: "Open mind. Electrical background. No fear. Don't be afraid of a challenge. When in doubt, walk away. Ask questions. Don't learn the hard way."

- **Cook, Hotel**: "Being able to work with people is the most important [thing] in any workplace. Get along with people instead of arguing. Know what you are doing. Stay focused. React quickly. Be a good listener. Try to learn from people who have been around awhile. The best way is to sit down with people who have been in the industry for many years."

- **Technical Trainer, Automotive Company**: "You must have an open mind. You must want to learn. Have a commitment to a higher standard of success."

- **Assistant Project Manager, Construction**: "Keep an open mind. Go in as an empty slate. You can learn from everyone. Learn how to deal with people. Be willing to make mistakes and learn from mistakes. Always do your homework. Read up on them. Ask. Use your resources to be a self-learner whenever possible. Keep your black book on you, keep your own diary. Learn to read people, learn about people's demeanor. Read body language. Be aware of your surroundings. Know the company's do's and don'ts and unspoken do's and don'ts. Get someone to confide in."

- **Graphic Designer, World Wide Web Company**: "Employers should provide enough learning resources (such as quality trainer, equipment, etc.) to train the right person that needs the training. Give a good reward or an opportunity for promotion."

- **Senior Editor, Publishing Company**: "It takes an open mind in this job. One plus one does not always equal two. There are many moments when you can't possibly know everything, and that what you enjoy may not be what another person enjoys. You have to consider yourself a helper in the process—you can't change the authors' feelings and stance. Learning in this job is something you can't do enough of—there's always something new, so you always have to build on your learning and your experiences to be the best at doing the job. Learning never ends."

Technicians/Trade, Transportation, & Communications

- **Computer Technician, Software Company**: "Work hard to satisfy the customer. Put the job as your number one priority—even over the financial part of it."

- **Automotive Technician, Auto Repair Shop**: "Be patient and careful."

Sales Workers/Trade, Transportation, & Communications

- **Office Manager and Service Writer, Auto Repair Shop**: "Successful learning in the workplace is dependent on the employer-company relationship. First, the company must screen employees when hired. Prospects should be told the importance, availability, and participation in company training programs and policies. In larger companies another method is to blend your more experienced with new employees who have potential. My experience is to require some training and motivate employees to participate in additional training. Training or learning need not be career-specific. Learning skills such as assertiveness training, first-aid, CPR benefit the company as well as the individual."

- **Classified Sales Representative, Newspaper**: "Don't be afraid to try things yourself. Ask questions. Have people walk you through things. Be confident."

- **Owner, Hobby Shop**: "You got to have an open mind. If you don't have an open mind, you can't learn anything. You have to be willing to understand that you can learn from everybody. If you don't have the desire to want to give as much as you can get and want to understand what it is you're doing for your job, you really don't learn. Maintain your own dignity. If you don't have the desire, you don't accomplish everything."

Office and Clerical/Trade, Transportation, & Communications

- **Office Operation Manager, Financial Services**: "Have a good attitude. Have a willingness to move forward. Be willing to take risks, calculated risks. Put the benchmark higher. Keep complacency at a minimum. Keep your value high."

- **Personnel Manager, Fiscal Person, Operations Manager, and Education Coordinator, Small Business**: "Have a good attitude. Keep an open mind and a willingness to succeed. Keep a desire to move forward. With these pieces in place people will be able to work through. Take some calculated risks, put the benchmark a little higher than you are used to. Strive for something higher to prevent you from becoming complacent. People get real happy where they are at and they are not willing to move that next step forward. I always try to put myself a step higher than where you should be, because it gives me something to work towards. Otherwise life is not a challenge and you do not move forward. You stop your life-long learning process when you become very complacent with what you are doing and you don't move forward any more, you don't learn any more, you don't gain knowledge, and you don't become valuable to your company and yourself. You kind of spend your time instead of being valuable."

- **Office Manager, Environmental Contractor**: "You need to be a very good listener. Try not to put yourself above people."

- **Manager, Retail Store**: "You have to be patient. And just try to listen to people who are over you. I have to listen to the people under me. I try out [their] suggestions. If you listen and try that is a good idea. If it doesn't work then it doesn't work. Something I didn't think of. I think to keep eyes open and people feel comfortable to come and say we can do it. They feel a little more into work. They contribute to work. I think it's work in that way."

- **Secretary/Bookkeeper, Automotive Dealer**: "Look before you leap into a job. Make sure you know what kind of a situation (job) you are going to be working for. Make sure you have the organization hierarchy in order and let you do your job to the best of your ability."

- **General Contractor, Construction**: "It depends on the type of industry you are in. Not all workplace situations involve learning. However, if you want to be considered on the cutting edge, you do. You need to recognize the value or opinion of employees. 'Two heads are better than one.' So the more I can get resources from employees, the more probably the job will be better and the more proficiently the work will be done. The more satisfied employees do better jobs. Communicate with employees and get two-ways of communication. Let them feel pride in a job well done and hopefully it will get some work."

Craft Workers (Skilled)/Trade, Transportation, & Communications

- **Maintenance Supervisor, School District**: "Know how to get along with people. Know how to use them as learning resources."

- **General Contractor, Self-Employed**: "You have to have an open mind. The industry is always changing or certain products are changing. Customers should get what they want. Never take short cuts as they will come back to haunt you (I've rarely had callbacks). Make sure legally of what you are doing. Don't do anything without a change order or contract. Document everything. You can never learn enough. There is always someone who can do it better/cheaper. You have to keep up with the learning curve."

- **Paste-Up Artist, Auto Repair Shop**: "It takes patience. Don't be too anxious. Every company that offers ads is different, and what one can or will do is different from the next. It's funny because not every company is a company you can work with. It takes a while to learn the job."

Operatives (Semi-Skilled)/Trade, Transportation, & Communications

- **Welder, Self-Employed**: "Look at your work and see what you can do. Respect yourself. Respect what you do. The better your job, the better you feel about yourself. Be confident in your work. Be stingy and careful. Make quality work. Take pride!"

- **Bus Driver, School District**: "Have to be able to work with a variety of people. Students, parents, teachers, administrators, abled and disabled students, and parents."

- **Telephone Serviceperson, Phone Company**: "On the job training is the best way to learn. You should be in a job you like. It makes it easier to learn. It takes patience to be a good learner. You can't learn everything at once. Good basics in education are important. Be a good listener when people are explaining things. Be interested and have a willingness to learn."

- **Bus Driver, Private Bus Company**: "Be a good listener. Be able to take the boss's advice and teachings and the requirements needed to do the job correctly. Be willing to accept responsibility. Hauling people is not a task that comes naturally. Be a safe driver and handle people with respect. It takes a long time to do a job properly and accept responsibility."

- **Bus Driver, School District**: "Don't have a know-it-all attitude. Don't have a cocky 'I've got it under control' attitude. Recognize difficulties involved. Don't allow students to intimidate you. Be firm but gentle. Mean what you say. Don't be afraid of students or parents. Follow through. Experience is the best teacher. Sometimes better. You don't know it all before you start. Safety and responsibility are drilled into your mind, but no one tells you how to get along with others."

Laborers (Unskilled)/Trade, Transportation, & Communications

- **Dishwasher, Restaurant**: "I guess the main thing to be successful in workplace learning is basically to do your job the best you can. You have to take that seriously, since you are getting paid for it. You have to keep calm. You just have to listen to other people. Even if the work is hard, you have been working all day long, you get tired at the end of the day . . . keep your cool, follow orders, get along with as many people as possible so you don't get in trouble."

- **Cashier, Grocery Store**: "One thing [you must do] to be successful in workplace learning is really know how to work with people. And that can be anywhere you work, but you definitely have to know how to work with people. I think that to be successful in the workplace is essentially being able to get people to smile, to say 'hello,' 'how're you doing,' or to make them feel that they are important because everybody wants to feel important."

Service Workers/Trade, Transportation, & Communications

- **Service Representative, Paging Company**: "What I need is customer service skills. The most effective way is learning through experience of my own and experience of my colleagues. Some training is also necessary. But the training should be closely related to my daily work."

- **Cashier, Discount Retail Store**: "The successful way of learning at a job is definitely hands on training and experience. Because they can't tell you everything but until you're actually in the situation, you don't know how to deal with it. So the best learning method in the workplace is hands-on experience."

- **Passenger Service Agent, Airlines**: "To be successful in learning in the workplace, a worker must have a positive attitude. He/she must be willing to learn the basic concepts of the work being done, no matter how trivial. The person must be open to new possibilities and realize that he or she is learning constantly. I think that it is very important that the worker be aware of his or her environment and should spend time observing what others are doing and how they are doing it."

Behavioral Event Interview Guide to Assess Workplace Learning Climate

Directions to Interviewers: Follow the directions on this guide explicitly. Ask individuals only the questions that you have been given to ask. Tape record the interview and have signed releases from the individual and employer completed before the interview is conducted. When you finish, hand in this guide with any notes from the interview and your tape recordings. Make your notes as complete as possible.

Name of Individual Conducting the Interview (Interviewer's Name)	Name of Individual Interviewed (Confidential: For Use of One Interviewer Only)

RESPONDENT'S INDUSTRY & HIERARCHICAL LEVEL

Industry (*Check one only*)	**Hierarchical Level** (*Check one only*)
☐ Health and Human Services	☐ Officials and managers
☐ Office, Financial Services, & Government	☐ Professionals

☐ Accommodations & Personal Services	☐ Technicians
☐ Manufacturing, Agri-Business, Mining, & Construction	☐ Sales workers
☐ Trade, Transportation, & Communications	☐ Office and clerical
	☐ Craft workers (*Skilled*)
	☐ Operatives (*Semi-Skilled*)
	☐ Laborers (*Unskilled*)
	☐ Service workers

Today's Date	**Job Title of Individual Interviewed**

Employer of Individual Interviewed

BACKGROUND OF THIS STUDY

"Thank you for agreeing to participate in this study. How people learn in the workplace may or may not be different from how they learn in other settings. The purpose of this study is to identify the conditions that help or hinder learning. Please understand that the term *learning* refers to the way you change by mastering new knowledge and skills while you do your work or while you receive training to do your work. Workplace conditions refer to anything in your work setting that influences your ability to learn or apply what you learn. You will be asked about several major issues in this interview: (1) tell a story about a time when you were *discouraged from learning* in your organization; (2) tell a story about a time when you were *encouraged to learn* in your organization; (3) list *actions* that could be taken by the management of your organization that you believe would most encourage you to learn in the workplace; and (4) your opinion about the *most important changes* that are occurring in your work setting that require you to learn and to master new ways of doing things. Please be specific in your answers to the questions." Before participating in this interview, please read and sign the consent form.

RESPONDENT'S JOB REQUIREMENTS

QUESTION		NOTES ON THE ANSWER
1	What are your work requirements? Describe your work duties very briefly in a sentence or two.	*List work requirements and duties.*

CONDITIONS THAT *DISCOURAGE* WORKPLACE LEARNING

QUESTION		NOTES ON THE ANSWER
1	Think back to a time when you were asked to do something new and different in the work-place and you felt discouraged by conditions in	*What was the learning challenge?*

the organization that prevented you from learning. This can be considered a *learning situation*, whether it occurred during your work or during training about your work. It should have occurred while you were in your present job and with your present employer. It is important that you describe the situation in detail and explain specifically what happened that made you feel discouraged in learning something new. First, provide an overview of the situation. What was the learning challenge you faced? Then answer some background questions: When did this occur (*give approximate dates*)? Who was involved (*give job titles but not names*)? Where did this occur (*give approximate location*)?

When did this occur?

Who was involved?

Where did this occur?

		STEP BY STEP	WHAT WAS HAPPENING, AND WHAT WERE YOU DOING?	WHAT WERE YOU THINKING AS THIS WAS HAPPENING AND/OR AS YOU WERE DOING WHAT YOU WERE DOING?	WHAT WERE YOU FEELING AS THIS WAS HAPPENING AND/OR AS YOU WERE DOING WHAT YOU WERE DOING?
2	Tell me *what happened in this situation that made you feel discouraged about learning something new*. Be as specific as possible, describing what happened in the	1			

sequence that it happened. Be sure to explain what was happening, what you were doing, what you were thinking, and what you were feeling as events unfold.				
	2			
	3			
	4			
	5			
	6			
	7			

3	What do you believe were the conditions in the organization that *discouraged* your learning in this situation? Summarize or list those conditions in your own words.	*What were the conditions?*
		What is your summary of the conditions that discouraged your learning? List them:

CONDITIONS THAT *ENCOURAGE* WORKPLACE LEARNING

QUESTION	NOTES ON THE ANSWER
1	Think back to a time when you were asked to do something new and different in the workplace and you felt encouraged by conditions in the organization that encouraged you to learn. This can be considered a *learning situation*, whether it occurred during your work or during training about your work. It should have occurred while you were in your present job and with your present employer. It is important that you describe the situation in detail and explain specifically what happened that made you feel encouraged in learning something new. First, provide an overview of the situation. What was the learning challenge you faced? Then answer some background questions: When did this occur (*give approximate dates*)? Who was involved (*give job titles but not names*)? Where did this occur (*give approximate location*)?	*What was the learning challenge?*
		When did this occur?
		Who was involved?
		Where did this occur?

		STEP BY STEP	WHAT WAS HAPPENING, AND WHAT WERE YOU DOING?	WHAT WERE YOU THINKING AS THIS WAS HAPPENING AND/OR AS YOU WERE DOING WHAT YOU WERE DOING?	WHAT WERE YOU FEELING AS THIS WAS HAPPENING AND/OR AS YOU WERE DOING WHAT YOU WERE DOING?
2	Tell me *what happened in this situation that made you feel encouraged about learning something new.* Be as spe-	1			

cific as possible, describing what happened in the sequence that it happened. Be sure to explain what was happening, what you were doing, what you were thinking, and what you were feeling as events unfold.				
	2			
	3			
	4			
	5			
	6			
	7			
3	What do you believe were the conditions in the organization that *encouraged* your learning in this situation? Summarize or list those conditions in your own words.		*What were the conditions?*	
			What is your summary of the conditions that encouraged your learning? List them:	

YOUR OPINIONS

QUESTION		NOTES ON THE ANSWER
1	*What actions do you believe could be taken by the management of your organization to create conditions that would encourage people to learn more effectively in the workplace?* Make a list of things that could be done by your organization's management.	*List of actions that could be taken by company management:*
2	What is your opinion about the *most important changes* that are occurring in your work setting that require you to learn and to master new ways of doing things? Make a list of the trends or changes that require you to change and to learn new things at work.	

Thank You for Your Cooperation!

SELF-ASSESSMENT INSTRUMENT:

ASSESSING INDIVIDUAL WORKPLACE

LEARNING COMPETENCIES

Directions: Workplace learning competence is the ability to be effective in learning in real time in workplace settings. Use this instrument to rate your level of competence as a workplace learner. For each competency listed in the left column, rate your level of perceived competence in the right column. Use the following scale:

1 = Not applicable.

2 = I perceive myself to be functioning at a *less than effective level* in my present workplace on this workplace learning competency.

3 = I perceive myself to be functioning at a *somewhat effective level* in my present workplace on this workplace learning competency.

4 = I perceive myself to be functioning at an *effective level* in my present workplace on this workplace learning competency.

5 = I perceive myself to be functioning at a *highly effective level* in my present workplace on this workplace learning competency.

Then, in the far right column, place a number from 1 to 7 to indicate how important you believe it to be to improve this workplace learning competency. A 1 indicates that taking

action to build this workplace learning competency is of highest priority. A 7 indicates that improvement on the competency is of lowest priority.

WORKPLACE LEARNING COMPETENCY	YOUR PERCEIVED LEVEL OF COMPETENCE					HOW IMPORTANT DO YOU BELIEVE IT TO BE TO IMPROVE THIS WORKPLACE LEARNING COMPETENCY?
I BELIEVE THAT I AM ABLE TO:	NOT APPLICABLE 1	LESS THAN EFFECTIVE 2	SOMEWHAT EFFECTIVE 3	EFFECTIVE 4	HIGHLY EFFECTIVE 5	(Rate from 1 to 7, with 1 = Most important)

FOUNDATIONAL COMPETENCIES

1	*Reading skill*: Read to a level of proficiency appropriate for learning in a workplace setting.	1	2	3	4	5	☐
2	*Writing skill*: Write to a level of proficiency appropriate for learning in a workplace setting.	1	2	3	4	5	☐
3	*Computation skill*: Apply mathematics to a level of proficiency appropriate for learning in a workplace setting.	1	2	3	4	5	☐
4	*Listening skill*: Listen effectively and to a level of proficiency appropriate for learning in a workplace setting.	1	2	3	4	5	☐
5	*Questioning skill*: Pose appropriate questions to others and obtain meaningful and unambiguous answers to those questions.	1	2	3	4	5	☐

6	*Speaking skill:* Speak to individuals or present to groups with a level of proficiency appropriate for learning in a workplace setting.	1	2	3	4	5	☐
7	*Cognitive skills:* Think, draw conclusions, think creatively, make decisions, and solve problems.	1	2	3	4	5	☐
8	*Individual skills:* Demonstrate a willingness to accept responsibility and display self-esteem.	1	2	3	4	5	☐
9	*Resource skills:* Allocate such resources as time, money, people, and information appropriately to learn in the workplace.	1	2	3	4	5	☐
10	*Interpersonal skill:* Work cooperatively with others, carry out formal or informal training or mentoring of others, and maintain effective interpersonal relations with customers.	1	2	3	4	5	☐
11	*Informational and technological skill:* Acquire and analyze data from various sources.	1	2	3	4	5	☐

INTERMEDIATE COMPETENCIES

12	*Systems thinking:* View organizations and work from a systems perspective (Senge, 1994).	1	2	3	4	5	☐

13	*Personal mastery:* Show willingness to learn and take pride in learning (Senge, 1994).	1	2	3	4	5	☐
14	*Mental modeling:* Create, communicate, and critique ingrained (and otherwise taken-for-granted) assumptions, beliefs, or values (Senge, 1994).	1	2	3	4	5	☐
15	*Shared visioning:* Formulate, communicate, and build enthusiasm about shared views of the future (Senge, 1994).	1	2	3	4	5	☐
16	*Team learning skill:* Participate effectively and actively in workplace groups and use dialogue and other approaches to formulate, communicate, and test ideas generated by self or others (Senge, 1994).	1	2	3	4	5	☐
17	*Self-knowledge:* Demonstrate "awareness and understanding of self as learner" (Smith, 1982, p. 21).	1	2	3	4	5	☐
18	*Short-term memory skill:* Remember facts, people, and situations for short time spans, usually about 48 hours or less.	1	2	3	4	5	☐
19	*Long-term memory skill:* Remember facts, people, and situations for longer time spans, usually exceeding 48 hours.	1	2	3	4	5	☐

20	*Subject matter knowledge:* Possess a solid foundation of background knowledge on the issue or subject that I set out to learn about in the workplace.	1	2	3	4	5	☐
21	*Enjoyment of learning and work:* Display joy in the learning process itself and in the work that I perform.	1	2	3	4	5	☐
22	*Flexibility:* Show a willingness to apply what I know in new ways as conditions warrant their application.	1	2	3	4	5	☐
23	*Persistence and confidence:* Show determination to pursue new knowledge or skill, even when finding it or mastering it proves more difficult than expected.	1	2	3	4	5	☐
24	*Sense of urgency:* Display sensitivity to the importance of time to self and others.	1	2	3	4	5	☐
25	*Honesty:* Give information in a straightforward manner, free of deception, and elicit similar behavior from others.	1	2	3	4	5	☐
26	*Giving respect to others:* Defer to others with more experience or knowledge.	1	2	3	4	5	☐

THE PERCEPTIVIST ROLE

		1	2	3	4	5	
27	*Work environment analytical skills:* "Examine work environments for issues or characteristics affecting human performance" (Rothwell, 1996).	1	2	3	4	5	☐
28	*Sensory awareness:* Show sensitivity to stimuli received from the outside world based on the use of any one or all of the five senses.	1	2	3	4	5	☐
29	*Open-mindedness:* Demonstrate a willingness to see, to observe, and to internalize what the world presents and reinterprets it afresh.	1	2	3	4	5	☐
30	*Humility:* Display modesty about what I do or do not know, a willingness to listen to fresh perspectives without pretending to know when I do not know.	1	2	3	4	5	☐
31	*Analytical skill (synthesis):* "Break down the components of a larger whole and reassemble them to achieve improved human performance" (Rothwell, 1996, p. 19).	1	2	3	4	5	☐
32	*Intuition:* Show sensitivity to stimuli generated by myself from memory or from	1	2	3	4	5	☐

the application of nonverbal logic.						

THE INFORMATION-GATHERER ROLE

33	*Information-sourcing skill:* Identify the kind of information needed to satisfy curiosity and show an ability to locate such information from credible sources.	1	2	3	4	5	☐
34	*Information-gathering skill:* Collect information by talking to others, asking questions of others, facilitating groups to answer questions, and finding information from other sources.	1	2	3	4	5	☐
35	*Information-organizing skill:* Organize or structure information obtained from one or many sources and categorize it into schemes that permit recall, comparison, or creative reexamination.	1	2	3	4	5	☐
36	*Feedback solicitation skill:* Display an ability to solicit feedback on what I learned from others.	1	2	3	4	5	☐

THE ANALYST ROLE

37	*Willingness to experiment and gain experience:* Show an openness to try out new ideas or approaches, even when they are untested or	1	2	3	4	5	☐

		1	2	3	4	5	
	their results are unknown.						
38	*Internalization skill:* Translate general knowledge or information into specific information that can be immediately applied or tested.	1	2	3	4	5	☐
39	*Application of new knowledge skill:* Use new knowledge or skill in harmony with the way it was described or characterized from the original source(s).	1	2	3	4	5	☐
40	*Ability to adapt knowledge to new situations or events:* Use new knowledge or skill in creative, unusual, or novel ways.	1	2	3	4	5	☐

THE EVALUATOR ROLE

		1	2	3	4	5	
41	*Critical examination of information skill:* Reflect on what was learned critically, offering follow-up questions or new ideas based on the information.	1	2	3	4	5	☐
42	*Learning how to learn skill:* Reflect on how I acquired new information or knowledge and find ways to improve the acquisition and application of new knowledge or skill in the future.	1	2	3	4	5	☐

| 43 | *Self-directedness skill:* Display a willingness to be proactive about my own learning, to take action without needing to be directed to learn or to act by other people. | 1 | 2 | 3 | 4 | 5 | ☐ |

AN ASSESSMENT INSTRUMENT FOR

OTHERS TO ASSESS INDIVIDUAL

WORKPLACE LEARNING COMPETENCIES

Directions: Workplace learning competence is the ability to be effective in learning in real time in workplace settings. Use this instrument to rate the competence of a workplace learner who is known to you. For each competency listed in the left column, rate his or her level of perceived competence in the right column. Use the following scale:

1 = Not applicable.

2 = I perceive him or her to be functioning at a *less than effective level* in his or her present workplace on this workplace learning competency.

3 = I perceive him or her to be functioning at a *somewhat effective level* in his or her present workplace on this workplace learning competency.

4 = I perceive him or her to be functioning at an *effective level* in his or her present workplace on this workplace learning competency.

5 = I perceive him or her to be functioning at a *highly effective level* in his or her present workplace on this workplace learning competency.

Then, in the far right column, place a number from 1 to 7 to indicate how important you believe it to be for this person to improve this workplace learning competency. A 1 indi-

cates that taking action to build this workplace learning competency is of highest priority. A 7 indicates that improvement on the competency is of lowest priority.

WORKPLACE LEARNING COMPETENCY	YOUR PERCEIVED LEVEL OF COMPETENCE					HOW IMPORTANT DO YOU BELIEVE IT TO BE TO IMPROVE THIS WORKPLACE LEARNING COMPETENCY?
I BELIEVE THAT THIS PERSON IS ABLE TO:	NOT APPLICABLE 1	LESS THAN EFFECTIVE 2	SOMEWHAT EFFECTIVE 3	EFFECTIVE 4	HIGHLY EFFECTIVE 5	(Rate from 1 to 7, with 1 = Most important)

FOUNDATIONAL COMPETENCIES

1	*Reading skill:* Read to a level of proficiency appropriate for learning in a workplace setting.	1	2	3	4	5	☐
2	*Writing skill:* Write to a level of proficiency appropriate for learning in a workplace setting.	1	2	3	4	5	☐
3	*Computation skill:* Apply mathematics to a level of proficiency appropriate for learning in a workplace setting.	1	2	3	4	5	☐
4	*Listening skill:* Listen effectively and to a level of proficiency appropriate for learning in a workplace setting.	1	2	3	4	5	☐
5	*Questioning skill:* Pose appropriate questions to others and obtain meaningful and unambiguous answers to those questions.	1	2	3	4	5	☐

		1	2	3	4	5		
6	*Speaking skill:* Speak to individuals or present to groups with a level of proficiency appropriate for learning in a workplace setting.	1	2	3	4	5		☐
7	*Cognitive skills:* Think, draw conclusions, think creatively, make decisions, and solve problems.	1	2	3	4	5		☐
8	*Individual skills:* Demonstrate a willingness to accept responsibility and display self-esteem.	1	2	3	4	5		☐
9	*Resource skills:* Allocate such resources as time, money, people, and information appropriately to learn in the workplace.	1	2	3	4	5		☐
10	*Interpersonal skill:* Work cooperatively with others, carry out formal or informal training or mentoring of others, and maintain effective interpersonal relations with customers.	1	2	3	4	5		☐
11	*Informational and technological skill:* Acquire and analyze data from various sources.	1	2	3	4	5		☐

INTERMEDIATE COMPETENCIES

		1	2	3	4	5		
12	*Systems thinking:* View organizations and work from a systems perspective (Senge, 1994).	1	2	3	4	5		☐

13	*Personal mastery:* Show willingness to learn and take pride in learning (Senge, 1994).	1	2	3	4	5	☐
14	*Mental modeling:* Create, communicate, and critique ingrained (and otherwise taken-for-granted) assumptions, beliefs, or values (Senge, 1994).	1	2	3	4	5	☐
15	*Shared visioning:* Formulate, communicate, and build enthusiasm about shared views of the future (Senge, 1994).	1	2	3	4	5	☐
16	*Team learning skill:* Participate effectively and actively in workplace groups and use dialogue and other approaches to formulate, communicate, and test ideas generated by himself or herself or others (Senge, 1994).	1	2	3	4	5	☐
17	*Self-knowledge:* Demonstrate "awareness and understanding of self as learner" (Smith, 1982, p. 21).	1	2	3	4	5	☐
18	*Short-term memory skill:* Remember facts, people, and situations for short time spans, usually about 48 hours or less.	1	2	3	4	5	☐
19	*Long-term memory skill:* Remember facts, people, and situations for longer time spans, usually exceeding 48 hours.	1	2	3	4	5	☐

20	*Subject matter knowledge:* Possess a solid foundation of background knowledge on the issue or subject that he or she sets out to learn about in the workplace.	1	2	3	4	5	☐
21	*Enjoyment of learning and work:* Display joy in the learning process itself and in the work that he or she performs.	1	2	3	4	5	☐
22	*Flexibility:* Show a willingness to apply what he or she knows in new ways as conditions warrant their application.	1	2	3	4	5	☐
23	*Persistence and confidence:* Show determination to pursue new knowledge or skill, even when finding it or mastering it proves more difficult than expected.	1	2	3	4	5	☐
24	*Sense of urgency:* Display sensitivity to the importance of time to self and others.	1	2	3	4	5	☐
25	*Honesty:* Give information in a straightforward manner, free of deception, and elicit similar behavior from others.	1	2	3	4	5	☐
26	*Giving respect to others:* Defer to others with more experience or knowledge.	1	2	3	4	5	☐

THE PERCEPTIVIST ROLE

		1	2	3	4	5	
27	*Work environment analytical skills:* "Examine work environments for issues or characteristics affecting human performance" (Rothwell, 1996).	1	2	3	4	5	☐
28	*Sensory awareness:* Show sensitivity to stimuli received from the outside world based on the use of any one or all of the five senses.	1	2	3	4	5	☐
29	*Open-mindedness:* Demonstrate a willingness to see, to observe, and to internalize what the world presents and reinterpret it afresh.	1	2	3	4	5	☐
30	*Humility:* Display modesty about what he or she does or does not know, a willingness to listen to fresh perspectives without pretending to know when he or she does not know.	1	2	3	4	5	☐
31	*Analytical skill (synthesis):* "Break down the components of a larger whole and reassemble them to achieve improved human performance" (Rothwell, 1996, p. 19).	1	2	3	4	5	☐
32	*Intuition:* Show sensitivity to stimuli generated by him or her from memory or from	1	2	3	4	5	☐

the application of nonverbal logic.						

THE INFORMATION-GATHERER ROLE

33	*Information-sourcing skill:* Identify the kind of information needed to satisfy curiosity and show an ability to locate such information from credible sources.	1	2	3	4	5	☐
34	*Information-gathering skill:* Collect information by talking to others, asking questions of others, facilitating groups to answer questions, and finding information from other sources.	1	2	3	4	5	☐
35	*Information-organizing skill:* Organize or structure information obtained from one or many sources and categorize it into schemes that permit recall, comparison, or creative reexamination.	1	2	3	4	5	☐
36	*Feedback solicitation skill:* Display an ability to solicit feedback on what he or she has learned from others.	1	2	3	4	5	☐

THE ANALYST ROLE

37	*Willingness to experiment and gain experience:* Show an openness to try out new ideas or approaches, even when they are untested or	1	2	3	4	5	☐

	their results are unknown.						
38	*Internalization skill:* Translate general knowledge or information into specific information that can be immediately applied or tested.	1	2	3	4	5	☐
39	*Application of new knowledge skill:* Use new knowledge or skill in harmony with the way it was described or characterized from the original source(s).	1	2	3	4	5	☐
40	*Ability to adapt knowledge to new situations or events:* Use new knowledge or skill in creative, unusual, or novel ways.	1	2	3	4	5	☐

THE EVALUATOR ROLE

41	*Critical examination of information skill:* Reflect on what was learned critically, offering follow-up questions or new ideas based on the information.	1	2	3	4	5	☐
42	*Learning how to learn skill:* Reflect on how he or she acquired new information or knowledge and find ways to improve the acquisition and application of new knowledge or skill in the future.	1	2	3	4	5	☐

| 43 | *Self-directedness skill:* Display a willingness to be proactive about his or her own learning, to take action without needing to be directed to learn or to act by other people. | 1 | 2 | 3 | 4 | 5 | ☐ |

Notes

PREFACE

1. Alvin Toffler, *Powershift: Knowledge, Wealth, and Violence at the Edge of the 21st Century* (New York: Bantam Books, 1994).

2. William J. Rothwell, *ASTD Models for Human Performance Improvement: Roles, Competencies, Outputs* (Alexandria, Va.: The American Society for Training and Development, 1996); William J. Rothwell, Ethan Sanders, and Jeffrey G. Soper, *ASTD Models for Workplace Learning and Performance: Roles, Competencies, Outputs* (Alexandria, Va.: The American Society for Training and Development, 1999); and William J. Rothwell, editor, *ASTD Models for Human Performance: Roles, Competencies, Outputs,* 2nd edition (Alexandria, Va.: The American Society for Training and Development, 2000).

CHAPTER 1

1. William J. Rothwell and H. J. Sredl, *The ASTD Reference Guide to Workplace Learning and Performance,* 3rd edition, 2 volumes (Amherst, Mass.: HRD Press, 2000).

2. William J. Rothwell, *Beyond Training and Development: State of the Art Strategies for Enhancing Human Performance* (New York: AMACOM, 1996).

3. William J. Rothwell, Carolyn Hohne, and Steven King, *Human Performance Improvement: Building Practitioner Competence* (Woburn, Mass.: Butterworth-Heineman, 2000).

4. *The American Heritage Dictionary*, 2nd edition (Boston: Houghton-Mifflin, 1985), pp. 720–721.

5. William J. Rothwell, editor, *ASTD Models for Human Performance*, 2nd edition (Alexandria, Va.: The American Society for Training and Development, 2000).

6. Mary L. Broad and John Newstrom, *Transfer of Training: Action-Packed Strategies to Ensure High Payoff from Training Investments* (Cambridge, Mass.: Perseus Press, 1992).

7. William J. Rothwell and H. C. Kazanas, *Improving On-the-Job Training: How to Establish and Operate a Comprehensive OJT Program* (San Francisco: Jossey-Bass, 1994).

8. B. Joseph Pine, Stan Davis, and B. Joseph Pine II, *Mass Customization: The New Frontier in Business Competition* (Boston, Mass.: Harvard Business School Press, 1999).

9. See, for instance, Dale H. Shunk, *Learning Theories: An Educational Perspective*, 2nd edition (Englewood Cliffs, N.J.: Prentice-Hall, 1996).

10. Leonard Nadler, "A Study of the Needs of Selected Training Directors in Pennsylvania Which Might Be Met by Professional Education Institutions," *Dissertation Abstracts International* 24, 2 (University Microfilms No. 63-3766), 1962.

11. Ibid.

12. Ibid.

13. Neal Chalofsky and Carney Ives Lincoln, *Up the HRD Ladder: A Guide for Professional Growth* (Reading, Mass.: Addison-Wesley, 1983), p. 37.

14. Jerry Gilley and S. Eggland, *Principles of Human Resource Development* (Reading, Mass.: Addison-Wesley, 1989), pp. 310–311.

15. J. Kenny, "Core Competencies of a Trainer," *Canadian Training Methods*, Special Issue, 1976, pp. i–xvi.

16. Valerie Dixon, Kathleen Conway, Karen Ashley, and Nancy Stewart, *Training Competency Architecture* (Toronto: Ontario Society for Training and Development, 1995).

17. Ibid.

18. Chalofsky and Lincoln, *Up the HRD Ladder*, p. 65.

19. Ibid.

20. P. Pinto and J. Walker, "What Do Training and Development Professionals Really Do?" *Training and Development Journal* 32, 7 (1978): 59. See also P. Pinto and J. Walker, *A Study of Professional Training and*

Development Roles and Competencies (Madison, Wis.: The American Society for Training and Development, 1978).

21. Ibid., p. 65.

22. Chalofsky and Lincoln, *Up the HRD Ladder;* Gilley and Eggland, *Human Resource Development*; P. McLagan, *Models for HRD Practice*, 4 volumes (Alexandria, Va.: The American Society for Training and Development, 1989); P. McLagan and R. McCullough, *Models for Excellence: The Conclusions and Recommendations of the ASTD Training and Development Competency Study* (Washington, D.C.: The American Society for Training and Development, 1983); William J. Rothwell, *ASTD Models for Human Performance Improvement* (Alexandria, Va.: The American Society for Training and Development, 1996); and William J. Rothwell, *ASTD Models for Human Performance*, 2nd edition (Alexandria, Va.: The American Society for Training and Development, 2000).

23. P. McLagan and R. McCullough, *Models for Excellence.*

24. Gilley and Eggland, Human Resource Development.

25. McLagan and McCullough, *Models for Excellence.*

26. Gilley and Eggland, *Human Resource Development*, p. 318.

27. McLagan, *Models for HRD Practice.*

28. Ibid., p. 7.

29. Ibid., p. 69.

30. Ibid., p. 17.

31. Rothwell, *ASTD Models for Human Performance Improvement.*

32. Rothwell, *ASTD Models for Human Performance*, 2nd edition.

33. Pinto and Walker, *Professional Training and Development Roles and Competencies.*

34. McLagan and McCullough, *Models for Excellence.*

35. McLagan, *Models for HRD Practice.*

36. Rothwell, *ASTD Models for Human Performance Improvement*, p. 2.

37. Rothwell, *ASTD Models for Human Performance*, 2nd edition, p. 89.

38. George M. Piskurich and Ethan S. Sanders, *ASTD Models for Learning Technologies: Roles, Competencies, Outputs* (Alexandria, Va.: The American Society for Training and Development, 1998).

39. William J. Rothwell, Ethan Sanders, and Jeffrey G. Soper, *ASTD Models for Workplace Learning and Performance: Roles, Competencies, and*

Outputs (Alexandria, Va.: The American Society for Training and Development, 1999).

40. Ibid., p. 121.

41. B. Hergenhahn and M. Olson, *An Introduction to Theories of Learning*, 5th edition (Upper Saddle River, N.J.: Prentice-Hall, 1997), p. 5.

42. W. Zangwill, "Toward a Theory of Continuous Improvement and the Learning Curve," *Management Science* 44, 7 (1998): 910–920.

43. M. Barrick, "The Big Five Personality Dimensions and Job Performance: A Meta-Analysis," *Personnel Psychology* 44, 1 (1991): 1–26; N. Capon, "Determinants of Financial Performance: A Meta-Analysis," *Management Science* 36, 10 (1990): 1143–1159; M. Hirst, "The Effects of Setting Budget Goals and Task Uncertainty on Performance: A Theoretical Analysis," *Accounting Review* 62, 4 (1987): 774–784; D. Lee, "Job Challenge, Work Effort, and Job Performance of Young Engineers: A Causal Analysis," *IEEE Transactions on Engineering Management* 39, 3 (1992): 214–226; and L. Lerner, "An Empirical Study of the Predictors of Corporate Social Performance: A Multi-Dimensional Analysis," *Journal of Business Ethics* 7, 12 (1988): 951–959.

44. Rothwell, *Beyond Training and Development.*

CHAPTER 2

1. William J. Rothwell, Ethan Sanders, and Jeffrey G. Soper, *ASTD Models for Workplace Learning and Performance: Roles, Competencies, and Outputs* (Alexandria, Va.: The American Society for Training and Development, 1999), p. 21.

2. Ibid.

3. William J. Rothwell, *ASTD Models for Human Performance Improvement* (Alexandria, Va.: The American Society for Training and Development, 1996).

4. William J. Rothwell, Robert Prescott, and Maria Taylor, *Strategic Human Resource Leader: How to Prepare Your Organization for the Six Key Trends Shaping the Future* (Palo Alto, Calif.: Davies-Black, 1998).

5. Mark Van Buren and William Woodwell, Jr., *The 2000 ASTD*

Trends Report: Staying Ahead of the Winds of Change (Alexandria, Va.: The American Society for Training and Development, 2000).

6. H. Gardner, *Frames of Mind: The Theory of Multiple Intelligences* (New York: Basic Books, 1993).

7. Robert Havighurst, *Developmental Tasks and Education* (New York: David McKay, 1961).

8. M. Barrick, "The Big Five Personality Dimensions and Job Performance: A Meta-Analysis," *Personnel Psychology* 44, 1 (1991): 1–26; N. Capon, "Determinants of Financial Performance: A Meta-Analysis," *Management Science* 36, 10 (1990): 1143–1159; M. Hirst, "The Effects of Setting Budget Goals and Task Uncertainty on Performance: A Theoretical Analysis," *Accounting Review* 62, 4 (1987): 774–784; D. Lee, "Job Challenge, Work Effort, and Job Performance of Young Engineers: A Causal Analysis," *IEEE Transactions on Engineering Management* 39, 3 (1992): 214–226; and L. Lerner, "An Empirical Study of the Predictors of Corporate Social Performance: A Multi-Dimensional Analysis," *Journal of Business Ethics* 7, 12 (1988): 951–959.

9. Cyril O. Houle, *The Inquiring Mind* (Madison: University of Wisconsin Press, 1961).

10. See, for instance, William J. Rothwell, *The Action Learning Guidebook: A Real-Time Strategy for Problem-Solving, Training Design, and Employee Development* (San Francisco: Jossey-Bass/Pfeiffer, 1999).

11. R. Campbell and D. Monson, "Building a Goal-Based Scenario Learning Environment," *Educational Technology* 34, 9 (1994): 9–14.

12. See R. Brown, "Meta-Competence: A Recipe for Reframing the Competence Debate" *Personnel Review* 22, 6 (1993): 25–36; and J. Slabbert, "A Step Beyond Competence," *Aspects of Educational and Training Technology Series* 25 (1992): 112–119.

13. See, for instance, B. Bova, "Mentoring as a Learning Experience," in *Learning in the Workplace,* V. J. Marsick, editor (New York: Croom Helm, 1987), pp. 119–133; J. Carruthers, "The Principles and Practice of Mentoring," in *The Return of the Mentor: Strategies for Workplace Learning*, B. J. Caldwell and E. M. A. Carter, editors (Bristol, Pa.: Falmer Press, 1993), pp. 9–24; N. Chalofsky, "A New Paradigm for Learning in Organizations," *Human Resource Development Quarterly* 7, 3 (1996): 287–293; R. Durr, L. Guglielmino, and P. Guglielmino, "Self-Directed Learning Readi-

ness and Occupational Categories," *Human Resource Development Quarterly* 7, 4 (1996): 349–358; P. Guglielmino and D. Roberts, "A Comparison of Self-Directed Learning Readiness in U. S. and Hong Kong: Samples and the Implications for Job Performance," *Human Resource Development Quarterly* 3, 3 (1992): pp. 261–271; S. Kozlowski, "Organizational Change, Informal Learning, and Adaptation: Emerging Trends in Training and Continuing Education," *The Journal of Continuing Higher Education* 43, 1 (1995): pp. 2–11; A. Lomi, E. Larsen, and A. Ginsberg, "Adaptive Learning in Organizations: A System Dynamics-Based Exploration," *Journal of Management* 23, 4 (1997): 561–582; C. Manz and K. Manz, "Strategies for Facilitating Self-Directed Learning: A Process for Enhancing Human Resource Development," *Human Resource Development Quarterly* 2, 1 (1991): 3–12; V. Marsick, "Learning in the Workplace: The Case for Reflectivity and Critical Reflectivity," *Adult Education Quarterly* 38, 4 (1988): 187–198; V. Marsick and K. Watkins, "Approaches to Studying Learning in the Workplace," in *Learning in the Workplace,* V. J. Marsick, editor, pp. 171–198; C. Munnelly, "Learning Participation: The Worker's Viewpoint," in *Learning in the Workplace,* V. J. Marsick, editor, pp. 79–95; G. Ravid, "Self-Directed Learning in Industry," in *Learning in the Workplace,* V. J. Marsick, editor, pp. 101–118; A. Rusaw, "Learning by Association: Professional Associations as Learning Agents," *Human Resource Development Quarterly* 6, 2 (1995): 215–226; and R. Skruber, "Organizations as Clarifying Learning Environments," in *Learning in the Workplace,* V. J. Marsick, editor, pp. 55–78.

14. Dale Feuer, "Uh-oh . . . Second Thoughts About Adult Learning Theory," *Training* 25, 12 (1988): 31–39.

15. Darren Short and Rose Opengart, "It's a Free Agent World," *Training & Development* 54, 9 (2000): 60–66; Arnold Packer, "Getting to Know the Employee of the Future," *Training & Development* 54, 8 (2000): 39–43; and Shari Caudron, "Free Agent Learner," *Training & Development* 52, 8 (1999): 26–30; see also Daniel R. Tobin, *All Learning Is Self-Directed* (Alexandria, Va.: The American Society for Training and Development, 2000).

16. Malcolm Knowles, *The Adult Learner: A Neglected Species*, 4th edition (Houston: Gulf Publishing, 1990).

17. See http://wellspring.isinj.com/faq_dl.html.

18. Ibid.

19. Ibid.

20. Ibid.

21. Although much has been written about the EPSS, the classic treatment is still Gloria Gery, *Electronic Performance Support Systems: How and Why to Remake the Workplace Through the Strategic Application of Technology* (Boston: Weingarten, 1991).

CHAPTER 3

1. Vincent Miller, "The History of Training," in *The ASTD Training and Development Handbook: A Guide to Human Resource Development,* R. Craig, editor (New York: McGraw-Hill, 1996).

2. S. Merriam, "An Update on Adult Learning Theory," in *New Directions for Adult and Continuing Education* (San Francisco: Jossey-Bass, 1993).

3. P. Cooper, "Paradigm Shifts in Designed Instruction: From Behaviorism to Cognitivism to Constructivism," in *Emerging Issues in HRD Sourcebook,* W. Rothwell, editor (Amherst, Mass.: HRD Press, 1995), pp. 231–239 (reprint of 1993 article from *Educational Technology*).

4. D. Bullock, "Behaviorism and NSPI: The Erratically Applied Discipline," *Performance and Instruction* 21, 3 (1982): 4–8.

5. Cooper, "Paradigm Shifts in Designed Instruction," p. 231.

6. William J. Rothwell and H. J. Sredl, *The ASTD Reference Guide to Workplace Learning and Performance,* 3rd edition, 2 volumes (Amherst, Mass.: HRD Press, 2000).

7. Ibid.

8. Ibid.

9. David Jonassen, "Objectivism Versus Constructivism: Do We Need a New Philosophical Paradigm?" *Educational Technology Research and Development* 39, 3 (1991): 5–14.

10. Cooper, "Paradigm Shifts in Designed Instruction," p. 236.

11. R. Sperry, "Hemispheric Deconnection and Unity in Continuous Awareness," *Scientific American* 23 (1968): 723–733.

12. T. Buzan, *The Mind Map Book: How to Use Radiant Thinking to*

Maximize Your Brain's Untapped Potential (New York: Dutton, 1994); N. Herrmann, *The Whole Brain Business Book* (New York: McGraw-Hill, 1996); R. Ornstein, *The Psychology of Consciousness* (New York: Harcourt Brace Jovanovich, 1977); and E. Zaidel, "A Response to Gazzanga: Language in the Right Hemisphere: Convergent Perspectives," *American Psychologist* 38, 5 (1983): 542–546. For a description of how organizations are exploring with neural networks and using the brain as a model for them, see Jon Dodd, "Mapping the Mind for Knowledge," *Information World Review* 174 (2001): 27–28.

13. See, for instance, Eric Jensen, *Brain-Based Learning,* 2nd edition (Brain Store, 2000); Judy Stevens and Dee Goldberg, *For the Learner's Sake: Brain-Based Instruction for the 21st Century* (Zephyr Press, 2001); David A. Sousa, *How the Brain Learns: A Classroom Teacher's Guide*, 2nd edition (Corwin Press, 2000); and Marilee Sprenger, *Becoming a "Wiz" at Brain-Based Teaching: From Translation to Application* (Corwin Press, 2001).

14. R. Sperry. "Hemispheric Deconnection and Unity in Continuous Awareness," *Scientific American* 23 (1968): pp. 722–723.

15. Ruth Palombo Weiss, "The Mind-Body Connection in Learning," *T + D* 55, 9 (2001): 60–67.

16. Ibid.

17. Ibid.

18. Ibid., p. 60.

19. N. Dixon, D. Adams, and R. Cullins, "Learning Style," in *What Works: Assessment, Development, and Measurement,* L. Bassi and D. Russ-Eft, editors (Alexandria, Va.: The American Society for Training and Development, 1997), p. 55.

20. Ibid., p. 38.

21. D. Kolb, *The Learning Style Inventory* (Boston: McBer, 1976). See also William J. Rothwell, "The Rothwell Self-Directed On-the-Job Learning Assessment Instrument," in *The Sourcebook for Self-Directed Learning,* William J. Rothwell and Kevin Sensenig, editors (Amherst, Mass.: HRD Press, 1999), pp. 181–190.

22. Darin E. Hartley, *On-Demand Learning: Training in the New Millennium* (Amherst, Mass.: HRD Press, 2000); H. B. Long, *Self-Directed Learning: Consensus and Conflict* (Norman, Okla.: Oklahoma Research Center for Continuing Professional and Higher Education, 1991); and Raymond

Wlodkowski, *Enhancing Adult Motivation to Learn* (San Francisco: Jossey-Bass, 1993).

23. Wlodkowski, *Enhancing Adult Motivation to Learn.*

24. Ibid., p. 213.

25. K. Patricia Cross, *Adults as Learners: Increasing Participation and Facilitating Learning* (San Francisco: Jossey-Bass, 1981); and Malcolm Knowles, *The Modern Practice of Adult Education*, revised edition (Chicago: Follett, 1980).

26. Wlodkowski, *Enhancing Adult Motivation to Learn*, p. 217.

27. Ibid., p. 237.

28. Ibid.

29. Ibid., p. 240.

30. Jack Gordon, "Learning How to Learn," *Training* 27, 5 (1990): 51–62.

31. R. Smith, *Learning How to Learn* (Chicago: Follett, 1982).

32. Ibid.

33. Ibid.

34. Ibid.

35. R. Reading, "Metacognitive Instruction: Trainers Teaching Thinking Skills," *Performance Improvement Quarterly* 3, 1 (1990): 27–41.

36. A. Anderson et al. "Can You Teach Your People to Think Smarter?" *Across the Board* 33, 3 (1996): 16–27; Chris Argyris, "Teaching Smart People How to Learn," *Harvard Business Review* 69, 3 (1991), 99–109; M. Heiman and J. Slomianko, *Learning to Learn on the Job* (Alexandria, Va.: The American Society for Training and Development, 1990); K. Pijanowski, J. Johnson, and G. Roth, "Learning How to Learn in the Seventh Inning Stretch," *Performance & Instruction* 35, 3 (1996): 20–22; and William J. Rothwell, *The Self-Directed On-the-Job Learning Workshop* (Amherst, Mass.: HRD Press, 1996).

37. B. Collard, J. Epperheimer, and D. Saign, *Career Resilience in a Changing Workplace* (Columbus, Ohio: ERIC Clearinghouse on Adult, Career, and Vocational Education. ED 396, 191: 1996).

38. William Bridges, *Job Shift: How to Prosper in a Workplace Without Jobs* (Reading, Mass.: Addison-Wesley, 1994); and J. Rifkin, *The End of Work* (New York: Putnam, 1995).

39. Jack Gordon, "Learning How to Learn," *Training* 27, 5 (1990): 51–62.

40. Hartley, *On-Demand Learning,* pp. 24–27.

41. Barbara Van Horn and Laura Reed-Morrison, *Adult Learner Skills Competencies: A Framework for Developing Curricula in Adult Contexts and Linking Instruction to Assessment* (University Park, Pa.: The Institute for the Study of Adult Literacy, 1996–1997).

42. Ibid.

CHAPTER 4

1. See William J. Rothwell and H. C. Kazanas, *Mastering the Instructional Design Process: A Systematic Approach*, 2nd edition (San Francisco: Jossey-Bass, 1998).

2. Ibid.

3. William J. Rothwell, *The Action Learning Guidebook: A Real-Time Strategy for Problem-Solving, Training Design, and Employee Development* (San Francisco: Jossey-Bass/Pfeiffer, 1999).

4. K. Mellander, *The Power of Learning: Fostering Employee Growth* (Homewood, Ill.: Business One Irwin, 1993); and D. Russ-Eft, H. Preskill, and C. Sleezer, editors, *Human Resource Development Review: Research and Implications* (Thousand Oaks, Calif.: Sage, 1997).

5. Benjamin Bloom, *Taxonomy of Educational Objectives: The Classification of Educational Goals: Cognitive Domain* (New York: David McKay, 1956).

6. D. Krathwohl, B. Bloom, and B. Masia, *Taxonomy of Educational Objectives: The Classification of Educational Goals: Affective Domain* (New York: David McKay, 1964).

7. A. Harrow, *A Taxonomy of the Psychomotor Domain: A Guide for Developing Behavioral Objectives* (New York: David McKay, 1972).

8. Michael Lombardo and Robert Eichinger, *Eighty-Eight Assignments for Development in Place* (Greensboro, N.C.: The Center for Creative Leadership, 1989); and *The Teaching Firm* (Newton, Mass.: The Center for Workforce Development, Education Development Center, 1998).

9. Cyril O. Houle, *The Inquiring Mind* (Madison: University of Wisconsin Press, 1961).

10. Robert F. Mager, *How to Turn Learners on . . . Without Turning Them Off: Ways to Ignite Interest in Learning*, 3rd edition (Atlanta: The Center for Effective Performance, 1997).

11. Allen Tough, *The Adult's Learning Projects* (Toronto: Ontario Institute for Studies in Education, 1979), p. 1.

12. Ibid.

13. Ibid., p. 6.

CHAPTER 5

1. For a more complete description of role theory, see William J. Rothwell and H. J. Sredl, *The ASTD Reference Guide to Workplace Learning and Performance,* 3rd edition, 2 volumes (Amherst, Mass.: HRD Press, 2000).

2. R. Boyatzis, *The Competent Manager: A Model for Effective Performance* (New York: John Wiley, 1982).

3. See D. Dubois and W. J. Rothwell, *The Competency Toolkit*, 2 volumes (Amherst, Mass.: HRD Press, 2000); and W. Rothwell and J. Lindholm, "Competency Identification, Modelling and Assessment in the USA," *International Journal of Training and Development* 3, 2 (1999): 90–105.

4. C. K. Prahalad and G. Hamel, "The Core Competence of the Corporation," *Harvard Business Review,* May–June 1990, pp. 79–91; and G. Hamel and C. K. Prahalad, *Competing for the Future* (Boston: Harvard Business Press, 1994), p. 249.

5. P. McLagan, *Models for HRD Practice*, 4 volumes (Alexandria, Va.: The American Society for Training and Development, 1989), p. 7.

6. See Dubois and Rothwell, *The Competency Toolkit;* and Rothwell and Lindholm, "Competency Identification, Modelling and Assessment in the USA," pp. 90–105.

7. U.S. Department of Labor, *What Work Requires of Schools: A SCANS Report for America 2000* (Washington, D.C.: Superintendent of Public Documents, 1991).

8. Peter Senge, *The Fifth Discipline: The Art and Practice of the Learning Organization* (New York: Currency/Doubleday, 1994); and R. Smith, *Learning How to Learn: Applied Theory for Adults* (Chicago: Follett, 1982).

9. Senge, *The Fifth Discipline*.

10. Ibid.

11. Ibid.

12. Ibid.

13. Smith, *Learning How to Learn*, p. 21.

14. William J. Rothwell, *ASTD Models for Human Performance Improvement* (Alexandria, Va.: The American Society for Training and Development, 1996).

15. Ibid., p. 19.

16. McLagan, *Models for HRD Practice,* p. 77.

17. Rothwell, *ASTD Models for Human Performance Improvement;* William J. Rothwell, editor, *ASTD Models for Human Performance*, 2nd edition (Alexandria, Va.: The American Society for Training and Development, 2000).

CHAPTER 6

1. William J. Rothwell, Ethan Sanders, and Jeffrey G. Soper, *ASTD Models for Workplace Learning and Performance: Roles, Competencies, and Outputs* (Alexandria, Va.: The American Society for Training and Development, 1999), p. 43.

2. William J. Rothwell, *ASTD Models for Human Performance Improvement* (Alexandria, Va.: The American Society for Training and Development, 1996); and William J. Rothwell, editor, *ASTD Models for Human Performance*, 2nd edition. (Alexandria, Va.: The American Society for Training and Development, 2000).

3. Rothwell, Sanders, and Soper, *ASTD Models for Workplace Learning and Performance*, p. 43.

4. Ibid.

5. Ibid.

6. Ibid.

7. Ibid.

8. Ibid.

9. See William J. Rothwell and H. C. Kazanas, *Mastering the Instructional Design Process: A Systematic Approach*, 2nd edition (San Francisco: Jossey-Bass, 1998).

10. C. Hendry, "Understanding and Creating Whole Organizational Change Through Learning Theory," *Human Relations* 49, 5 (1996): 621–641.

11. D. Whitney, "Appreciative Inquiry: An Innovative Process for Organization Change," *Employment Relations Today* 25, 1 (1998): 11–21.

12. R. Gagné and K. Medsker, *The Conditions of Learning: Training Applications* (Fort Worth, Tex.: Harcourt Brace, 1996).

13. William J. Rothwell, *The Action Learning Guidebook: A Real-Time Strategy for Problem-Solving, Training Design, and Employee Development* (San Francisco: Jossey-Bass/Pfeiffer, 1999).

CHAPTER 7

1. Peter Senge, *The Fifth Discipline: The Art and Practice of the Learning Organization* (New York: Currency/Doubleday, 1994), p. 4.

2. William J. Rothwell, "Models for the Workplace Learner." Unpublished research report. (University Park, Pa.: The Pennsylvania State University, 2000).

3. Penny West, "The Concept of the Learning Organization," *Journal of European Industrial Training* 18, 1 (1994): 15–20.

4. D. Mark, "Organizational Learning: A Review of Some Literature," *Organization Studies* 14, 3 (1993): 375–394.

5. Joan K. Bennett, "The Building Blocks of the Learning Organization," *Training* 31, 6 (1994): 41–49.

6. Ibid.

7. B. Hedberg, "How Organizations Learn and Unlearn," in *Handbook of Organizational Design,* P. C. Nystrom and W. H. Starbuck, editors (New York: Oxford University Press, 1981), p. 6. © Oxford University Press 1981. Reprinted from *Handbook of Organizational Design: Volume 1, Adapting Organizations to Their Environments* edited by Paul C. Nystrom and William H. Starbuck (1981) by permission of Oxford University Press.

8. Nancy Dixon, "Organizational Learning: A Review of the Literature with Implications for HRD Professionals," *Human Resource Development Quarterly 3, 1*(1992): 29.

9. C. Argyris and D. Schön, *Organizational Learning: A Theory of Action Perspective* (Reading, Mass.: Addison-Wesley, 1978).

10. Ibid., p. 329.

11. Hedberg, "How Organizations Learn and Unlearn," p. 3. © Oxford University Press 1981. Reprinted from *Handbook of Organizational Design: Volume 1, Adapting Organizations to Their Environments* edited by Paul C. Nystrom and William H. Starbuck (1981) by permission of Oxford University Press.

12. Ibid., p. 5.

13. Ibid., p. 18.

14. P. Shrivastava, "A Typology of Organizational Learning Systems," *Journal of Management Studies* 1 (1983): 8–28.

15. Argyris and Schön, *Organizational Learning*, p. 18.

16. Senge, *The Fifth Discipline*, p. 8.

17. B. Levitt and and J. March, "Organizational Learning," *Annual Review of Sociology* 14 (1988): 319–340; J. March, "Exploration and Exploitation in Organizational Learning," *Organizational Science* 2 (1991): 71–87.

18. S. Clegg, "Globalizing the Intelligent Organization: Learning Organizations, Smart Workers, Clever Countries and the Sociological Imagination," *Management Learning* 30, 3 (1999): 259–280.

19. D. Chang, "Implementation of JIT in the USA and Its Impact on Organizational Performance: An Empirical Study." Unpublished dissertation (Lincoln: University of Nebraska, 1992).

20. J. Dahlgaard, A. Norgaard, and S. Jakobsen, "Styles of Success," *European Quality* 4, 6 (1997): 36–39.

21. R. F. Herley, "Innovation, Market Orientation, and Organizational Learning: An Integration and Empirical Examination," *Journal of Marketing* 62, 3 (1998): 42–54.

22. G. Richards and S. Goh, "Implementing Organizational Learning: Toward a Systematic Approach," *The Journal of Public Sector Management*, Autumn 1995, pp. 25–31.

23. B. Virany, M. Tushman, and E. Romanelli, "Executive Succession and Organization Outcomes in Turbulent Environments," in *Organizational*

Learning, M. D. Cohen and L. S. Sproull, editors (London: Sage, 1992), pp. 302–329.

24. L. Bassi, L. Buchanan, and S. Cheney, *Trends That Affect Learning and Performance Improvement: A Report on the Members of the ASTD Benchmarking Forum* (Alexandria, Va.: The American Society for Training and Development, 1997).

25. U.S. Department of Labor, *The Road to High Performance Workplaces* (Washington, D.C.: Office of the American Workplace, 1994).

26. Senge, *The Fifth Discipline,* p. 4.

27. David D. Dubois and William J. Rothwell, *Developing the High-Performance Workplace: Administrator's Handbook* (Amherst, Mass.: Human Resource Development Press, 1996); and David D. Dubois and William J. Rothwell, *Developing the High-Performance Workplace: Data Collection Instrument* (Amherst, Mass.: HRD Press, 1996).

28. Senge, *The Fifth Discipline,* p. 14.

29. Ibid., p. 7.

30. Ibid., p. 8.

31. Ibid., p. 9.

32. Ibid., p. 10.

33. Rothwell, "Models for the Workplace Learner."

34. Ibid.

35. William J. Morin, *Trust Me: How to Rebuild Trust in the Workplace* (San Diego: Harcourt Brace, 1990).

36. Malcolm Knowles, *The Adult Learner: A Neglected Species,* 4th edition (Houston: Gulf Publishing, 1990).

37. William J. Rothwell and H. C. Kazanas, *Human Resource Development: A Strategic Approach,* revised edition (Amherst, Mass.: HRD Press, 1994).

38. David D. Dubois and William J. Rothwell, *The Competency Toolkit,* 2 volumes (Amherst, Mass.: HRD Press, 2000).

39. Richard L. Bunning, "Skill-Based Pay," *Personnel Administrator* 34, 6 (1989): 65–70; Edward E. Lawler, *Rewarding Excellence: Pay Strategies for the New Economy* (San Francisco: Jossey-Bass, 2000); and Michael White, "Linking Compensation to Knowledge Will Pay Off in the 1990s," *Planning Review* 19, 6 (1991): 15–17.

40. J. Clabby, "Psychological Barriers to Learning: Approach Using Group Treatment," *Small Group Behavior* 16, 4 (1985): 525–533; J. Dhillon, *Perception of Barriers to Learning by College Students* [ERIC No. ED129148]

(Columbus, Ohio: The Eric Clearinghouse, 1975); D. DiMattia, R. Yeager, and I. Dube, "Emotional Barriers to Learning," *Personnel Journal* 68, 11 (1989): 86–89; C. Evans, "Breaking Through Barriers to Adult Learning," *Equity and Excellence* 24, 3 (1989): 28–29; M. Even, "Baggage Barriers," *Lifelong Learning* 11, 4 (1988): 29–30; A. Hanson, "Facilitators and Barriers to Pharmacists' Participation in Lifelong Learning," *American Journal of Pharmaceutical Education* 55, 1 (1991): 20–29; and D. Richter, "Barriers to Adult Learning: Does Anticipation Match Reality?" *Journal of College Student Personnel* 25, 5 (1984): 465–467.

41. M. Poole, *Women's Career Development: Barriers to Learning Within the Traditional Workplace* [ERIC No. ED374250] (Columbus, Ohio: The Eric Clearinghouse, 1994); A. Vowles, "Gaining Competitive Advantage Through Organizational Learning," *CMA Magazine* 67, 3 (1993): 12–14; and D. Watts, "Disorder and Contradiction: An Empirical Perspective on Self-Organization," *Human Systems Management* 9, 4 (1990): 239–248.

42. Rothwell, "Models for the Workplace Learner."

CHAPTER 8

1. Rob Altmann, "Forecasting Your Organizational Climate," *Journal of Property Management* 65, 4 (2000): 62.

2. Rob Altmann, "Start Minimizing Your Workforce Problems: Understand the Organizational Climate," *The Canadian Manager* 25, 2 (2000): 15.

3. A. E. Reichers and B. Schneider, "Climate and Culture: An Evolution of Constructs," in *Organizational Climate and Culture,* B. Schneider, editor (San Francisco: Jossey-Bass, 1990), p. 22.

4. Mark A. Shadur, Rene Kienzle, and John J. Rodwell, "The Relationship Between Organizational Climate and Employee Perceptions of Involvement," *Group & Organization Management* 24, 4 (1999): 479–503.

5. Ibid.

6. Ibid.

7. Ibid.

8. See E. H. Schein, *Organizational Culture and Leadership: A Dynamic View* (San Francisco: Jossey-Bass, 1985).

9. See Richard A. Krueger and Mary Anne Casey, *Focus Groups: A*

Practical Guide for Applied Research, 3rd edition (Thousand Oaks, Calif.: Sage, 2000).

10. Bill Gillham, *The Research Interview* (New York: Continuum, 2000).

11. For recent examples, see G. Douglas Lipp and Clifford H. Clarke, "Managing Culture," *Executive Excellence* 17, 12 (2000): 12; Bob Woods, "Creating an Employer Culture, Seven Steps at a Time," *Chief Executive*, July 2001, p. 15; and Denis St. Amour, "Successful Organizational Change," *The Canadian Manager* 26, 2 (2001): 20–22.

12. See, for instance, Beth Ann Holden, "Winning Strategies: Tell Me a Story," *Incentive* 173, 2 (1999): 65–66; Faye L. Smith and Joann Keyton, "Organizational Storytelling," *Management Communication Quarterly* 15, 2 (2001): 149–182; and Alden Solovy, "Once Upon a Culture," *Hospitals & Health Networks* 73, 5 (1999): 26.

13. Matthew B. Miles and A. Michael Huberman, *Qualitative Data Analysis: An Expanded Sourcebook*, 2nd edition (Thousand Oaks, Calif.: Sage Publications, 1994).

CHAPTER 9

1. For a description of the roles of—and differences between—a CLO and a CKO, see William Powell, "Higher Learning," $T+D$ 55, 7 (2001): 51–54. For a sample job description of a CLO, see Ruth Stadius, *ASTD Trainer's Toolkit: Job Descriptions in Workplace Learning and Performance* (Alexandria, Va.: The American Society for Training and Development, 1999).

2. See Patrick Connor and Linda K. Lake, *Managing Organizational Change* (Westport, Conn.: Praeger, 1994). See also Jeanie Duck, "Managing Change: The Art of Balancing," *Harvard Business Review* 71, 6 (1993): 109–118.

3. See W. Rothwell, R. Sullivan, and G. McLean, "Models for Change and Steps in Action Research," in *Practicing Organization Development: A Handbook for Consultants,* W. Rothwell, R. Sullivan, and G. McLean, editors (San Diego: Pfeiffer & Co., 1995), pp. 47–74.

4. See Robert J. House, "A Path-Goal Theory of Leadership Effectiveness," *Administrative Science Quarterly*, September 1971, pp. 321–339.

5. See William J. Rothwell, *The Evaluator* (Alexandria, Va.: The American Society for Training and Development, 2000).

6. W. James Smith and Jack A. Tesmer, "Adoption," in *Practicing Organization Development: A Handbook for Consultants,* W. Rothwell, R. Sullivan, and G. McLean, editors, (San Diego: Pfeiffer & Co., 1995), pp. 369–394.

7. See William J. Rothwell, *Beyond Training and Development: State-of-the-Art Strategies for Enhancing Human Performance* (New York: AMACOM, 1996).

8. William J. Rothwell, Carolyn Hohne, and Steven King, *Human Performance Improvement: Building Practitioner Competence* (Woburn, Mass.: Butterworth-Heineman, 2000).

9. Robert Mager, *Analyzing Performance Problems or You Really Oughta Wanna: How to Figure Out Why People Aren't Doing What They Should Be, and What to Do About It,* 3rd edition (Atlanta: The Center for Effective Performance, 1997).

10. William J. Rothwell, editor, *ASTD Models for Human Performance,* 2nd edition (Alexandria, Va.: The American Society for Training and Development, 2000).

CHAPTER 10

1. See W. Rothwell, R. Prescott, and M. Taylor, *Strategic Human Resource Leader: How to Prepare Your Organization for the Six Key Trends Shaping the Future* (Palo Alto, Calif.: Davies-Black, 1998).

2. William J. Rothwell, Carolyn Hohne, and Steven King, *Human Performance Improvement: Building Practitioner Competence* (Woburn, Mass.: Butterworth-Heineman, 2000).

3. See C. Wick and L. Leon, *The Learning Edge: How Smart Managers and Smart Companies Stay Ahead* (New York: McGraw-Hill, 1993).

4. John Heron, *The Facilitator's Handbook* (New York: Kogan Page, 1995); Dale Hunter, Anne Bailey, and Bill Taylor, *The Art of Facilitation* (Tucson, Ariz.: Fisher Books, 1995); Dennis Kinlaw, *Facilitation Skills: The ASTD Trainer's Sourcebook* (New York: McGraw-Hill, 1996); and R. Schwartz, *The Skilled Facilitator: Practical Wisdom for Developing Effective Groups* (San Francisco: Jossey-Bass, 1994).

5. See William J. Rothwell, *The Just-in-Time Training Assessment Instru-*

ment: Administrator's Handbook (Amherst, Mass.: HRD Press, 1996); and William J. Rothwell, *The Just-in-Time Training Assessment Instrument: Data Collection Instrument* (Amherst, Mass.: HRD Press, 1996).

6. For a competency model of learning facilitators in keeping with this discussion, see the description of research on facilitation competence in William J. Rothwell, *The Action Learning Guidebook: A Real-Time Strategy for Problem-Solving, Training Design, and Employee Development* (San Francisco: Jossey-Bass/Pfeiffer, 1999).

7. Ibid.

8. See, for instance, George Collison, Bonnie Elbaum, Sarah Haavind, and Robert Tinker, *Facilitating Online Learning: Effective Strategies for Moderators* (Madison, Wis.: Atwood Publishing, 2000); and Susan Schor Ko and Steve Rossen, *Teaching Online: A Practical Guide* (Boston: Houghton-Mifflin, 2000).

9. David B. Peterson and Mary D. Hicks, *Development First* (Minneapolis: Personnel Decisions, Inc., 1995); and David B. Peterson and Mary D. Hicks, *Development First Workbook* (Minneapolis: Personnel Decisions, Inc., 1999).

CHAPTER 11

1. See, for instance, Beverly Kaye and Devon Scheef, "Mentoring," in *Info-Line*, Stock no. 250004 (Alexandria, Va.: The American Society for Training and Development, 2000).

2. C. Hendry, "Understanding and Creating Whole Organizational Change Through Learning Theory," *Human Relations* 49, 5 (1996): 621–641.

APPENDIX A

1. U.S. Department of Labor, *What Work Requires of Schools: A SCANS Report for America 2000* (Washington, D.C.: Superintendent of Public Documents, 1991).

2. Ibid.

3. Lyle Spencer and Signe Spencer, *Competence at Work: Models for Superior Performance* (New York: John Wiley, 1993).

Index

About the Author

William J. Rothwell is professor of Human Resource Development in the Department of Adult Education, Instructional Systems, and Workforce Education and Development in the College of Education on the University Park Campus of The Pennsylvania State University. He is also president of Rothwell and Associates, Inc., a private consulting firm specializing in a comprehensive approach to human performance improvement with a client list including some thirty-two multinational corporations. Previously assistant vice president and management development director for the Franklin Life Insurance Company in Springfield, Illinois, and training director for the Illinois Office of Auditor General, he has worked full-time in human resources management and employee training and development from 1979 to the present, combining real-world experience with academic and consulting experience.

Rothwell's most recent publications include *Building Effective Technical Training* (2002 with J. Benkowski); *Creating In-House Sales Training and Development Programs* (2002, in press, with W. Donahue and J. Park); *Planning and Managing Human Resources*, 2nd edition (2002, in press, with H. Kazanas); *The Manager and Change Leader* (2001); *Effective Succession Planning*, 2nd edition (2000); *The Complete Guide to Training Delivery: A Competency-Based Approach* (2000, with M. King and S. King); *Human Performance Improvement: Building Practitioner Competence* (2000, with C. Hohne and S. King); *The ASTD Reference Guide to Workplace Learning and Performance: Present and Future Roles and Competencies*, 3rd edition, 2 volumes (2000, with H. Sredl); *The Analyst* (2000); *The Evaluator* (2000); *The Intervention Selector, Designer and Developer, and Implementor* (2000); *ASTD Models for Human Performance*, 2nd edition (2000); *The Competency Toolkit*, 2 volumes (2000, with D. Dubois); *Building In-House Leadership and Management Development Programs* (1999, with H. Kazanas); *ASTD Models for Workplace*

Learning and Performance (1999, with E. Sanders and J. Soper); *The Action Learning Guidebook: A Real-Time Strategy for Problem Solving, Training Design, and Employee Development: Sourcebook for Self-Directed Learning* (1999, with K. Sensenig, as editors); *Creating, Measuring and Documenting Service Impact: A Capacity Building Resource: Rationales, Models, Activities, Methods, Techniques, Instruments* (1998); *In Action: Improving Human Performance* (1998, with D. Dubois, as editors); *Strategic Human Resource Leader: How to Help Your Organization Manage the Six Trends Affecting the Workforce* (1998, with R. Prescott and M. Taylor); *In Action: Linking HRD and Organizational Strategy* (1998, as editor); *Mastering the Instructional Design Process: A Systematic Approach,* 2nd edition (1998, with H. Kazanas).

Rothwell is the American editor for the *International Journal of Training and Development,* an international academic journal published by Blackwell's of England. He is also coeditor of the Jossey-Bass/Pfeiffer series *Practicing Organization Development: The Change Agent Series in Group and Organizational Change* (see www.practicingod.com) and coeditor of another book series, the Jossey-Bass/Pfeiffer series *Using Technology in Training and Learning.*

He can be contacted at 647 Berkshire Drive, State College, PA 16803. His e-mail address is wjr9@psu.edu, and his personal Web site is at www.rothwell-associates.com.